SUPERPOWER?

SUPERPOWER?

The Amazing Race between China's Hare and India's Tortoise

Raghav Bahl

Portfolio / Penguin

PORTFOLIO / PENGUIN
Published by the Penguin Group
Penguin Group (USA) Inc., 375 Hudson Street,
New York, New York 10014, U.S.A.
Penguin Group (Canada), 90 Eglinton Avenue East, Suite 700,
Toronto, Ontario, Canada M4P 2Y3
(a division of Pearson Penguin Canada Inc.)
Penguin Books Ltd, 80 Strand, London WC2R 0RL, England
Penguin Ireland, 25 St. Stephen's Green, Dublin 2, Ireland
`(a division of Penguin Books Ltd)
Penguin Books Australia Ltd, 250 Camberwell Road, Camberwell,
Victoria 3124, Australia
(a division of Pearson Australia Group Pty Ltd)
Penguin Books India Pvt Ltd, 11 Community Centre, Panchsheel Park,
New Delhi – 110 017, India
Penguin Group (NZ), 67 Apollo Drive, Rosedale, North Shore 0632,
New Zealand (a division of Pearson New Zealand Ltd)
Penguin Books (South Africa) (Pty) Ltd, 24 Sturdee Avenue,
Rosebank, Johannesburg 2196, South Africa

Penguin Books Ltd, Registered Offices:
80 Strand, London WC2R 0RL, England

First American edition
Published in 2010 by Portfolio / Penguin,
a member of Penguin Group (USA) Inc.
1   2   3   4   5   6   7   8   9   10

Library of Congress Cataloging-in-Publication Data

Bahl, Raghav.
Superpower? : the amazing race between China's hare and India's tortoise / Raghav Bahl.
p. cm.
Includes bibliographical references and index.
ISBN 978-1-59184-396-2
1. China—Relations—India. 2. India—Relations—China. 3. Great powers. 4. Geopolitics. 5. Social change—China.
6. Social change—India. 7. China—Economic conditions—2000– 8. India—Economic conditions—21st century. 9.
China—Social conditions—2000– 10. India—Social conditions—21st century. I. Title.
DS740.5.I5B34 2010
951.06—dc22
2010029658

Printed in the United States of America

*Dedicated to my late grandparents and my late father
for teaching me the virtues of ambition and excellence
and to my mother
for being an embodiment of resilience*

CONTENTS

ACKNOWLEDGEMENTS

I owe a debt of gratitude to several people who have contributed their invaluable time and effort to make this book possible. Without question the biggest one is due to my colleague, Vivian Fernandes, who was my Executive Editor on this project. Vivian was a friend, philosopher, guide, researcher and critic through the effort—without him, this work would not have come to fruition. Vivian is an outstanding journalist with a painstaking devotion to detail and excellence; his contribution is particularly compelling in chapters 4 and 5. I also owe a lot to my research associate, Renu Sharma, for her dogged and intelligent pursuit of facts and nuggets. I am also grateful to the professional and focussed team of young economists at AssignmentBuddy, led by Nishant Mehra and ably supported by Vidhi Pant. I simply cannot forget the intellectual energy that Shalini Iyer brought to her legal research on the two countries. I am also hugely thankful to Shagun Khare (entrepreneurship), Teshu Singh and Cheryl Jacob (colonial history) for assisting me with specific areas. Raja Rajeshwari, my redoubtable colleague at CNBC-TV18, was the last port of call on all bits and pieces of information. Finally, I thank my publishers Penguin India and my editor Udayan Mitra for taking a bet on a first-time author. I hope I have not let anybody down—while the credit for this work belongs to everyone who's helped out, the errors and weaknesses are entirely mine.

I would like to end by acknowledging the moral and material support I have received from several colleagues and family members.

Deepti Jain, my assistant, was indefatigable about searching Google, keying in data and taking printouts. Rajneesh Singh (Head of HR at Network18) and Saurabh Khandelwal (his assistant) were unstinting in their efforts to put together a research team; Ajit Andhare tracked potential publishers, Kshipra Jatana helped out with legal contracts and Piyush Jain managed the post-manuscript phase; Indrajit Gupta led the *Forbes India* team in designing the jacket; frankly, without all of them it would have been a no-go.

Last, and certainly not the least, I am deeply grateful to my family. My sister Vandana has always been around to see me through stressful times; my wife Ritu, daughter Tara and son Vidur were, as usual, pillars of strength. Ritu was there to egg me on whenever I got afflicted by doubt, and the kids happily adjusted their dinner time to accommodate my nocturnal stints in the study. Ultimately, their infectious smiles got me to the end.

I hope this book adds at least a sliver to your understanding of our world. I would then consider it a worthwhile effort.

Preface

WHY DON'T THEY GET INDIA?

A lot of Indians believe in rebirth and transmigration of the soul. While it is an intellectually rich philosophy, its quick and everyday version simply means that a person's second, third, fourth or nth life is influenced by his actions, or *karma*, in previous ones. By this simplistic yardstick, I must have been a foreign investor in at least a couple of my earlier births!

Ever since I began my entrepreneurial life in the early 1990s, I have dealt, rather pleasantly, with foreign investors of all hues, shapes and sizes. One foreign investor or the other sits atop every key milestone. In the early days, there were venture capitalists just coming to grips with the 'maddening complexities' of India. I was, in their lingo, a person with 'promising intellectual capital' in a 'virgin consumer-focused business' which was likely to witness 'explosive growth as India's GDP shifted gears and consumer aspirations stretched beyond the needs of daily survival'. In other words, I was a poor but bright fellow, bereft of any financial capital, brimming with special media skills and ideas, capable of creating 'value' as the country's television content business was 'unleashed'. So if they gave me $5 million in cash and a chunk in equity, I could build a team of professionals and a company which could become a leader in 'India's nascent media industry'. That's the first kind of foreign investor I encountered way back in 1993.

I must hand it to these guys for getting it somewhat right. Frankly, if I had $5 million in those days, I would have kept it under the mattress, but never given it away to a struggling thirty-two-year-old who barely had enough money to buy a second-hand car. But these guys did bet on us, and I daresay, made plenty of money. As our operations grew, we took bigger bets—and ran into even weightier foreign investors! The early-stage venture capitalist gave way to the late-stage private equity chap, who now gave us $20 million, but took a smaller chunk of equity, simply because 'start-up risks had been mitigated, and proof of concept was visible in our growing operations'. These fellows would visit us once every quarter, sit through board meetings, see some fancy graphics, meet our key people, tour the facilities, and round off with plenty of spirits at the Dublin bar. Their excitement about India was always subdued, tinged with an edge of scepticism, if not outright disbelief. Why does your government take so long to give approvals? Why is your foreign investment policy so restrictive? Why are your airports in such a shambles? How come your hotels are so good, when the roads leading to them are so potholed? How do you speak such good English? Why do you have so many newspapers? Why are so many of them in English? How are they able to survive? Why don't you lower your voice when you make fun of your politicians? How come your licence was not cancelled after you did such a tough interview with the finance minister? Why are there no malls here? Why are your cinema halls so rundown? Why don't Indian consumers pay for services?

Every conversation would end with some variant of the same observation: 'You know what, it's not like that in China—or Korea, or Thailand, or Dubai.'

As we acquired commercial muscle, our confidence and market share soared. From foreign investors who gave us equity capital, we moved 'up the value chain' to do deals with 'foreign strategic players'— large American media groups who bet their brand, programming and reputations with us. Our first joint venture was with CNBC to launch a twenty-four-hour business news channel in India. We made all the investments, took all the risks, and paid them a royalty. We followed through with another deal with CNN, to launch a twenty-four-hour general news channel in India. Again, we made all the investments, took all the risks and paid them a royalty. We then bought 50 per cent of Viacom's India operations, including such iconic brands as MTV India, Nickelodeon India and VH1 India. We put in slightly over $100 million to launch Colors, a general entertainment channel; the venture was led by our CEO, delighting our foreign partners with its spectacular success. Next on our rollcall was Forbes, as we set about publishing *Forbes India*.

In less than five years, we had put together a pantheon of the world's leading media brands on the same Indian balance sheet. Who would have imagined, or dared, to bring such competing American media groups—CNBC, CNN, MTV, Nickelodeon, VH1, Forbes—under a single owner? I am often asked: 'How did you pull that off?' My answer is a shrug; how do I say that I must have been a foreign investor in at least a couple of my previous births?

The colour of money changed from 'financial' to 'strategic', but the scepticism never ceased. Why is the Indian market so small? Why are Indian regulations so weak and confusing? Why is there no protection for intellectual property rights? Why does the Indian consumer steal our signals? Why do Indian courts take so long to decide anything? Why do Indians prefer tacky Bollywood films to Hollywood's masterpieces? Why are Indian commentators and politicians so free with their words and criticism? Why don't you have stricter libel and defamation laws? Why do we have to use Indian satellites only? Why are long overdue policy decisions put on hold by ever-so-frequent elections? Why is India's bureaucracy so timid? Why are India's bankers so conservative? Why are the interest rates so high? Why are all policies made in English? How do Indians speak such good English? Why does such abject poverty coexist with such immense amounts of corporate wealth in India? Why don't you want more dollars to come into your country? How come you have built such an efficient capital market? But then, why don't you have a bond market? Why do you control the prices of oil and cable TV? Why is the government trying, but failing, to ban jeans in colleges? Why do your social clubs insist on western attire? Why don't you allow more foreign players in your cricket league? Why do you have such old politicians in key ministries?

Invariably, almost every such 'why conversation' would end with: 'Oh, but it's not like that in China—or Korea, or Thailand, or Dubai!'

Frankly, I could never escape the feeling that India was just a 'hedging instrument' for the investors. While they put serious money and conviction into China, Korea, Thailand and Dubai, their attitude towards India was, to use their terminology, somewhat 'derivative' or 'collateral'. India was a bit too complex and inexplicable for them, yet India had some of the dynamics which could, one odd day, make for an economic superpower. So even if they couldn't, or wouldn't, understand the country, they dared not bypass it, since India had mysterious potential: it could be the quaint outlier, or 'multi-bagger', in their portfolio. It made sense to 'play blind' on India—put in some money, but not bother too much with it. If you were dealt a good hand, you could make a killing; otherwise, your 'max downside' was to simply write off the investment as a 'hedging cost' for bets taken elsewhere in Asia.

A question began to beg for an answer: do these foreigners even 'get India'?

I was twenty-two when I first set foot on foreign soil, in February 1982. It was under extraordinary circumstances. I was flown into New York for emergency medical treatment. Our plane landed in a city buried under a severe snowstorm. Muscular attendants pushed my stretcher past immigration and loaded it on to a howling ambulance. Everything was a blur of ceiling lights and whizzing corridors. It was my first brush with American efficiency, and I was wide-eyed with admiration. The traffic into midtown Manhattan was exceptionally heavy, but we made generous use of the howler. Cars would part with magical discipline, clearing the way for my ambulance to race to the hospital. I was checked in and tucked into a rather comfortable bed. I spent the whole evening answering questions from friendly *male* nurses (the whole experience was full of firsts!).

I spent the next four months in hospitals, clinics, hotels and sub-leased apartments. I would run into guards, housekeepers, lift attendants, nurses, all of whom, without exception, would ask me one cheerful question: 'You from Pakistan?' India simply did not exist in popular consciousness. That was the year *Gandhi* swept the Oscars. I was often asked 'if that guy was for real?' Another question would pop up with unerring regularity: 'How come you speak such good English? Have you studied in London—you have such a British accent! Does every Indian speak such good English?'

At the end of four months, I was convinced about two things: Americans are a terrific people to deal with, but India is simply not on their radar. It was an astonishing revelation, since the streets, universities and hospitals were crammed with Indians. Yet we did not exist, as a nation, or a real, tangible, identifiable entity.

One question has troubled me for nearly three decades now: why don't foreign investors really, I mean *really*, get India? Why can't they figure us out?

A couple of years ago, one of our crucial foreign bankers asked me to address their top leadership on 'any topic that could keep a hundred bankers interested for about an hour before cocktails begin'. The bank was flying in its overseas board and management council to India for their annual summit. It was a first for them, and for India. These were people who had led businesses in America, Europe, Asia, Africa, and every other important place on earth. Most of them were visiting Asia—forget India—for the first time. They were nothing but top drawer. I am usually economical about accepting such invitations, but in this case I agreed readily. For one, a good entrepreneur never says no to his banker. For another, I was curious to use this gathering as a laboratory to test some of my fledgling theories about 'Why don't they get India?'

I stuffed some half-baked thoughts into my jacket, and reached the hotel in downtown New Delhi. Slowly, through a rambling forty-minute talk, punctuated with a few animated questions and exchanges, I laid out a 'theory'. I had given my talk a working title: 'Why the West Can't Figure Out India: A Gut-level Assessment of India's Political/ Economic Legacy'.

I started by rewinding to India's independence movement. The West's inability to 'get its arms around a complex India' began right there. India's struggle for independence was led by lawyers who were steeped in the liberal democratic traditions of the West. Mahatma Gandhi, Jawaharlal Nehru, Sardar Patel and many others were students at Oxford or Cambridge who had lived in London in their youth, worn the trendiest western attire and often indulged in the finest luxuries that money could buy on Bond Street. Yet they had led a movement of impoverished farmers and artisans, given up western luxuries, at least at home, and identified almost completely with the aspirations of the 'starving millions'. Their leadership was not symbolic or synthetic; they did not lead double lives, austere in public view but soft and indulgent in private. They were intellectually honest leaders, whose words broadly matched their deeds. They created a genuine democracy, based on free and equal citizens. Of course it suffered from critical flaws, cradled as it was within an imperfect society with deep prejudices and historical fissures.

Yet Indian democracy survived, giving the West its first brush with an 'incomprehensible' India. Country after newly independent country was aborting its experiment with democracy. Rulers of many newly-liberated countries were becoming autocrats. But India stood apart in persisting with democracy, however flawed and imperfect it might have been.

This triggered indifference—or worse, suspicion—in the West. Those who reluctantly accepted India's democracy, but failed to comprehend it, took easy refuge in indifference ('since we can't understand it, let's keep a precious distance from it'). Others were convinced that India was doing a fiddle, using a skin-deep democracy as a subterfuge to hide a totalitarian state; they became deeply suspicious, preferring to keep their precious distance. Inevitably, India became remote, inaccessible, distant—an object of indifference or suspicion.

This indifference or suspicion hardened as India embraced Soviet-style socialism. The contradiction now was sharp, almost gratifying, for western leaders who were already questioning India's credentials. A democracy which is wedded to the Soviets! Hah, gimme a break! A country which preaches equality and freedom, but stifles its entrepreneurs and nationalizes assets? No way!

So the '50s and '60s were decades of estrangement from the West. India's first prime minister, Jawaharlal Nehru, was a vocal and articulate fan of Soviet-style planning. He used catchy language, calling government-owned steel plants and hydroelectric dams the 'temples of modern India'. He was passionate about putting the 'commanding heights of the economy' in public ownership, most of it created with Russian technology and rouble financing. India also created the classic insular economy: high tariff walls, pegged exchange rates and crippling entry barriers via industrial licensing. Private enterprise got emaciated and entrepreneurship virtually extinguished. A massive illegal—or 'black'—economy flourished. All through this, India's political leaders delighted in getting themselves photographed at the Kremlin, in a fraternal clinch with Soviet officials. These images of a 'left-leaning, communist-worshipping India' stuck in western consciousness, obliterating the massive doses of democratic reform that were positively convulsing an ancient and feudal society.

That was the paradox of India under Nehru. He created visible symbols of stiff state controls on the economy. At the same time, he unleashed forces of democracy and change which should have been music to western ears—universal adult suffrage, equal fundamental rights for citizens of any gender or class or caste, substantially fair elections, a daringly free press, a genuinely autonomous judiciary, a bustling entertainment and information society, a strong English-speaking middle class, a high-quality technological and education infrastructure and a culture of liberal thought, all as early as in the 1950s, when large swathes of a newly-liberated world were regressing towards authoritarian rule. The West could not handle this paradox; India's communist tilt was visibly black, its democratic efforts should have been sparklingly white, but the resultant grey was a bit too amorphous for the West to figure out. Black was an easy colour to understand, communism was an easy target to trash. And since a highly walled-off India was not even a profitable quest for western capital, it just made sense to flow with the obvious. The West was happy to leave India alone and not give a damn.

The estrangement of the '50s hardened into the palpable bitterness of the late '60s and '70s. India fought two wars, with China in 1962 and with Pakistan in 1965. These pushed India into a tighter embrace with the Soviets. India used Russian-built tanks and MIG-25s, while Pakistan used Pattons and F-14s. In perception terms, it was a proxy war between America and USSR. From indifference or suspicion, the West was now getting adversarial about India.

Two years after Jawaharlal Nehru's death in 1964, his daughter, the populist and shrilly leftist Indira Gandhi became prime minister. She nationalized banks, hiked marginal income taxes to nearly 100 per cent, forced multinational companies to disinvest majority stakes, fought another war with Pakistan in 1971 to liberate Bangladesh, thumbed her nose at Henry Kissinger and glared at President Nixon, called the American bluff over the 42nd Fleet in the Indian Ocean, showed undisguised affection for General Secretary Leonid Brezhnev, detonated a test nuclear device, and took an assertive pro-South/anti-US line at international conferences. For the West, it was QED; India was virtually a renegade state, to be given a wide berth or bitterly opposed.

Ironically, the '60s and '70s saw a contiguous blossoming of a liberal democracy within the country. The political opposition rose as a credible force, even dethroning Indira Gandhi's government in 1977. It was the first party-switch of a national government, after nearly thirty years of independence. At the provincial level, an effective two-party system emerged, with governments changing every five years. The middle class soared into a new political consciousness. The free press stood against the tyranny of Indira Gandhi's short-lived, failed 'emergency rule'. Indian cinema flowered as bold themes were explored. A conservative society began to flirt with a fresh sexual and consumer proclivity. Ordinary Indians—sportspersons, film stars, authors, astronauts—became icons, ejecting political leaders from a perch that was hitherto reserved for them. The country continued to churn out doctors, engineers and other high-calibre professionals with surprising dexterity. An astonishingly affluent class of 'non-resident Indians' emerged, whose intellectual prowess was feted in America and Europe. Yet the West missed all of this. It stopped at India's Iron Curtain, oblivious of an emerging urban society that was as free, vocal and choice-oriented as its own.

Then came the '80s, and the first whiff of a promise; it was now the turn of Rajiv Gandhi, Indira Gandhi's son and Jawaharlal Nehru's grandson, to be elected prime minister. He rode the crest of a sympathy wave generated by his mother's assassination. He got a four-fifths majority in parliament, larger than what his grandfather or mother had ever managed. He was a young, forty-year-old commercial pilot, with a mind for modern technology. He became a champion of computers and telecoms. He loosened a few hidebound socialist laws, creating a climate in which private enterprise could be resuscitated.

The country witnessed its first equity boom, as stock prices multiplied with bull-market frenzy. Rajiv also opened up to the West, his Italian wife a natural asset in that quest. In any case, the Soviets were declining in influence. Finally, it seemed that India was reaching out and the West was responding to dismantle decades of indifference, suspicion and bitterness. But that was not to be; once more, India and the West missed their date with each other. Rajiv Gandhi's regime got entangled in a web of corruption charges and political intrigue; it was voted out in 1989, and India's brief dalliance with the West was nipped in the bud.

The government that was elected in 1989 was notoriously short-lived. It was also very notorious. It indulged in politicking of the worst kind, unleashing caste wars and religious strife. Globally too, the world was shredded by crisis. Kuwait was invaded, oil prices spiralled, and India bungled its politics and economics. The 1989 regime was replaced by another rag-tag coalition, which was even more opportunistic and short-sighted. The country was on the verge of its first international loan default. It had to infamously pledge its gold reserves with the IMF to tide over that commitment. Mercifully, the second coalition too collapsed, and India was hurled into a mid-term election within two years. But destiny was not yet done with it. Rajiv Gandhi, widely fancied to ride back to power, was assassinated in the middle of electioneering; once again his party got elected on a sympathy wave, led this time by an old political warhorse, P.V. Narasimha Rao.

Rao was the seventy-three-year-old successor to the young Rajiv Gandhi. He was acutely aware of the financial crisis that could have swallowed his government. Rao trotted out the redoubtable Dr Manmohan Singh as his finance minister. Singh was an internationally admired economist who had spent long years in government, including a stint as the RBI (Reserve bank of India) chief in the '80s. The brief to Singh was succinct: save India from going over the edge. Rescue India from bankruptcy.

Singh moved with alacrity. In June 1991, he sharply devalued the rupee. By India's timid standards, it was a bold and shocking move. Singh followed through with revolutionary policy changes. Industrial licensing was abolished. Shares of public sector companies were sold. Multinational companies were allowed to set up factories and businesses. The currency was made near-convertible. Stock markets were thrown open to foreign capital—they leapt with joy. India's animal spirits were unleashed. Hundreds of first generation entrepreneurs, including yours truly, leveraged their skills and chutzpah to raise millions of equity dollars to launch new enterprises. Satellite television beamed unbridled images of western consumerism into middle-class Indian homes. Aspirations soared. Consumer credit became easily available. Fancy cars, mobile phones and private airlines took to the skies. India's much-vaunted technology firms got listed on NASDAQ. Old, bulky, family-owned businesses got buried under an avalanche of mint-fresh entrepreneurial energy. The survivors were forced to severely restructure their operations and attitudes as urban India flung away decades of socialist paralysis.

The West sat up and took notice. Bitterness dissipated. Suspicion was tamed. But indifference was not quite replaced by excitement. For one, political instability continued to dog India. M/s Narasimha Rao and Manmohan Singh were voted out in 1996, to be replaced by a coalition which, mercifully, was not regressive. But it was unstable. One anonymous prime minister was replaced by another weak candidate within months. The West, which was enjoying India's unfolding economic spectacle, continued to be deeply suspicious about its fragile governance. Another reason for the West's muted response was its excitement about China, Brazil and Russia—especially China which was mounting an altogether new curve of explosive growth.

That's how India was poised towards the end of the twentieth century. After decades of invisibility, it had managed to create a blip on the western radar, but China was the sexy one. Exploratory droplets of western capital had fallen into India, but that was meagre compared to the torrential pouring into China. I remember what one of my legendary foreign investor friends told me around that time: 'China's got a real J-curve of growth. It's the classic hockey stick. Demand simply takes off after a couple of years, whether it's demand for cars or internet connections or refrigerators. You guys are darn slow, mate. Your J-curve is just so f-l-a-a-a-t. It stays horizontal for years and years, and just when you are about to give up, it shows a small upturn. Just why does you consumer take so long to change his habits? Why is he so brutal about paying low prices? Just why do you guys take so bloody long to decide about anything?'

Clearly, even now, after nearly a decade of being in business, India struggled to get itself understood—or perhaps, the West continued its struggle to unravel India. And since China provided a sexy and instantly profitable diversion, it required just too much effort to figure out the mysteries of India's f-l-a-a-a-t J-curve. Throw in India's unstable polity, and it's not difficult to imagine why the West still did not bother to 'get India', even as the twentieth century crawled to a close.

But 1999 was a turnaround year. India finally got itself a stable government. It wasn't one-party rule, but the country's politics was gelling around two coalitions. The group in power, with over 60 per cent majority in parliament, could be described as right of centre, while the opposition space was occupied by parties with a marked leftist tilt, but with sufficiently credible free-market genes. India's Republicans and Democrats, Conservatives and Labourites, were acquiring political form. The West had cause to rejoice, to look at India with fresh energy. A big question mark over the country, its inherently unstable parliament, was giving way to a grudging two-party system. The western world's flirtation with India could have bloomed into a full-blown romance.

Alas, one more time, destiny willed otherwise. The right-wing government detonated India's second nuclear device after twenty-five years of non-testing, triggering sharp global sanctions. Barely a year later, world markets were buried under the debris of dotcom stocks, followed by 9/11 which shook the world in 2001. The world seized up in fright. Afghanistan was bombed. Western money put South Asia on hold.

Once again, India was like the bride that was all dressed up and ready to go, but its western suitors were now too scared to woo her.

By 2003, faint marriage bells had begun to ring again. The wounds of 9/11 were scarring. India's macroeconomics was beginning to allure. Historically low inflation, taxes and interest rates had kickstarted a domestic consumption boom. Equity markets were pulling out of a trough. Investment demand, particularly in middle-class housing, was accelerating. A youthful India was going suburban with aplomb, thronging malls, buying cars and goodies. Cellphone users were zooming. Urban India was enjoying boom-like conditions. A left-of-centre government, now headed by Dr Manmohan Singh, the academician finance minister who had switched on India's economic revolution in 1991, took office in 2004. His finance minister was a

Harvard-trained lawyer who had, seven years earlier, in another government, slashed taxes and become the darling of corporate India. Foreign capital began pouring in. Equity markets doubled, then trebled. GDP leapt by 9 per cent in 2005. India was finally taking off. And this time, the West was keen to join the party. It was finally 'getting India'!

I paused. My audience of globetrotting bankers was rapt in attention. I had been speaking for forty minutes. A gentle 8 p.m. breeze was seductive and the bar was open. I expected to hear polite coughs, suggesting that I wind up and try a cocktail. But the air seemed pregnant with unasked questions. I needed a drink. It was time to conclude. 'Now, only a solitary wrinkle remains for India. It is still not considered as sexy as China, because India's policymakers are still too timid, cowed down by decades of socialism and risk aversion. They underestimate India more than anybody else does. On the one hand, young India is supremely confident, entrepreneur India is straining at leashes, foreigners are gung ho—but there is only one constituency, India's own policymakers, that needs to come on board, needs to have the same confidence in their own country that others do. Once that happens, this last wrinkle will go, and India will be as sexy, if not more, as China.' I ended by waving my arms, hoping to signal via bodily motion that I had ended on a flourish.

The applause was a bit scattered. The audience had concentrated intensely through my talk; then why such a tepid acknowledgement? They still seemed lost in thought. Most got up and sauntered towards the bar, talking in low but animated tones. Clearly, I had triggered some introspection, some soul-searching, perhaps even plenty of disbelief and some disagreement.

I sat down to dinner at the head table. The global CEO pumped my hand and thanked me for 'taking the trouble'. He congratulated me, on cue, for an 'illuminating talk' (what else could he say?). Then, as an afterthought, he asked, 'So, when is the book coming? When are you going to publish all of this? It will be a bestseller.' I muttered some inanity, picked up my wine, took a sumptuous gulp, and got busy with the first of many delectable courses.

That was in 2005. Over the next couple of years, India rocked. The economy grew 9 per cent on the trot, markets doubled again, and it was pink champagne all the way. While China still swung the sweepstakes, at least a few foreign voices had begun to say that 'a democratic India could outperform China'. These voices were scattered, lonely, and quite the exception—but at least India was in the game. The only guys still out of it were India's politicians. In golf-speak, they continued to hit bunkers, playing well over their already modest handicap.

If I was a foreign investor in a couple of my previous births, I must have been a civil servant in at least two others before that, because next to foreign investors, government policymakers and bureaucrats have ruled my horoscope ever since I became an entrepreneur. Just imagine how often one had to run to them for approvals: to bring in foreign investment, to pay royalty dollars, to buy overseas companies, to uplink satellite signals, to give board rights to joint venture partners, to list a company on the stock exchanges, to offer shares on a rights basis to your own shareholders, to pay bonuses to oneself . . . the list is virtually endless. Every few weeks, entrepreneurs in India have to sit across the table with civil servants, and plead for approvals; that's the reality, like it or stuff it!

The Indian civil servant is enormously intelligent. He is among the brightest in the land. He gets it quickly. He is usually articulate and accessible. He can see through a problem and understand solutions. But he often lacks the gumption to 'just do it'. He is trained to see the glass as half empty, never half full. His instinct is to push a decision, not take it. He is a champion of the 'middle route', the 'golden mean'. He stays clear of anything that is even remotely controversial, breakthrough or bold. He uses 'consensus' and 'consultation' as a shield to 'protect his backside'. His favourite phrase is that 'government decisions are process- not result-oriented'. Of course there is that exceptional officer who goes against the grain, who innovates and takes risks, but to borrow another favorite phrase, 'by and large' these guys like to hedge their bets to the point of inaction.

Try this example: Many years ago, the government made a bold policy change. It allowed Indian companies to 'automatically remit foreign currency equal to twice their net worth'. So if you had the cash, and an auditor's certificate of your net worth, you only had to go to your bank, and ask them to send out the dollars to a contracting party. This was dramatic stuff; until then, foreign exchange transactions were so tightly monitored that a dozen approvals were required before even a single dollar could be remitted. Companies like ours heaved a sigh of relief. We thought we were free. Imagine our consternation when a government-owned bank refused to believe the new regulation! I went and spoke to the chairman. I showed him the new rules, written in clear, unambiguous English, in black and white. The chairman nodded, 'Yes, Mr Bahl, I agree with you. The law indeed *seems* to say that no approval is needed. But how can I believe it? How could it have become so liberal overnight? It has to be a misprint. I am afraid I can't take this call. I will have to refer it to the Reserve Bank of India.' I couldn't believe what I was hearing. The man, a senior and experienced banker, was refusing to believe his own eyes, was refusing to believe that the world had changed, but was willing to believe that the government could have wrongly published its policy! It was frustrating, but there was nothing I could do. The matter was referred to the RBI, who simply laughed it back at the chairman. 'Can't you read the new guidelines? This is not required to come to us anymore.' The chairman turned scarlet when I met him with the RBI's order.

Here's another one. In the early 2000s, the government changed FDI rules for news broadcast companies. Foreigners were allowed a maximum of 26 per cent 'direct plus indirect' equity. But big problems arose in the definition of 'indirect foreign equity'. We 'humbly submitted' to the government that our shareholders changed every minute since we were a publicly traded company, so this whole business of 'indirect foreign equity' was 'ab initio indeterminable'. Simply put, no one could ever 'certify' the quantum of 'indirect foreign equity' because a) you did not have a fixed register of shareholders; and b) even if you did, you had no way of knowing how much foreign equity existed on the balance sheet of that shareholder. I thought our arguments were so completely based on common sense that they would be accepted in an instant. To my complete disbelief, it took nearly eight years for this principle to become policy!

But I must also hasten to add that most regulators are utterly accessible, polite and intelligent people (I mean that sincerely). They fully understand issues; what's more, they are sensitive to the damage being caused by the delay. Unfortunately, they are just completely bound by rigid procedures. Ironically, so many of them have told me, off the record, 'Why did you even come to us? But now that you have, both of us are trapped. You need a quick decision, but I will have to consult half a dozen ministries before I can tell you that your action is not correct, but it is right!'

Now imagine similar incidents playing out with hundreds of millions of ordinary entrepreneurs and citizens, at thousands of government offices, day after day. The waste and delay is so teeth-gnashingly pointless.

There is an even more damaging impact of this 'play safe' attitude. It breeds a lack of confidence, which crawls into one's DNA, lowering ambition, lowering self-worth and creating an inferiority complex. India's policymakers certainly feel that way about China. Try this with an Indian politician or civil servant. Tell him about China's gargantuan strides, show him how hopelessly behind India is on several scores, praise China's vision, boldness, and execution—then watch how defensive the Indian gets. 'My friend, it's easy for you to praise China. Remember, they don't have to deal with parliament. They don't have to face elections every five years. They can simply send tanks into Tiananmen Square and massacre hundreds of protestors. We can't even hang murderers and dacoits—instead, we make them ministers.' When you counter that with the examples of the US, UK, Germany, Israel, Japan and other democracies which have successfully negotiated 'obstacles', yet notched bigger triumphs than China, the defensive Indian policymaker retreats even further into his shell: 'My friend, you are making an odious comparison. These are rich countries. Have you ever gone into India's villages? Have you seen the grinding poverty? Most Indians live on less than a dollar a day.' He then throws his hands up in despair, confident that he has won the argument, confident that India's obvious poverty is a good enough reason to keep it poor!

I have often been asked, 'You are such an India bull, what do you believe is the biggest risk to the India story?' This is one question I have answered without the slightest hesitation. There is only one risk for India, and that's the lack of confidence that India's own leaders have in its abilities and destiny. Every other disability stems from this endemic, ingrained complex that our policymakers suffer from. They peg India lower than an Indian can stretch to. They force India to punch below its weight. They are content being in the upper quartile, never quite believing that India has what it takes to be at the top, not just *near* the top. They delight in small achievements and celebrate the climb to the base camp, secure in their conviction that India cannot scale the peak. They are so incremental and risk averse that they pitch India much lower than what young India is yearning for, aspiring for, and increasingly, is impatient for.

I am not an academician, nor an economist, nor a policymaker—I am a simple editor and entrepreneur. The book I am asking you to read is largely a work of instinct, intuition and experience. Today there is a transformational opportunity for India to do what China has done–lift hundreds of millions of its people out of poverty. Between India and China, the odds are fifty-fifty. It's an amazing race between China's hare and India's tortoise—one that China need not automatically win, and India should not believe it is bound to lose.

Prologue

CHINA AND THE ART OF
ESCAPE VELOCITY

N apoleon once said, 'Let China sleep, for when China wakes up, she will shake the world.'

China has woken up—as predicted, its economic growth has shocked and awed the world. While several factors are responsible for this miracle, the principal thrust has come from capital spending on a scale unknown to mankind. China has built schools, hospitals, roads, railways, airports, bridges, ports, ships, skyscrapers, factories, malls, technology parks and new cities with an ambition that can only be described as spectacular and brutally effective—and I use 'brutal' in a largely positive sense. There is simply no other word that can capture the mind-numbing ambition and scale on which China has marshalled its investment machine There is a saying in the Red Army that quantity has a quality all its own; that quality is now on show for the whole world to gasp at.

China today is investing nearly half its GDP, something that's simply unprecedented. No other economy, at no other time in history, has invested capital on that scale. At the peak of its economic miracle, Japan was investing only 30 per cent plus of its GDP; but China is investing 50 per cent! Roy Ramos of Goldman Sachs paints a graphic picture of China's credit expansion, estimating that in less than ten

1

months in 2009–10 it added 'the equivalent of India's banking industry *twice* over'.

Over 200 years of economic experience tells us that hyper-investment creates a bubble and ends in a dreadful collapse. Even common sense should tell us the same thing. If you spend trillions of dollars in creating mammoth bridges, malls, plants and ports, the immediate impact is nice and invigorating. The economy expands, people earn more, they spend more, factories hum with production, and wealth gets created. But problems begin when ports go half empty (because they are larger than needed) or roads fall short of toll revenue targets (because fewer cars are being driven). It's what economists call 'over-capacity' created by 'hyper-investment'—in common sense terms, it's simply a case of building a palace when all you needed was a five-bedroom dwelling (ask the Emir of Dubai). The trouble begins when you have to keep extra guards, gardeners, electricians and housekeepers to tend to the unused parts of the palace. Sooner or later, you begin to feel the pinch of all that wasteful maintenance of unused rooms and hallways. That's when you cut your losses and abandon unused parts of the palace which eventually fall into ruin; the feel-good bubble gets pricked, and wealth is destroyed.

But China has consistently defied all such prophesies of doom. Too many smart people—for very cogent and rational reasons that are steeped in economic logic and theory—have been predicting that China's bubble has to burst. But it's not happened, and shows no real signs of happening, yet. True, there have been bumps along the road: China has weathered a few storms and some small bubbles have been pricked, but nothing that can be called an epic disaster caused by an epic spree of hyper-investing. Actually, the time has come to acknowledge a truth: either conventional economic theory will have to be rewritten, or China will eventually collapse. The two cannot co-exist. China cannot defy 200 years of economic laws with such ease and facility; either its defiance will end in tragedy, or conventional economic theory has become irrelevant and hit a dead end.

Frankly, it's not too bizarre to believe that China could be scripting a new economic logic. I would venture a 50 per cent wager on China actually trumping conventional theory. Why do I say that? Because by investing on a scale hitherto unknown and untested, China may have defined a new 'escape velocity' of capital spending. Traditional theory says that investment should be 'sustainable', that is, it should be 'matched' by rising consumption. But what if you pump so much capital into your economy—similar to putting extra fuel into a rocket—that you 'escape' the gravitational pull of low thresholds? Especially if the bulk of your capital is spent on infrastructure (roads, railways, schools, hospitals, ports), as against factories which produce toys and televisions? This could be the Chinese masterstroke, the single discontinuity which could defeat 200 years of economic wisdom. Big factories may create over-capacity, but mammoth infrastructure could trigger higher productivity and the ability to create wealth. So it may be a fatal mistake to look at China's investment spree in a single lump of factories-plus-infrastructure. Perhaps big factories create waste, while big infrastructure, especially life-enhancing social assets, empowers people. By rapidly educating your workforce, by brilliantly executing immensely large projects, by importing expertise and dollars in a shrinking world, you could create a 'shower of wealth and productivity' such that consumption 'trickles through' quickly into the bubble. The sheer scale of your activities could end up swelling the tide in which everybody and everything rises together; a new model of 'tidal wave investing' could buoy the whole ocean to a much higher watermark.

China's final and ultimate repudiation of conventional theory may be the apparent neutralizing of democracy. Two hundred years of political economy have taught us that genuine enterprise and innovation take place only when people are free, when individual genius soars unfettered. Look around you—America, Europe, Japan, Israel, South Korea, Brazil, India, Australia, the bulk of the world's wealth resides and flourishes in a democracy. But China is challenging that axiom; once again, it is using ambition and infallible execution to trump democracy. It believes that people will trade wealth for freedom; for nearly three decades, this belief has held good and gathered in strength. So will China drive the final nail into the coffin of history? Can real wealth be shared and sustained if ordinary people live in constant fear and threat? Sooner or later, won't the will to create wealth break down, or a revolution of rising expectations overturn the rule? However much China may protest otherwise, the jury is truly out on this one.

Clearly, China is crafting a new economic wisdom which has stood textbook material on its head. It's spending unbelievable amounts of capital under an 'escape velocity' model as opposed to the 'sustainable investment' theory of conventional economics. It is betting on consumption 'trickling through' as against 'matching investment' under traditional economics. It is using mandated prices of foreign currency, wages and land, as against free market discovered prices, and finally, it is doing all of this in a rigidly controlled quasi-democracy (many wouldn't bother with such semantics, and call it a plain authoritarian state, but that could be missing a few nuances of China's extraordinary story). Will it succeed? As I've said before, I wouldn't wager more than 50 per cent on this happening. But what about the other 50 per cent?

Now look at India: that's a classical textbook case. India's structure is an uncanny prototype of a 'promising' economy. Well above half its GDP—nearly 58 per cent—is consumed by over a billion people (another 11 per cent is consumed by the government), giving it the kind of organic strength that transformed the economies of the US, UK, Germany and Japan. Just its rural economy is made up of 800 million people spending over $425 billion. This when agriculture's share is declining, manufacturing is rising, and services are already more than half the GDP—again, a classically attractive mix (although India needs to have higher manufacturing and even lower agriculture, but the lines are moving in the right direction). Like China, India saves nearly 40 per cent of its GDP, but the bulk comes from households (as against China, where state-owned corporations with somewhat contrived accounting contribute more than households). India's resource consumption has decreased for every incremental dollar of GDP since 1991 (as against China, which was using three times more resources per dollar of GDP than India). India's economy is healthily private, with state-owned corporations accounting for less than a tenth of the output. Its stock exchange was set up in 1875, the oldest in Asia—it is also perhaps the most digitized in the world. At slightly over a trillion dollars, its stock market capitalization is about equal to its GDP—another beautifully balanced economic attribute. Its foreign reserves are over a quarter of a trillion dollars, neither uncomfortably high, nor low. Its bank credit is roughly equal to half its GDP (as opposed to 150 per cent for China), while bad loans are at an astonishingly low 2-3 per cent in a world devastated by toxic financial assets (recall that China's bad debts are precariously estimated at between 30-50 per cent, the large range itself betraying a huge risk of fuzzy estimates). Indian banks had virtually zero exposure to the sub-prime paper that ravaged America and Europe. About 40 per cent of the economy is exposed to global trade (exports and imports)—low enough to escape world crises, yet high enough to remain an open, competitive economy. The Indian rupee largely floats against world currencies, in contrast to China's yuan, which is globally pummelled for being artificially undervalued. The rupee danced in a 25 per cent band after Lehman's collapse, without disrupting anything. A red rag is India's weak government budget and rather high public debt at 80 per cent of GDP—but here again, the highly vulnerable dollar loans are paltry by Asian standards. India is in a very sweet demographic spot, being the youngest country in the world: half a billion Indians are less than twenty-five years old, giving it a unique 'demographic dividend' among peers. Ten of the world's thirty fastest-growing cities are in India; its urbanization rate, at 30 per cent, is accelerating. With 350 million people displaying a reasonable proficiency in English, it's the largest English-using country in the world. Its judicial system is robustly based on English common law. It's a genuine, albeit imperfect, democracy.

To repeat, India is a classical textbook case. If 200 years of economic theory is sound, then India simply must succeed in creating an America- and Japan-like miracle. Continuing to infuse physics into economics, India's growth is like the 'wave theory': closer to the epicentre, the waves are tiny, densely packed, and look really small. But as they spread outward, they pick up cascading strength, making larger and stronger concentric ripples. It starts as an undetectable wobble, but soon becomes a ring of thrusting circles, growing in size and strength with each outward lunge. That could be India's model—dotted with micro changes, the atoms picking up energy from each other, pushing and jostling those around them to move faster, until all the particles begin whizzing around kinetically, pumping up a balloon of spreading prosperity.

So, if China's got the all-new, not-yet-fully-tested model of 'escape velocity' capital investments, India's going with the rather established 'wave theory' of inaudibly permeating growth.

I also stumbled upon a fascinating piece by Nobel Laureate Paul Krugman called *The Myth of Asia's Miracle: A Cautionary Fable*. It was written in the early '90s—therefore, it can be interpreted with the luxury of hindsight. Krugman analysed two earlier economic races: one between the US and Soviet Union ('50s through to the '80s), and another between the US and Japan ('70s and '80s). He cited plenty of popular commentary from those days which read ominously like today's obituaries. By way of example, he quoted Calvin Hooper (1957) who had predicted that 'a collectivist, authoritarian state was inherently better at achieving economic growth than free-market democracies (and) the Soviet economy might outstrip that of the United States by the early 1970s'. Others asserted that 'Japan would overtake the United States in real per capita income by 1985, and total Japanese output would exceed that of the United States by 1998'.

According to Krugman, these predications were bound to fail because they ignored the intangible force-multipliers of innovation, technology and competitive efficiency. He added that similar predictions were also being made then (do remember that 'then' was the early '90s!) about the US and China. 'The World Bank estimates that the Chinese economy is currently about 40 per cent as large as that of the United States. If China can grow at 10 per cent annually, by the year 2010 its economy will be a third larger than ours.' Of course, at that time Krugman concluded that this comparison too could fail. Today we are in 2010, and we know that Krugman was right. Forget about being a third larger, the Chinese economy continues to be less than 40 per cent of the US even today.

Krugman's fallacies have a crucial bearing on who will ultimately breast the tape, China's hare or India's tortoise. Perhaps the answer will not be quite as simple as who is investing more and growing faster today. You will have to put your arms around a few intangibles: Who has superior innovation? Who has more entrepreneurial savvy? Who is grappling with and expanding in intensely competitive conditions?

Finally, there is another, enormously enigmatic factor at work here. It's not about China versus India, but China *and* India versus the rest of the world. During their peak growth decades, countries like Great Britain, the US, Germany, Japan or South Korea added trillions of dollars in income to hundreds of millions of people. But it's for the first time in human history that trillions of dollars are being added to *billions* of people. Now imagine this contrast playing out on the ground—for instance, America and China have roughly the same land mass, but China has thirteen times more people than what America had a century ago when it began its economic miracle. So today's China (or India, for that matter) could be cradling several countries, or sub-economies, at different points of transition; its rich coastal sub-economy is perhaps the equivalent of a Japan or Germany, while parts of the hinterland could be similar to a Brazil, South Korea, Australia or Bangladesh. As soon as the top 150-200 million Chinese hit a Japan- or Germany-like living standard, the growth impulse could be moving to another sub-economy which is mimicking a Brazil or Australia, and finally, perhaps three quarters of a century later, to the 'Bangladesh-like sub-economy'.

Earlier, in 50–150 million people countries like the US, Japan or Germany, many people would get very rich quite rapidly. Now billions more are getting somewhat rich (but not 'very rich') at a reasonable clip (but not 'rapidly'); as soon as one sub-economy becomes rich, the growth wave moves to the next-in-line poorer one. Earlier, the smaller rich economies made a 'one-time transition' over a few decades; but China and India, because of their large numbers, could see 'serial transitions' as one sub-economy after another hits higher living standards. This could make their growth stories far more elastic, with repeated 'rebounds' from 'slowdowns', as one sub-economy plateaus but another begins firing on all cylinders. What's more, this uncharted dynamic could be happening simultaneously across both countries in a contiguous part of Planet Earth. The centre of economic gravity could be shifting from some point in the Pacific Ocean to a dot near Mount Everest.

Earlier, each transforming country had a somewhat predictable economic graph, with a thin two-dimensional line rising along an 'S curve'. Today, China's and India's income curve is more three-dimensional, thickening and flattening out over billions of people in several sub-economies. It is a wave without known coordinates, one that cannot be mapped on any prior experience in human civilization. Will this dynamic create many more happy, better off, better educated and motivated citizens, workers and consumers? Or will it create a larger constituency of relatively deprived, worse off, more dissatisfied people (compared to peers in smaller countries that became wealthy much earlier)? Will a slower accumulation of wealth encourage them to patiently strive for more, or make them impatient and angry? How differently will these billions of 'comparatively lesser mortals' work, play, consume, save and invest versus their historical counterparts?

So what's my wager now? If I put 50 per cent on China, would I put more on India? No, I would still venture no more than a 50 per cent bet on India, because we are at a critical crossroads in economic history. In stock market parlance, China is the 'beta stock': it could give wildly high returns, or it could sink like a stone. India is the 'defensive scrip' which may not leap to the stratosphere, but is also unlikely to fall too much from where it is. If China scales the summit, it will force a rewrite of economic textbooks. If India ascends to the top, it will reinforce the strength of conventional wisdom.

But which way will history turn?

China's spectacular sweep, compared to India's relatively mild rise, could tempt an easy answer, but it would be wise to remember that history unfolds over several decades, perhaps even in fractions of centuries. So it truly may be too early to call this match. Do also remember that China and India were the quickest to bounce back after the Lehman crisis. China's rebound, however, was accompanied by huge debt and deflation, as prices (and therefore demand) were weak. India's turnaround was sturdier, caused by lower debt and modest inflation. So in economic terms, India's nominal GDP grew twice as fast as China's for a few quarters on the trot—the first time that this happened in nearly three decades. This is what economists call a 'lead indicator': in simple language, it could be the one swallow which makes the summer, an early signal of change. But before we spring to quick conclusions again, do remember that China is so far ahead that India's fledgling momentum could easily get snuffed out. The imponderables are far too many; China's ambition and confidence are, unfortunately, equalled by India's poor governance and self-doubt. China could yet re-write economic theory, and India could yet blow its chances.

As with all good games of chance, there's a joker in the pack. What if India were to graft some of China's ambition and determination? Or, what if China were to adopt some of India's democracy? Now the game gets really interesting, because the odds then move, from comparing economic structures, to figuring out which country can do what more easily. Can India fix its governance more easily than China can repair its politics? Whoever gets this one right will win the biggest wager of the twenty-first century.

A BRIC-by-BRIC Shift of Civilizations

India, who? That's largely how the world ignored India's economic liberalization in the early '90s. To be sure, there were some who took early bets on the 'India story'. You could call them gold-diggers, explorers, punters—sheer risk takers who always like to buy some chips when a new casino opens. But big-ticket institutional investors, those who managed unfathomable amounts of western capital, simply chose to stay focused on China, Brazil, Russia, Mexico, the Middle East and East Asia's Tiger Economies. India was too complex a country, its problems too myriad, its policy changes too riddled with half-steps. It was a mysterious, mythical subcontinent buried under the weight of its own anonymity; global risk capital simply chose to ignore this half-asleep, half-stirring tortoise–elephant.

Then one day in 2001, a missive from Goldman Sachs in New York changed the game. It coined an acronym, BRICs; B stood for Brazil, R for Russia, I for India and C for China. Hyphenating India with China as the economic locomotives of the twenty-first century, the report startled the world by suggesting that India could become the world's third largest economy by 2050, ahead of Japan and Germany, just behind the US and China.

At the time this prediction was made, BRICs were less than 15 per cent of G6 economies (the US, Japan, Germany, France, Italy, UK) but held a quarter of the earth's land mass and 40 per cent of its population. Using demographics, capital accumulation and productivity growth, the model projected BRICs would become half of G6 by 2025 and bigger in less than forty years, and this with just some steady policies, without doing any 'miracle economy' cartwheels. BRICs' growth would be most dramatic in the first thirty years; two-thirds would be real growth, while a third would come from a rapid appreciation of currencies against the US dollar, by 300 per cent in fifty years.

By 2050, Goldman Sachs said, only the US and Japan would figure in the six largest economies of the world. While growth for Brazil, Russia and China was expected to slow down significantly, India would be the only country growing at above 3 per cent by 2050. It would also be the only one whose population would grow throughout the fifty years. However, except for Russia, citizens of BRICs would be poorer than individuals in G6 countries—China's $30,000 per capita income would be far lower than America's $80,000 in 2050. India's per capita income would multiply thirty-five times in US dollars, yet it would be lower than any of the other key countries.

While these predictions were startling, they were equally rooted in history. Japan's GDP had grown eight times in the thirty years from 1955 to 1985, while the yen appreciated by 300 per cent against the US dollar. Similarly, Korea's GDP had increased by nine times between 1970 and 2000.

Three years later, in October 2004, the team at Goldman Sachs released a follow-up report. It claimed that 800 million people in BRICs would cross the $3,000 annual income level in about a decade, 'equivalent to the addition of a new America and Europe to the global consumer class'. In two decades, 200 million BRICs citizens, more than the population of Japan, would have annual incomes above $15,000. Within twenty years, China would overtake the US as the world's largest car market (incidentally, a resurgent China achieved this feat for a few months in 2009, over a crisis-ridden America). Over the same time, BRICs could increase their share of global equity markets by over five times, to 17 per cent—close to Europe's share—causing a tectonic shift in world capital markets.

The BRICs idea has now caught a momentum far beyond the catchy corporate acronym popularized by Goldman Sachs. It's almost become a geo-political platform, akin to G6, G20 and G77. The foreign ministers of BRICs met for a political summit at Yekaterinburg in Russia, the city in which Tsar Nicholas II was executed. They promptly crafted an agenda to 'promote energy and food security, fight terrorism and reform global political and financial bodies'. The ministers were fully aware of their eco-political weight. China and India are the two fastest growing economies. Russia is the world's second largest oil producer, while China is the second biggest consumer. Other items on the 'economic might' list are virtually endless, inspiring hushed suggestions about 'replacing the US dollar as the world's reserve currency'. While that may be an unrealistic ambition at this stage, the very fact that it is even being contemplated speaks volumes about the burgeoning clout of BRICs.

The post-Lehman recession caused a swifter shift of economic power away from the West. Writing towards the end of 2009, Jim O'Neill (the principal author of BRICs) said, 'We often felt that the durability of the BRICs concept needed to be tested through an economic shock. Indeed, these days we think that the combined GDP of the BRICs might exceed that of the G7 countries by 2027, about ten years earlier than we initially believed.'

Jim O'Neill has always been particularly excited about India's prospects: 'With the BRICs dream, India has the greatest potential of the four. We estimate that by 2050, India's GDP could be $25 trillion, fifty times bigger than it is today. (But) India is the lowest of the BRICs; this means that India has the biggest potential but also the most to deliver.'

What's fascinating in the BRICs study is the shift of civilizations embedded in all the mathematics. Both China and India were giants in the seventeenth and eighteeenth centuries; according to economic historian Angus Maddison, together they accounted for over 50 per cent of world GDP in 1600 (China had 28 per cent, and India 23 per cent). But two hundred years of colonial domination shrunk their economies and political space on the globe. Over the last few decades, both countries are beginning to rear again, the initial swell of a giant tidal wave that made its last crest in 1770.

Colonial Twins by the Bend in the River

On 31 December 1600, a group of London businessmen banded together to create a quaintly named company, Governor and Company of Merchants of London Trading into the East Indies. A royal charter gave it all privileges of trading in that part of Asia. Little did these gentlemen realize that their British East India Company (known better under this popular shorthand) would unleash a dynamic whose reverberations would ripple across the world 300 years later. The Company was the common womb from which two stepchildren, British India and colonial China, sprang to become non-identical Asian twins.

The Company smacked into a dilemma as it began trading with China and India. There were few buyers for British broadcloth and other European goods in Asia, but large buyers in Europe for tea, silk and porcelain from the East. The Company soon realized that it needed political power to oust Portuguese competitors and control the terms of trade with native Indians. In China, it ran into another problem; Chinese traders were unwilling to sell unless they were paid in silver. British merchants had to move with devil's speed to plug this one-sided drain of gold and silver. They devised an elaborately devious plot to trade opium at auction in Calcutta, mix it with tobacco, smuggle it across the seas into China, and finally use these illicit earnings to pay for Chinese exotica.

Since opium imports were banned in China, Emperor Daoguang sent a polite but firm protest to Queen Victoria. Unfortunately, the letter was whisked midway and it never reached the queen; history may have been different if an informed queen had clamped down on the British East India Company's illegal intentions. In 1839, after a decade of aborted anti-opium campaigns, the Chinese monarch ran out of patience. He confiscated and destroyed 20,000 chests of ill-gotten opium and detained an entire foreign community. The events escalated into the world's first drug war, known as the First Opium War (1839–42), between the Qing dynasty and the British East India Company. The Chinese were pummelled into submission and forced to sign the first of many unequal treaties which rankle ordinary citizens to this day. The 1842 Treaty of Nanjing granted an indemnity of 21 million dollars to the Company and opened the ports of Canton, Amoy, Foochow, Ningpo and Shanghai to opium imports. Tariff was brought down to 5 per cent and British nationals were granted 'extraterritoriality'; earlier, the 'brutal violence and beastly intemperance' of British sailors would attract stiff Chinese penalties, but now Chinese laws were not applicable on foreign nationals who could not be taxed, nor arrested, nor tried by Chinese authorities. Even today, China calls the ensuing century full of 'national humiliations'.

France, Russia and the United States jumped in to rain more blows on a down and out country. All of them forced China to sign similarly unequal treaties at Tianjin in 1858, giving rights to new 'treaty ports', access to the hinterland and lower tariffs. The opening of the Suez Canal in 1869 allowed America to ship military assistance to Japan via the shortened route, emboldening Japan to rout China in the 1895 war. The Sino–Japanese treaty went beyond trade, allowing foreigners to freely set up industries in China. Within two years, thirty cotton and silk mills had sprung up in several provinces. The colonial powers 'carved up the Chinese melon' with undisguised relish; the Russians got Port Arthur, the British got the New Territories around Hong Kong, the Germans got Shantung, and the Americans pushed strenuously for an 'Open Door Policy' in 1899.

Ultimately, the burden of humiliations became too heavy to carry for the Qing rulers; led by Sun Yat-sen, the Chinese Revolution of 1911 put paid to the monarchy.

Surprisingly, the British East India Company authored an utterly different edition of colonial rule in India. Perhaps the two situations were not comparable to begin with. In China, one dynasty was ruling over the entire country, and several colonial powers vied to carve the 'single' melon on offer. India's situation was a mirror image of this: Great Britain was the single colonial power, but India was carved up into hundreds of intrigue-ridden, weak 'kingdoms'. It was a lush but unguarded orchard of ripe 'cherries', easy to sweep away into a tidy political basket.

Strangely, India and China are today known by a number of animal analogies—hare, dragon and panda for China, and tortoise, elephant and peacock for India. But back then, both were known as differently sized fruit. The bend in the river occurred at this watershed moment in their histories, flinging Indian cherries and the Chinese melon along totally different trajectories.

The British East India Company set up its first trading post at Surat on India's west coast in the early seventeenth century. While its primary export of British broadcloth did not find eager buyers in India, the reverse trade—of Indian goods being sold in Great Britain— was extremely lucrative. Fortuitously for the British, India's mighty Mughals began declining after Emperor Aurangzeb's death in 1707.

Over the next century, the loose federation of tiny monarchies built by the Mughals crumbled into a fractious bunch of local 'kingdoms'. The Company seized this opportunity to wield political power and control the terms of trade with native Indians. Its first conquest was in Bengal, on India's east coast. Egged on by French colonialists, Siraj-ud-Daula, the nawab of Bengal, foolishly attacked Fort William, the British settlement in Calcutta. His misadventure collided against Robert Clive's cunning political management. Clive, a most mercurial Company official, lured Mir Jafar to defect from Siraj's camp at the Battle of Plassey in 1757 (incidentally, 'Mir Jafar' has become a byword for 'back-stabber' in several Indian languages). Robert Clive defeated Siraj and planted Mir Jafar as the puppet ruler of Bengal.

Clive had plucked the first 'cherry', installing himself as the Governor of Bengal. Ironically, more than two-thirds of Clive's 2,900-strong troops at Plassey were native Indians, known as 'sepoys' of the British East India Company. He wrote to his directors in London: 'I can assert with some degree of confidence that this rich and flourishing kingdom may be totally subdued by so small a force as two thousand Europeans . . . (The Indians are) indolent, luxurious, ignorant and cowardly beyond conception . . . (They) attempt everything by treachery rather than force.'

A triumphant Company extracted the Treaty of Allahabad from the weak Mughal emperor, gaining administrative control over Bengal, Bihar and Orissa. It won the right to earn over 2 million sterling every year by taxing over 20 million people. The Company had tasted blood; it realized that the 'business of government' was far more lucrative than trading in exotic goods. Robert Clive went on an 'unrepentant plunder of Bengal', leading to miserable casualties (10 million people) in the 1770 famine.

Robert Clive was replaced by the far more moderate Warren Hastings, who admired Indian culture and was fluent in Persian and Hindi. He set up the institution of 'District Collector', an official who exercised a mixture of judicial and executive powers (this job survives even today, and is among the most coveted by young, educated Indians). This was a benign period during which a hybrid society emerged, especially in Bengal. For instance, James Skinner was the offspring of an inter-marriage between a Scotsman and a Rajput princess. He had at least seven wives and almost eighty children, and raised two cavalry regiments, 1st Skinner's Horse and 3rd Skinner's Horse, and founded St James' Church. A thousand miles across in South India, Colonel Kirkpatrick married Khair-un-Nissa, the daughter of a court noble—he dyed his beard and behaved like a Muslim nobleman.

As the British East India Company plucked more 'cherries', annexing territories and small princely states, English became the language of power. In 1774, English replaced Persian as the official language of the Supreme Court. Yet it was confined to the occupying British elite and a few English schools in Calcutta, Bombay and Madras. A separate legal system was created, confirmed by the case of the Indian Chief (1800): wherever Europeans settled or created factories, those settlements became an 'imaginative geography' governed by laws made by the British Crown and the East India Company.

Back in London, a brilliant young English lawyer, Thomas Babington Macaulay, stood before his parliament in 1833. He made an impassioned appeal, saying the role of British colonizers was to 'give good government to a people to whom we cannot give a free government'. Later that year he set sail to India, charged with two gigantic tasks: of codifying the law and revamping the educational system. History may have taken an entirely different course if Macaulay had set sail to China with the same missionary zeal, but in China, the colonizers were happy to protect their watering holes, imbued by no such spirit to 'civilize' a war-torn country.

Macaulay created a new charter for the British East India Company which completely transformed India's legal edifice. An all-India legislative council replaced regional legislatures. Law-making powers were taken away from the provincial governments in Bengal, Bombay and Madras Presidencies. One set of laws and courts were established for everybody. In his other task, Macaulay's famous Minute on Education (1835) brought English out of its imperial closet; with one stroke of his powerful pen, he made English the official language of India and the medium of instruction in all educational institutions. His objective was to create 'interpreters between us and the millions whom we govern, a class of persons, Indian in blood and colour, but English in taste, in opinions, in morals and intellect'. By 1882, over 60 per cent of the primary schools were teaching the Queen's language. English was called the 'milk of tigress', creating a new energy and opportunity for the natives. Several publications sprung to fill the need of a swelling readership, the *Englishman*, the *Friend of India*, the *Asiatic Mirror*, the *Calcutta Advertiser*, the *Bengal Gazette*, and the *Madras Courier*, among others. At the time of Independence in 1947, over 6 million people in India knew English.

But the First War of Independence in 1857 (which British historians call a 'sepoy', or soldier, mutiny) was a bloody scar of history that altered the character of the British Raj . On 2 August 1858, the British parliament proclaimed Queen Victoria as India's ruling monarch; 'in conceptual terms, the British who had started their rule as "outsiders" became "insiders"'. They now strengthened what was called the steel frame of the British Indian Empire: the Indian civil service (ICS), the police and the army.

Earlier, 'fifty to sixty extended (British) families contributed the vast majority of civil servants who governed India'. For instance, John Cotton was the sixth generation in an unbroken male line to join the ICS. But soon the rules were changed to introduce a competitive entrance examination in London. Satyendranath Tagore (elder brother of Nobel Laureate Rabindranath Tagore) became the first Indian to pass the exam in 1863. By 1871, three other Indians had qualified, but all of them had to go to London to take the exam. After nearly half a century of struggle, Great Britain conceded a separate local recruitment exam in Allahabad in February 1922. By 1941, there were more Indians than Europeans among the ranks of ICS officers. The British Indian army, dominated by men recruited from Punjab, Nepal and North-West Frontier Provinces, cloned several traditions of the parent country. Clubs and gymkhanas created an aura of British social etiquette for India's English-speaking upper classes.

The dining table replaced the floor in middle-class homes; people began to use spoons, knives and forks, instead of hands, to pick food from plates. European food habits were voraciously localized, for example, English pork chops were still grilled, but marinated in spices and chillies. Soups and salads became part of an Indian menu— mulligatawny soup, for instance, comes from the Tamil words 'malagu tunni', meaning 'pepper water', or a western version of 'rasam'. Cutlets, cakes, sausages, croquettes, puddings, jams and biscuits became as Indian as curry and rice. Football, tennis and cricket became a rage with sporty locals.

It was perhaps an accidental symmetry, but Mahatma Gandhi took charge of India's civil disobedience movement at around the same time that Sun Yat-sen led the Chinese Revolution in 1911. The bend in the river became a hairpin turn at this moment in history: while China got trapped in merciless strife among Chiang Kai-shek's nationalists, Mao Zedong's communists and Japanese invaders, India's political movement nudged it ever closer to a Westminster-style democracy.

As the self-rule ideal gathered momentum in India, Gandhi recast the Congress into a 'parallel government like' structure (in another instance of truth being stranger than fiction, Gandhi's Indian National Congress was set up in 1885 by an Englishman, Allan Octavian Hume; little did Hume know that his organization would lead the movement to end British rule in India). The central working committee began to function like the de facto 'national cabinet', and provincial Congress committees were reorganized along linguistic lines. The first attempt at setting up an Indian Constitution was the Nehru Report of 1928 for Dominion rule. It spoke of common electorates with seats reserved for religious minorities. The people were given a set of fundamental rights. The British ignored the proposals, but these came in handy for the Congress when it agreed to contest elections under the Government of India Act of 1935. The country had its first brush with widespread electoral democracy.

Over the Himalayas, an anguished students' movement erupted against China's weak response to the Treaty of Versailles and the end of the First World War in 1919. Called the May Fourth Movement, it turned into a nationalist agitation. Ultimately, the Chinese Civil War broke out in 1927 between the Nationalist party and the Communist party. Mao Zedong orchestrated the Long March, a military revolt against Chiang Kai-shek's Kuomintang Nationalists. The Japanese army jumped into this cauldron in 1937; the second Sino–Japanese War lasted until the end of the Second World War in 1945. Mao Zedong led a fierce guerrilla resistance to the Japanese invasion. But the civil war between Mao's and Chiang's forces continued even after Japan had been ousted from the mainland. Ultimately, in 1949, Chiang's Kuomintang was defeated; Chiang fled to modern Taiwan, politically separating it from mainland China. (Later, in 1954, Mao planned to invade and liberate Taiwan. But the Soviets gave half-hearted support, and America threatened to use nuclear weapons against Mao's forces; eventually, Mao abandoned the military adventure.)

Finally, China's and India's destinies converged, for a fleeting moment in history, in the late 1940s. The British parliament passed the Indian Independence Act, 1947, and royal assent was granted to free India from colonial rule on 15 August 1947. Barely over two years later, on 1 October 1949, Mao founded the People's Republic of China at a massive rally in Beijing.

History's tangential moment was all too brief. China became a totalitarian state. India became a parliamentary democracy. Once again, these ancient civilizations—the non identical twins—were flung irretrievably apart. The British would often pompously describe their rule as one which 'civilized' India; it has to be admitted that they 'adopted' India as a subordinate state, transferring several institutional strengths. On the other hand, China's colonial history was far more turbulent under several rapacious rulers, without a similar 'institutional osmosis'. But could this also explain China's stout confidence and India's self-doubt? Did centuries of wars and strife make China's leaders tougher, more martial, bigger risk-takers? As against this, have the 'civilizing' niceties of British domination made India's leaders more timid and less confident? As the British themselves would say, it's worth a thought, old chap!

Today, in the twenty-first century, China and India are locked in a love–hate embrace. Actually, a bit more hate than love. Half a century ago, they fought a bruising war over disputed land. China claims nearly 150,000 sq. km as land expropriated by British rulers (1914) and annexed to then British-ruled India. In 1962, an under-prepared Indian army was soundly thrashed in the war, giving Indians an inferiority complex that the country is yet to recover from. Both the countries are also deeply suspicious about each other. India's first prime minister, Jawaharlal Nehru, who presided over the disastrous war, once told his ambassador, 'It is difficult to know what is in their mind. They smile while saying the most callous and ruthless things. Mao told me with a smile that he was not afraid of an atomic war.'

China tested a nuclear weapon in October 1964. India followed a decade later with its own nuclear implosion in 1974. China has the world's largest standing army; India trails America with the third largest. China is wary of India, like a stronger and richer sibling usually is—it knows that India is perhaps the only country that can challenge the emerging US–China superpower duopoly, converting it into a 'cluttered' three-way equation by 2050. China is the fastest growing, and India the second fastest growing economy in the world. Trade between the two is bounding up at nearly $60 billion every year. Both will soon have nearly 1.5 billion people each. But China is growing rapidly older, while India will remain young for several more decades. Both compete for America's attention: while China evokes fear, India seems to get the smiles.

Stephen Cohen, a veteran of China–India dynamics, has the most perceptive commentary on offer. According to him, 'relations are greatly affected by China's generally dismissive views of India'. China regards India as a soft power which can be made to fall in line, if not totally dominated. China is convinced that 'its civilization is older and greater than India's ... With its modest accomplishments, (India) should behave in a suitably modest fashion; Indian assertiveness, the Chinese believe, does not seem to be justified, given New Delhi's feeble economic and strategic record.' Indians respond to this with 'intrigue and fright'. The perceptions at both ends are 'mired in stereotypes', and awareness about each other is 'abysmal'. Many Indians also suffer from a siege mentality, believing that China is out to encircle it by building alliances with Pakistan and Nepal.

This mutual suspicion has survived over generations. Even as the Chinese hare has taken off on steroids, building a huge lead, the Indian tortoise has been lumbering behind, only recently building some muscle into its legs. It's a fable that should be reinvented and retold in the twenty-first century.

The Hare and the Tortoise: A Twenty-first Century Fable

In this twenty-first-century version of the fable, both the hare and the tortoise were at the starting line in 1978. The hare took off, bounding forward on shots of adrenaline. But the tortoise was forced to stay put at the starting line. For thirteen years, the hare sped forward, on shot after shot of steroids, even as the tortoise stayed chained. Eventually the chained tortoise was cut loose in 1991, and he took a slow, lumbering step forward. At that point in time, the hare was talking to the wind, the drug coursing through his blood. The tortoise started moving faster too, but alas, he was a tortoise, and his 'speed' was laughed at. Suddenly, Lehman-lightning struck in 2008. The hare, flying high, was struck harder; he fell to the ground with a loud thump. His adrenaline-pumped body had weakened after thirty years of a relentless chase. He was getting old, very old. The lightning struck the tortoise too, but his softer underbelly cushioned the fall. The tortoise picked himself up quickly, and began to move faster. By a strange quirk of time, he was getting younger. The hare, on the other hand, refused to pull himself up until he was given another shot. He was now getting old really fast. The doctor was hesitant, having seen the hare's damaged innards and advancing years. But the hare was adamant; he ultimately got his way, and began to fly again. He bounded from one air pocket to another, yet kept on going. The tortoise was having a surprisingly smooth, and quicker, ride. He continued to get younger. The finish line was visible on the far horizon.

Who made it across first? Did the air pockets abate? Did the hare's steroid-affected, ageing body recover its earlier strength? Or did the youthful tortoise beat the hare, as in the original fable?

China has already given an answer. Reacting to the hare and tortoise comparison, a Chinese official laughed it off. 'In the fable, the tortoise wins only because the hare went to sleep. We will ensure that this hare never does that, so the tortoise can forget about victory.'

No Indian official has reacted, perhaps waiting for the matter to be debated in its fractious parliament before it can draft its response.

And before all of us get carried away by a fable (even one that has enthralled children for decades), we must remember that the hare we are talking about is a $5 trillion gorilla, while the tortoise is a $1.50 trillion cub. Can the slow tortoise beat an ambitious and agile hare? The odds are difficult, but sometimes, miracles do happen. Of course, the tortoise will have to huff and puff a lot harder for the miracle of the fable to occur in reality.

One

THE RACE BEGINS

The Pillars of a Post-Lehman World

September can be called the month of Armageddon in the twenty-first century. Two terrorist-controlled aircraft crashed into New York's twin towers on 11 September 2001. American stock exchanges shut for business for four days, reeling under the impact of a strike whose geopolitical severity perhaps matched that of the Second World War sixty years ago. Going against the panic, Indian stock exchanges opened for trade on 12 September, the very next day.

Seven years later, a commercial Armageddon hit the world when Lehman Brothers collapsed on 15 September 2008. Nine Fifteen, when the global financial system seized up in fright. As markets plummeted, regulators across America, Britain, France, Germany, Switzerland, Australia, Taiwan, South Korea, Canada—and even Ireland, Greece and Indonesia—banned short-selling in stocks. Once again, India went against the panic, allowing investors to short. It wasn't as if India's stock markets were too small to matter at this stage, doing over $15 billion in daily trading. China, whose stock markets had not even introduced the concept until then, chose to go ahead with a trial experiment in short-selling just a month later.

Why have I compared two earth-shaking world events with relatively minor economic actions in India and China? It's not as if these countries were not affected by the global crises. Of course they were. But they were able to get on with it, take the crises in their stride without having to shut shop. In fact, there are dozens of other markers which prove that China and India are crafting unique—to use a more fashionable phrase, 'de-coupled'—economic destinies in the twenty-first century. For instance, almost every large economy in the world contracted after Lehman's crash. World GDP, running fulsome at $64 trillion until Nine Fifteen, fell by a shocking $3 trillion in barely twelve months. But China and India *added* nearly half a trillion dollars to their combined GDP in this very traumatic period, kindling the hope that these two Asian giants could become the shock absorbers of a distraught globe.

President Barack Obama, styled as America's first Asia Pacific president, acknowledged the new reality when he met the leaders of China and India in the same week in November 2009. He set the pecking order by first visiting President Hu Jintao in Beijing; but within five days, he had deftly equalized any perceived imbalance when Prime Minister Manmohan Singh became his first visiting head of state. The Indian prime minister virtually inaugurated Thanksgiving week festivities in Washington, adding a tinge of extra warmth. India's economic prowess and democracy were feted at every opportunity, culminating in a 400-guest celebrity ball on the lawns of the White House. As against this, the Beijing trip was uncomfortably thin on atmospherics. The usual Obama 'rock star' ebullience was missing; in fact, an inordinate amount of restraint, whether voluntary or imposed by his hosts, was visible. 'No hoops with Chinese basketball stars, no mingling with the Chinese people, and no roundtables with NGO leaders or activists,' rued Elizabeth Economy of the Council on Foreign Relations. Questions were not permitted at his joint press conference with President Hu. A top editor of *Southern Weekend* was demoted for an Obama interview which was more candid than authorized. China also refused to give way on the yuan, forcing America to delete the words 'exchange rates based on the economy'. China's $800 billion debt seemed to have pushed America on the back foot, putting the meeting 'at eye level' (a euphemism for China having got the better of the engagement). Some of his harshest critics called Barack Obama the 'pied piper of American retreat in the world'.

Clearly, the Indian visit had the laid-back celebratory veneer of an equity partnership, not the lean-forward tension of an indebted person talking to his lender. India's economist prime minister further buoyed Uncle Sam's spirits by saying America's economic woes were 'temporary', and the dollar would remain the world's reserve currency. The latest Pew survey had also thrown up a surprising affinity between the two countries: 76 per cent of Indians (higher than Israel's 71 per cent) now look favourably at America, up from 66 per cent in 2008. As against this, the mood in China was souring a bit. The bestseller *China Is Not Happy* chafes at an increasing overdependence on the US. Even President Obama's China visit seemed like a taut creditor–debtor engagement, in which the lender (China) was not-too-subtly extracting a price for bailing out the borrower (America) with an $800 billion lifeline.

It's quite usual for the world to be in awe of China's stupendous economic expansion, thought to be even stronger than the fabled American growth decades of 1820–70. Which country has grown at 9 per cent every year for thirty years? Which country has increased its per capita income by eleven times in such a short period, pulling 400 million people out of abysmal poverty? Which country holds the largest horde of cold cash, a full $2.5 trillion? Which country spends $1 billion every day to develop world-class infrastructure? Which country can spend $1 trillion to add the equivalent of 100 Channel Tunnels in five years? Which country consumes half the world's cement, a third of its steel, and a quarter of its aluminum? Which country can take only a decade to build Pudong in rice paddies and marshlands outside Shanghai (a suburb that is eight times the size of London's Canary Wharf and almost equal to Chicago's sprawl)? Which country runs the fastest train in the world covering a 700-mile journey in five hours (by comparison, America's Amtrak takes eighteen hours to cover the same distance between New York and Chicago)? Which country could soon have more Starbucks than America? Which country got Steven Spielberg to choreograph the opening ceremony of the Beijing Olympics in 2008, a coming out party to the world? Which country bought more cars and light trucks than America in 2009? And also bought 185 million units of refrigerators, washing machines, air-conditioners and other kitchen appliances, a third more than America? Which country can add 105 GW of power in one year, equal to the entire generating capacity of a large country like India? Which country is the world's largest producer of power from renewable energy? Which country could build fifty new nuclear reactors by 2020, while the rest of the world adds only fifteen? Which country produces 95 per cent of rare-earth metals like yttrium and lanthanum that are needed for everything from iPods to precision-guided weaponry? And which country has the gumption to further its 'resource nationalism' by insisting that producers who want to use these rare metals must set up plants in China? Clearly, all the encomiums that are heaped on China's economic miracle are more than richly deserved.

In the post-Lehman crisis too, China surprised everybody by bouncing back quickly. As growth fell from the red-hot 13 per cent to single digits, some people had begun to worry if China would be able to hold on. 20 million people were laid off in Guangdong; elsewhere too, social unrest caused by widespread job losses was becoming inflammable. But much to everybody's relief, China bounced back from 6 per cent, and started accelerating again. Yet a curious concern was evident in this relief. Earlier, every incredible Chinese achievement would be greeted with whoops of joy and unbridled admiration. This time, the whoops were muted by words of caution, even outright apprehension. In late 2009, *Newsweek* carried a show-stopping cover, 'Everything You Know about China Is Wrong', with an upside down portrait of Mao.

Inside, the story exploded six 'myths' about China's economy. 'China has become an economy driven almost entirely by state investment, which in the first half of 2009 accounted for 88 per cent of GDP growth—a share for which it is hard to find any parallel, in any country, at any time,' *Newsweek* noted. But far from being brilliant economic managers, Chinese leaders could be wasting the massive stimulus package on 'bridge to nowhere' projects. Over 95 per cent of the stimulus capital had been cornered by state-owned companies. China's public debt, once negligible, could have gone up to 70 per cent of GDP (if one correctly adds $1.5 trillion in off-balance-sheet debt owed by city and provincial governments). Contrary to popular belief, capitalism was not flourishing, as over 2 million private enterprises were forced to shut shop by a predatory state which starved them of credit, even as it favoured its own enterprises with generous, often undeserved, 3 per cent loans. The Chinese state continued to own two-thirds of all fixed assets like telecommunication lines, power plants, and real estate. The article accused Beijing of 'meddling' with the market by encouraging companies to renege on derivative contracts with western banks, or arresting the managers of an Australian mining company after it 'jilted' a merger with a local outfit. 'Entrepreneurs don't feel safe; there are many examples of the government taking over private businesses or changing the legal landscape, so they can take their profits as quickly as they can,' the article quoted Ming Huang, a finance professor at Cornell University. It should not come as any surprise that the average size of a private business in China has been 'flat-lined' at thirty employees for nearly two decades now.

The six-page *Newsweek* centrespread went on to add that China's export success was overhyped, since it virtually imports all the inputs, and adds very little value before exporting them; for example, it imports over $142 of components for an iPod which it eventually wholesales at $150 from its assembly plants, adding only $7.50 of value to that 'exported' piece. The article debunked the myth that Chinese companies will rule the world, since they have yet to display any real innovation or branding ability. It warned about an ideological rupture within the Communist party, and ended the sobering article with the potentially crippling environmental threat facing China.

A new Chinese phrase was catching currency: *guojin mintui*, meaning 'the state advances and private sector retreats'. It captured the popular anger simmering against the second wave of nationalization triggered by the post-Lehman collapse. Buoyed by large chunks of stimulus cash and excessively cheap credit, state-owned companies had turned predatory, forcing private businesses to sell out. Rizhao, the largest private steel company, was coerced into parting with majority equity to Shandong Iron and Steel. COFCO extracted a 20 per cent stake in Mengniu Dairy. Over 1500 private coal mines in Shanxi were ordered shut, or sold at very low prices to state companies. (Lian Zuqian's predicament created a splash in Chinese media. He had invested $37 million in buying mines in Linfen, but was being instructed to sell them for less than $16 million.)

The biggest fear was that China could be blowing up a US-like property bubble with consequences spookily similar to the collapse that ravaged America and the world (although China believers argue that most property purchases are being financed by savings, not credit; as against 56 per cent in America, only 17 per cent of total bank loans have gone to property buyers and developers, so the Chinese bubble could be far less dangerous). But the problem in China was a bit more tangled—unlike America's culprit banks and mortgage sellers, it was the government and its companies in China that were flipping assets amongst themselves at unreal prices to pump-prime the bubble. For instance, Tianjin had already built a quarter century's requirement of prime office space. State companies were buying and selling office towers in Beijing for $400 per square foot, despite there being no tenants. Ninety-nine per cent of South China Mall, the second largest in the world, was empty.

Very credible voices were rising, warning about the crimps in China's economy. Morgan Stanley's chief economist and once diehard China optimist, Stephen Roach, cautioned that China's leaders may have become 'overly complacent', which could make its miracle 'surprisingly fleeting'. Elsewhere, it was highlighted that the share of household income and consumption had fallen sixteen and eleven percentage points of GDP over the last decade. Geng Xiao of Brookings Institution lamented that China's asset price inflation and volatility may be 'extremely difficult to resolve'. Criticizing China's weak-yuan policy, Dominique Strauss-Kahn, the IMF chief, warned: 'If you have wrong prices, you make wrong decisions, especially concerning investment in the long run.' Nobel laureate Paul Krugman urged 'China's government to reconsider its stubbornness (in keeping a cheap yuan). Otherwise, the very mild protectionism it is currently complaining about will be the start of something much bigger (in ugly trade wars).' But Premier Wen Jiabao was unmoved, saying China will 'absolutely not yield' to calls for strengthening the yuan. America retaliated by virtually threatening to label China a 'currency manipulator'; this finally softened Beijing a bit, with its central bank chief admitting that pegging the yuan to the dollar was a crisis measure that would be withdrawn 'sooner or later'. But hopes of a quick or significant revaluation were belied.

The much respected Austrian economist, Jim Walker, minced no words at all when he said that 'the quality of China's growth in the last year is probably among the lowest in history—excess capacity being built on excess capacity—but no one cares'. For example, China could have added 60 million tons of steel capacity in 2009, when over 150 million tons was unutilized in the previous year. Just its excess cement capacity is thought to be greater than the combined consumption of the US, Japan and India. The country is using only 70 per cent of its available wind power, but continues to set up new turbines at a furious pace. (China's defenders argue that the capital stock per person in China is only 5 per cent of what it is in the US and Japan, so a temporary overcapacity is fine since China has plenty of headroom to grow further.) According to Minxin Pei, reckless Chinese bank lending has created a 'potential tidal wave of future non-performing loans'. James Chanos, the hedge fund whiz who had foretold the Enron bust, warned that China's hyper-stimulated economy was on a 'treadmill to hell; they can't afford to get off this heroin of property development, it's the only thing that keeps the economic growth numbers going'. The numbers were a bit chilling: China's total debt (government plus private) had climbed to 160 per cent of GDP. At this rate it could touch 200 per cent by 2011, which would be menacingly close to the level from which Japan fell off the precipice in 1991.

Northwestern University's Victor Shih told *Forbes* that China's loan binge is 'a Ponzi scheme whose head is the central bank'. Andy Xie called it a 'pure debt game much worse than previous ones'. The article concluded that 'assuming China's reckoning does arrive some day, it's impossible to say whether it might presage Japan-style deflation, Russian-style hyperinflation or American-style stagnation'.

Something counter-intuitive was happening here. And something counter-intuitive was happening with India too.

Everybody expected India's growth to halve from the 9 per cent notched up in the pre-Lehman days. But India surprised the world by turning around at the 'China watermark' of 6 per cent and gradually accelerating from there. For the very first time in recent history, India had out-performed China by bouncing back after a much shorter episode of pain compared to what its largest neighbour had to suffer. China had fallen from 13 to 6 per cent before recovering while India had fallen by less than half that. China's stock markets were down nearly 50 per cent from their peak; India's had fallen only 25 per cent. What's more, India's nominal GDP had grown twice as fast as China's for a few quarters in a row, even though its banks were lending at half the pace of China's banks. To Jim Walker, this proved that 'India is generating a much larger bang for each loan-growth buck than China'. UBS, the Swiss investment banking firm, called this 'a golden period' for India's economy. For Stephen Roach, a world 'fixated on China' could be missing India's 'dirty little secret ... India has long had a much better micro story than China: a large population of world-class companies, a well-educated and IT-competent workforce, relatively sound financial markets and banks, a well-entrenched rule of law, and democracy'. On the other hand, the *Economist* pointed out how 'arduous' it was for foreign companies to access China's domestic market: 'Publishing, telecommunications, oil exploration, marketing, pharmaceuticals, banking and insurance all remain either fiercely protected or off-limits to foreigners altogether, (who) complain about subsidized competition, restricted access, conflicting regulations, a lack of protection for intellectual property and opaque and arbitrary bureaucracy.' Nineteen American trade groups and companies wrote to Cabinet members in Washington, slamming 'systematic efforts by China to develop policies that build their domestic enterprises at the expense of US firms and US intellectual property'. The American commerce secretary concurred that US companies were 'significantly disadvantaged' in bidding for $85 billion of Chinese government contracts.

Legatum Institute is a London-based think tank that publishes a Prosperity Index of 104 countries, covering 90 per cent of the world's population. It's a young index, started in 2007. In the first two years, the focus was on straight economic variables. Not surprisingly, China outflanked India by a wide margin. But in 2009, the Prosperity Index expanded the list to seventy-nine variables to go beyond the monotheism of a country's GDP. Besides parameters like economic fundamentals and entrepreneurship, it included softer issues like personal freedom and trust. India leapt to the forty-fifth slot, way above China's seventy-fifth. While China continued to outbid India on major economic variables, including health, education and innovation,

India more than made up on the intangibles. India was thirty-sixth on 'domestic institutional maturity' to China's 100th. In 'governance', India clocked in at forty-first to China's ninety-third. In 'personal freedom', India notched up forty-seventh to China's ninety-first And in 'social capital', which measured the trust and support among various communities, India came in at a spectacular fifth to China's seventieth. This one was truly surprising. China is a largely homogenous society, while India is a cauldron of ethnic and religious plurality. Was India's democracy calming its people, and China's opaque politics breeding mistrust? By trumping India on economic parameters, China clearly seemed more pro-business, while India appeared to be giving a much better deal to people. What would happen if India became more business-friendly, in addition to running a European-style welfare state?

India's ability to rival China's economic miracle was first recognized in the pioneering BRICs model developed by Goldman Sachs in 2001. The model predicted that China would overtake the US in a few decades to become the world's largest economy. By 2050, India would become the world's third largest economy, overtaking Japan, and trailing only China and the US. More importantly, India was seen to have 'the potential to show the fastest growth over the next thirty and fifty years. While growth in the G6, Brazil, Russia and China is expected to slow significantly over the next fifty years, India's growth rate remains above 5 per cent throughout the period.' Five years after the initial study, Jim O'Neill, the lead author of the BRICs document, claimed that 'within the BRICs story, India has the best long-term growth potential, not least due to its fantastic labour force dynamics'.

A follow-up study to the original BRICs report was published in January 2007. It upped India's rank on the sweepstakes. Expansively titled 'India's Rising Growth Potential', the study concluded that the Indian economy can 'sustain growth rates of 8 per cent until 2020, significantly higher than the 5.7 per cent that we projected in our original BRICs paper ... The implications of this are that India will overtake the G6 economies faster than envisaged in our earlier BRICs research. India's GDP (in US dollar terms) will surpass that of the US before 2050, making it the world's second-largest economy. From 2007 to 2020, India's GDP per capita in US dollar terms will quadruple (one-third higher than the original BRICs projection). Indians will also consume about five times more cars (up from 3.5 times) and three times more crude oil (up from 2.3 times).'

This was truly counter-intuitive. Somehow, the world had got used to the fact that India would be far more modest and restrained, compared to China's bristling aggression. And this assessment was justified, as India had been taking baby steps to change its economic architecture, long dominated by state control and socialist ideology. Inevitably then, every Indian achievement in the past would create some excitement, but much more disappointment. The continuing refrain would be that India is a reluctant reformer: that it grudges privatization, is suspicious of a free market, and does everything half-heartedly.

The conventional equation was that China would shock and awe the world with its speed and ambition, but India would barely move the needle. This was how global discourse was poised until Nine Fifteen (despite the certificate of good conduct from the BRICs study). However, a subtle shift in this discourse took place as the world economy gingerly picked up after the Lehman debacle. The world was now toasting China's splendid recovery, but spending much more time on its weaknesses. Even as it was patting China on the back, it was pointing towards the concerns and challenges that China ought to be tackling with greater intent. It was throwing the spotlight as much on China's misses as on its hits.

For example, the world had stood and applauded the spectacular 2008 Beijing Olympics. But in 2009, an equally spectacular 60th anniversary parade in the same city drew as much scepticism as admiration. The made-in-China weaponry on display was fierce, and the smartly uniformed goose-stepping soldiers showed off a nation marching resolutely forward. But the world questioned the need to keep local residents behind closed doors, prohibited from stepping into their balconies. Kite-flying was banned; even homing pigeons had to be confined to their cages. Why was a resurgent nation so scared and paranoid?

And beyond the parade, why should a modern state allow religious activities only in government-controlled places of worship? Why was China being so squeamish about two dissidents at the Frankfurt Book Fair? Being the guest of honour, China had trotted out over 2,000 writers, publishers and artists to dazzle the world of intellectuals. But when Chinese officials learnt that two dissidents had been invited to speak at a pre-fair symposium, they retaliated with an 'either us or them' threat. 'We did not come to be instructed about democracy,' an official said testily. Eventually, China got its way and the dissidents were asked to stay away.

In 2005, China banned the practice of *yidi baodao* or 'reports from non-local places'. Earlier, journalists would travel to distant cities and write hard-hitting exposés on corruption and social unrest (they felt freer away from their local censors and minders). Ching Cheong, a reporter for Singapore's *Straits Times*, had laid his hands on transcripts of conversations with the late Zhao Ziyang, who had opposed the Tiananmen crackdown. Ching was formally charged with spying for Taiwan. Zhao Yan, a *New York Times* researcher, was held on suspicions of leaking state secrets. Shi Tao was sentenced to ten years in prison for leaking censorship details at his paper. Earlier, China had opened a tiny crack for international news broadcasters like CNN International, which was allowed to transmit into hotels (through the state-run China International Television Corporation). But in August 2005, even that small opening was closed, as new rules asserted that 'no more foreign satellite TV stations were to be granted landing rights in the country with immediate effect'.

According to the *New York Times*, 'after many years of fervent lobbying and deal-making in China, American media companies have little to show for their efforts there and are increasingly shifting their attention instead to India. Media executives still believe that Chinese audiences are receptive to Western culture—*SpongeBob SquarePants* is a big hit in China—but many companies have been pulling back out of frustration over censorship, piracy, strict restrictions on foreign investment and the glacial pace of its bureaucracy.'

'Unrestricted internet access is a source of strength,' President Obama told students in Shanghai. But his town hall meeting was telecast only locally in the city, and a suspiciously slow feed hit the internet. The worldwide web has always been an Achilles' heel for China. In 2008, the US embassy had set up an air-quality monitoring site on its grounds, sending pollution readings on Twitter, often to validate (or negate) 'tempered' official data put out by the state before the Beijing

Olympics. China flew into a rage, accusing the US of interfering in its internal affairs. Eventually, Twitter was blocked nationwide. 'Internet has become an important avenue through which anti-China forces infiltrate, sabotage and magnify their capabilities for destruction,' wrote the public security minister. Under a programme called Green Dam Youth Escort, China tried to install filtering software on all new computers, but withdrew the order after an outcry by users.

Just weeks later, a simmering face-off with Google erupted in full public view. Google threatened to pull out since it had detected a 'highly sophisticated and targeted attack' on its computers 'originating from China'. Google said the hackers wanted to gain access to the e-mail accounts of Chinese human rights activists on gmail: 'We have decided that we cannot participate in censorship anymore.' China hit back saying Google had engineered the whole thing to cut losses (since it was badly trailing Baidu, the local Chinese search engine). President Obama countered saying he was 'troubled', and Hillary Clinton jumped in with a cold war style warning about a descending 'information curtain'. The Chinese government asked her to 'stop using the so-called internet freedom question to level baseless accusations'. China's bloggers hyperventilated on the drama, but unlike other crises, their reflexive nationalism was muted. In fact, Google emerged the darling underdog in the Chinese blogosphere. Did the government pick up this signal and back off a bit? Perhaps so did Google—so the fracas hung in an uneasy truce until Google pulled the plug on its Chinese website in March 2010.

Ironically, China is the world's fastest-growing internet market—in 2008 it surpassed America as home to the largest internet-using population—yet it uses a sledgehammer to stamp out the faintest criticism of its communist state. Typically, China continues to block embarrassing searches on Google and Yahoo. YouTube, Wordpress and Blogspot cannot be reliably accessed; circumvention sites like anonymizer.com and proxify.com are also blocked. Cybercafes that could enable anonymous communication and networking among citizens are tightly licensed. Privately owned portals can only re-post news reports already published in approved mainland sources. Bloggers cannot write under pseudonyms, or they face huge fines.

But in a somewhat inexplicable strategy, China does allow raging debates to take place on a few issues of internal reform. A female pedicurist was accused of murdering a local official who tried to rape her; over 4 million posts erupted on the internet, protesting against the injustice. She was let free. A nineteen-year-old was convicted of operating an illegal taxi; he chopped off his finger to excite sympathy and rage on the web. The strategy worked: he was pardoned, and his finger was surgically restored. It was yet another triumph of what is being called 'internet justice' in China. This uneven approach to internet censorship begs a question: will China's leaders slip, or walk comfortably across the treacherous tightrope that a half-democracy is?

Even as China has been routinely criticized for its authoritarian political systems, nobody had ever felt the need to question the strength of its rulers. The Communist Party was once considered impregnable, an efficient, fortress-like political machine. Even a whiff of dissent was anathema and kept tightly under wraps. Today, open questions are being asked: *Newsweek* reported that the Communist Party is split between the Populists who 'want to improve China's social safety net, introduce greener policies and balance development between the east coast and poor western hinterlands' and the Elitists who favour the old policies of unbridled growth keeping 'money flowing into export-oriented coastal enclaves'. Why are the Populists openly accusing the Elitists of 'rigging' economic figures in the first half of 2009, to show an illusory bounce to the world? The Populists are considered 'sons of the soil', while the Elitists are 'princeling children of high-ranking Chinese officials'; will their schisms widen into an 'ugly rupture'? Is there a danger of history repeating itself, as the liberals and conservatives had clashed in the Tiananmen bloodshed of 1989?

Questions are also being asked whether ethnic conflict could sear China's resource-rich border regions. Urumqi continues to simmer after the July 2009 riots that killed 200 and wounded over 1,000 people in bloody clashes between Han Chinese and Uighur Muslims. Early in 2010, China's conscience was savaged by half a dozen brutal attacks by poor, middle-aged, lonesome men, hacking to death at least eighteen and injuring over 100 schoolchildren; popular blogger Han Han posted that 'one of the great causes of these murders is social injustice and unfairness'; Prime Minister Wen Jiabao felt the 'need to solve the deeper reasons behind this issue'. The UK-based Maplecroft has ranked China worst on the 'judicial effectiveness index' of the Human Rights Risk Atlas 2010, along with outcast nations like Burma, Somalia and North Korea. Fifty-three-year-old Akmal Sheikh, a British citizen suffering from bipolar disorder (manic depression), was executed in China for smuggling heroin; it was the first known execution of a European since the 1950s. A usually restrained Prime Minister Gordon Brown exploded saying he was 'appalled that our requests for clemency were not granted'. According to the *Economist*, China might have 'executed 1,700 convicts in 2008 or nearly five each day'!

Liu Xiaobo is a former literature professor who authored Charter 08, which demanded the right to free speech, open elections and the rule of law. He was held in secret detention for more than a year, and his lawyers were given just two weeks to prepare their defence. His wife was not allowed to attend the courtroom where his trial lasted less than three hours; he was sentenced to eleven years in prison, and deprived of his political rights for an additional two years. An official of the US embassy was highly critical, saying 'persecution of individuals for the peaceful expression of political views is inconsistent with internationally recognized norms of human rights'.

Australian mining giant Rio Tinto also had to face China's judicial wrath; its officials were summarily arrested for 'spying' without any access to counsel. Earlier, Rio Tinto had refused to sell equity to China Aluminum. The arrests were widely seen as a retaliatory punishment for that rebuff.

Doubts are being raised over China's investment sweep across Africa and East Asia. China's outbound FDI was over $50 billion in 2008, doubling from the previous year. Its creeping economic hegemony over Sudan, Zimbabwe and other African territories is awesome. But whispers are getting louder about Chinese arms and reconnaissance devices finding their way into the hands of the ruling juntas. *Time* reports that a Chinese state-owned manufacturer of security scanners has been charged with bribing local officials to win a $55 million contract in Namibia (until 2008, President Hu Jintao's son was heading this company, although he has not been implicated in this case). It talks about China Metallurgical's $1.4 billion investment into nickel mines in Papua New Guinea. The locals panic about losing their land,

and are miffed by rumours that China will use their nickel for a secret weapons' programme. Anti-China riots have broken out 'from the Solomon Islands and Zambia to Tongo and Lesotho'.

China has always reserved its friendliest face for Asia, its primary sphere of influence. It used the 1997 financial crisis skilfully to make friends with South Korea, Indonesia, Singapore and Thailand. In 2007, it even held joint military exercises with ASEAN countries. On New Year's Day in 2010, it inaugurated the world's third largest free trade area with ten South-East Asian nations. But China's artificially low yuan is now hurting ASEAN exports. Vietnam devalued its currency 5 per cent to keep it competitive, and Indonesia is having second thoughts about the free trade pact with China. Indonesia's troubled nails industry has invoked WTO rules on unfair trade, but an official threw up his hands in despair, saying 'China is China, you know. Even the US cannot talk to China.'

The tone, tenor and texture of the global discourse around China are clearly changing from a virtually unqualified acceptance to a set of searching, doubting questions. This is not to say that the world is repudiating China's remarkable progress. It simply cannot be anybody's case that China's achievements are puny or suspect. It's just that the unalloyed admiration of the pre-Lehman days is giving way to a more balanced and probing assessment.

The exact reverse seems to be happening for India. India's successes are being greeted, not with the scepticism of earlier years, but with whispers, if not whoops, of joy. Earlier, commentators would spend far more time on India's missed opportunities; now, they are throwing the spotlight on its potential expectations.

India had come to be seen as the trade union leader of poor countries. Frankly, the epithet was deserved, as India loved playing the renegade, the outlier, the do-gooder who would obstruct the 'mercenary' intentions of wealthy countries. Whether it was trade talks, or nuclear treaties, or climate change negotiations, India enjoyed taking a Robin Hood stance in international politics. It delighted in leading the Group of Have-nots. But with a rising, globalizing trillion dollar economy under its belt, India's body language began to change. It jettisoned its trade unionism to become the 'bridge' between rich and poor nations. It voted along with the US at the International

Atomic Energy Agency against Iran, a former third world ally. It moderated its once shrill objections to the Doha round of trade talks. *Newsweek* hailed it as an 'emerging power that can say yes'. Some quick concessions were made in climate change negotiations. India agreed to cap its emissions at developed country norms. It committed itself to the threshold of 2 degrees centigrade of global warming above pre-industrial levels; at Copenhagen, it even agreed to do this on the basis of 'equity', which could mean a potentially binding commitment of emission cuts in the future. (As against this, the *Economist* called China 'churlish' for insisting that all 'numerical targets be stripped out of the final accord, even those that did not apply to China'.) India also abandoned its earlier opposition to a 'peaking' date from where emissions have to come down—although no year has been mentioned yet. Finally, it volunteered to curtail emissions by up to 25 per cent by 2020, even if western countries refused to compensate in cash. India seemed to be getting convinced that 'whether the issue is liberalizing world trade, building a more stable financial architecture, reducing global warming or reigning in nuclear proliferation, Indian leadership is required', applauded *Newsweek*.

Winston Churchill had warned against freeing India, saying the country would 'fall back quite rapidly through the centuries into the barbarism and privations of the Middle Ages'. Two decades after Independence, India's 1967 elections were especially troubled and fractured; a British newspaper sang the dirge saying it was India's last election. For a while, especially in the ravaged '90s, it seemed that India was atomizing into colliding regional and ethnic sub-identities (not unlike the hundreds of tiny monarchies that had fallen like 'cherries' to the British). National political parties had shrunk to half the seats in parliament; the other half was occupied by dozens of 5–20 member parties, each pandering to a narrow constituency of caste, region, language or religion. None of these sectarian parties had a national vision or outlook; they were happy stoking petty and inflammatory issues to keep their vote banks surcharged. In a span of ten years, India held five general elections, and scores of provincial polls. Most threw up rickety and dangerous 'coalitions' which would collapse in months. What use is it to talk of governance when even the formation of a government is in doubt!

Suddenly, just as everybody was losing hope, the Indian voter reared up, as if to say 'enough is enough'. He finally gave a stable majority to a right wing alliance in 1999. National parties (ruling plus opposition) won over 60 per cent of the seats in parliament. The pattern was repeated in 2004 when the right wing coalition was replaced by a left–centre combine. Another five years later (2009), India's parliamentary democracy finally came of age when the incumbent central government was re-elected by a much larger majority. A leading commentator wrote that the incumbent's 'gamble of distancing itself from regional players with personalized agendas has paid handsome dividends'. Another said that 'Verdict 2009 is an unambiguous, comprehensive and titanic rejection by the country of extremist politics'. National parties increased their seats to over 75 per cent in parliament. The space occupied by the 'ultras' among the smaller parties was squeezed even further.

For three elections in a row, the fight had been between a right wing and centre–left alliance, giving shape to India's own multi-hued version of a western two-party democracy. In 2009, even the provinces saw a wave of incumbent victories for performing leaders. Political analyst Pratap Bhanu Mehta saw an end to the 'vicious cycles of knee-jerk anti-incumbency'; according to him, 'the scale of government spending is making possible a shift away from the politics of identity to the politics of development'. Rhetorical, rabble-rousing politicians had bitten the dust, while sober and competent ministers were getting re-elected. Political historian and journalist M.J. Akbar said, 'The language of conflict has passed its sell by date. The poor want to be part of the India Rising story.'

Clearly, the chemistry and adjectives of global discourse are changing. Now, China is capable of doing a few things wrong—and India is capable of doing some things right.

Why has the discourse changed? Perhaps because China is a hare on steroids, while India is a tortoise building some muscle into its legs.

A Hare on Steroids

Premier Wen Jiabao had the courage to admit that China's growth had become 'unstable, unbalanced, uncoordinated and unsustainable'. Such a frank and publicly spoken assessment was quickly labeled 'the four un's', winning the premier many admirers among western think tanks. For long, China's leaders have been correctly worshipped for their determination and execution skills. For thirty years, they got things done on an unprecedented scale, at an unprecedented pace. It was only natural to expect the same 'can do' spirit in fixing the problems.

The structure of China's economic success is unparalleled in human history. Four-fifths, or a full 80 per cent, of China's GDP is made up of investments and exports. Simply put, it has invested huge sums of money in creating factories, buildings, railways, roads, ports and airports to produce and send goods for consumption by people outside China. This has made it vulnerable to the fortunes of non-Chinese consumers. This is the biggest imbalance, and perhaps one that China knowingly created in the early years of its growth. In fact, China adroitly used a number of imbalances. When orchestrated together, these put strong tailwinds behind its take-off. It took land away very cheap from its people, and gave it away cheap to foreign investors. It kept its currency artificially cheap too. Finally, it gave these investors very cheap labour. Multinational corporations used this 'triple subsidy windfall' to make China the manufacturing factory of the world. Western consumers leapt for joy. They were paying far less to get familiar American brand names, with American guarantees on quality. They began to devour cheap China-made but America-branded products which were flooding their malls. China began to earn American dollars in sacks. It further sweetened the deal by lending these dollars back to America. That was a masterstroke: it allowed China to keep its currency cheap, and America to fuel the appetite of its consumers with cheaper and cheaper credit.

Cheap land, cheap currency, cheap labour, cheap interest rates, cheap American debt, high American consumption and high Chinese investment in factories, buildings, roads, ports and airports to keep infrastructure cheap for foreign investors—such an adroitly managed structure of very cheap costs and very high expenditure created the Chinese miracle. It injected ever higher doses of adrenaline into the Chinese hare.

To top it all, China's leaders executed their plan with ruthless precision. China unapologetically plumped for quantity and scale;

fortuitously, or perhaps because of China's unique model, this coincided with an almost unbelievable expansion of global trade. The jury is out on the cause and effect here, on who created what, but China's export thrust occurred at a time when the share of global trade in world GDP went up from 24 per cent to 31 per cent. China was at the right place at the right time with the right ambition and determination.

Economists are happy to 'forgive', even applaud, China's play for quantity over quality in the early stages of its growth. Most are happy to give the benefit of doubt to China's planners. After all, aggressive privatization of state-owned enterprises had thrown 60 million people out of jobs. If China had not scaled up quickly and dramatically, it could have derailed the entire country. So China ignored the imbalances; it furiously acquired land from poor peasants, spent hordes of cash in creating infrastructure at breakneck speed and on an outlandish scale, and encouraged foreign capital to set up huge factories. The result was an explosive growth in the economy.

The result was also an explosive growth in bad loans. Twenty years of aggressive (and loose) lending had pushed China's banking system into an unholy mess. The bad loan estimates swung between 20 to 50 per cent if overdue loans were included; Moody's painted an even scarier picture of 35–70 per cent for 1996. Four asset management companies were created to take over nearly $200 billion of bad loans, a fifth of the banks' portfolio at that time. Eight years later, a mere 20 per cent of these eroded loans had been recovered—which meant that a large part of the assets created in the early '90s had become complete junk.

An alarmed state set about repairing its banks. Sweeping changes were made in 1998. Banks were freed from the hegemony of local officials. Loan approvals were benchmarked to international practices. Cost of borrowing was increased to ensure viable recoveries. But change was slow and stubborn. Local communist control was replaced by a less intrusive, yet quite vested, central bureaucracy. Soon, earlier ills began to resurface on balance sheets, with bad loans jumping again to 26 per cent by 2002. The government was forced to use $60 billion of its foreign reserves to create Huijin, a new holding company, to recapitalize three of the largest commercial banks. Another $100 billion of bad loans was transferred to asset management corporations. The private Bank of Communications had to be bailed out with $5 billion. By 2004, virtually all of the 34,000 tiny regional cooperative or city banks were in severe distress.

Another peculiar problem began to rear its ugly head; in 1997, the National Bureau of Statistics (NBS) unearthed 60,000 reporting discrepancies. Popular media pounced on it, calling it a 'statistical fraud'. A study had shown how a pyramid of exaggerations was contaminating national economic data. For instance, all provincial estimates together exceeded the national growth number. Similarly, the sum of all regions exceeded the number for their province, and an addition of local city or town estimates was invariably ahead of their regional estimate. A specific census in 2005 showed how provinces were exaggerating their growth by nearly 4 per cent. In January of that year, the Chinese government banned its provinces from publishing any economic numbers before the National Bureau of Statistics (NBS) put its estimates out.

China's rigid communist hierarchy, with its inscrutable rewards system, was almost primed for such fraud. Since communist cadres ruled everywhere, being town mayors, enterprise CEOs and provincial governors, they did not have the stomach to miss targets set by party bosses. Not surprisingly, most of them 'exceeded' their targets. According to Gan and Li, 'Whenever the leaders have insisted on accelerated growth or when accelerated growth becomes the content of evaluation, then the wind of overstatement flourishes. Because statistical figures have become one of the main items used for evaluating outcomes and for graduating leaders, statistical falsification has become universal.'

Another somewhat suspicious facet of China's GDP growth was the extraordinarily high component of 'unexplained, unaccounted or residual' elements. While this is high for all early-stage, fast-growing economies, it was about one and a half times the average for Japan and Korea in similar phases. The World Bank said China was adjusting current price data by a deflator which was much lower than its consumer price inflation. Economists like Angus Maddison recommended even more severe adjustments to show that China's growth rate between 1978 and 1995 was 7.48 per cent, a whole 2 percentage points lower every year than official figures. While other economists, like Holz, have challenged Maddison's findings as too conservative, nobody denies a large element of overestimation in China's growth numbers.

Thomas Rawski was a professor at the University of Pittsburgh when he published a series of contentious articles in 2001 and 2002. He questioned how China's GDP could have gone up by 25 per cent when its energy consumption fell 13 per cent between 1997 and 2000. How could industrial production in 1998 have gone up by nearly 11 per cent when fifty-three out of ninety-four components suffered an absolute decline and only fourteen elements grew at more than 10 per cent? How could total fixed investment grow almost 14 per cent in a year in which steel and cement increased only 5 per cent? Rawski concluded that China could have grown at a mere 2 to 4 per cent in those slowdown years, far from the official growth numbers. But Rawski was dismissed as a 'troublemaker' by the Chinese government. Curiously, China later revised several data points relating to energy and other resources for this four-year period, making the growth appear more credible in hindsight.

China's economy had also become vulnerable to a couple of other fault lines. Local governments had begun to exercise powers which are usually reserved for central or large provincial governments in other countries. They were taking all major investment decisions and were free to raise finances, including foreign direct investment. Nearly 75 per cent of total national expenditure was being done by such 'licentious' city authorities (compared to about 30 per cent in developed countries). Minxin Pei has called this phenomenon the Decentralized Predatory State, where local officials delighted in making excessive investments. It was easily the most 'controllable' way of creating an illusion of prosperity for their people. Jobs, bribes, value added taxes, turnover taxes—local officials took credit for everything. The other crimp was China's critical dependence on booming property prices, forcing the state, consciously or unconsciously, to keep inflating the bubble. Nearly half of all early infrastructure investment in China may have been done by extracting (even extorting) a surplus on land values. So China needed to keep its property markets in good cheer—then it could take land away cheap from farmers and sell at high prices to developers. Bank of America estimated that 'proceeds from land sales may have financed at least 25–30 per cent of investment in infrastructure in recent years'.

These were the warts that had begun to erupt, prompting Wen Jiabao to call his country's growth 'unstable, unbalanced, uncoordinated and unsustainable'. In the words of its then deputy environment minister, 'We are using too many raw materials to sustain this growth. To produce goods worth $10,000, for example, we need seven times more resources than Japan, nearly six times more than the US, and perhaps most embarrassingly, three times more than India.'

Infrastructure was growing at an unbelievable 25 per cent per annum, and investment spending was threatening to touch 50 per cent of GDP. This was a spectacular repudiation of prudent economics. Even at its comparable peak, Japan's investment had never gone above 30 per cent plus of GDP. China was now consuming twice the oil per unit of GDP as the rest of the world. It had seven of the world's top ten polluted cities. Banks were lending at negative interest rates; effectively, that meant capital was free and could be splurged on assets that were never going to be profitable. Services made up just a third of the GDP, the lowest for any economy of this size. Domestic consumption, considered the bedrock of all prosperous countries, had fallen to its lowest at 35 per cent (from 46 per cent in 2000). The share of household income in GDP had declined 16 percentage points over the last decade. Chinese consumers, feeling scared and helpless at the absence of retirement and health benefits, preferred to save than spend. Lifestyle benefits were available to just the top ten cities in China; the rest of the country felt vulnerable. A third of the economy was completely under the state's sway, making market forces puny and ineffective. China's act was in danger of spinning out of control.

But the world had great faith in China's never-say-die leaders. The problems were known, and so were the solutions. China needed to change the structure of its economy. It had done a wonderful job in taking investments and exports to astronomical levels; it now should have made services more attractive than manufacturing, by jacking up prices of energy, water, electricity, land and capital. More businesses needed to be privatized (but the exact opposite has happened). The *hukou* system should have been relaxed, allowing rural migrants to take their families to permanently settle in cities; but for now, the government has only pledged to 'study' the problem, 'push for urbanization in an active and steady manner' and 'solve the *hukou* problem of migrant workers'. The state has also remained intolerant of even the slightest criticism on this score. When thirteen major newspapers published a synchronized editorial asking for urgent *hukou* reforms—'We hope that decades of Chinese government maladministration can end with this question'—the chief author was fired and the editorial promptly removed from all websites.

China should have urgently created confidence among its consumers to spend. Not willing to take risks, Chinese consumers had stashed nearly $4 trillion dollars in bank deposits. The state had to create a massive social security net which would convince Chinese consumers that they would be looked after in illness and old age. Today, they are covered for just a few hundred dollars every year in lifetime pension. Health and unemployment insurance are next to nothing. Economists were expecting China to hike this manifold, in their characteristically bold and devil-may-care style. But China has been a bit coy here.

Perhaps all would have been fine if Lehman had not bitten the dust. Chinese consumption had begun to grow at 15 per cent every year. If only for a few months, China had beaten America to become the world's largest car buyer. It overtook Japan as the world's second largest diamond market by sales, and pushed India to the second spot in consuming gold. Retail sales continued to be robust. China's model of 'trickle-through consumption' was beginning to work. Perhaps China's leaders would have delivered a restructured economy to their critics, silencing them yet again with their ability to pull a hare out of the hat. But they were stopped dead in their tracks by the global meltdown of 2008. It was, in a sense, the first spell of bad luck for China's 'lucky generals', the first time that the stars had not aligned in their favour.

Much to the despair of economists, China's leaders recoiled at the crisis. Instead of persisting with the arduous effort required to U-turn their supertanker economy, they let go the wheel, opened the throttle, and allowed the vehicle to hurtle along a direction they had sworn to turn away from. In other words, they regressed to exactly what had worked for them earlier. They decided to invest their way out of trouble, vowing to spend $585 billion over two years in building more railways, power grids, rural assets, highways and airports. A quarter of this money was to be spent on the Sichuan earthquake reconstruction effort.

This strategy had worked like a charm in the global crises of the mid-'90s and early 2000s. Massive internal spending had filled up the hole left by falling global demand. Once the global economy had recovered, China had bounced back smartly on both occasions. But this strategy may prove to be third time unlucky. Compared to the current financial armageddon, the earlier global crises were a walk in the park on a pleasant summer day. This time the western consumer has been ravaged, and is unlikely to turn over his wallet in a tearing hurry.

China may have made things worse for itself by instructing state-controlled banks to open the debt floodgates. Chinese banks lent a trillion dollars in just the first six months of 2009, twice the amount that was given out in the whole of 2008. Bank credit jumped to an alarming 150 per cent of GDP. (Just to get a proper sense here, be aware that Indian banks have lent only a little over 50 per cent of GDP to date. To wit, bad loans for Chinese banks have historically been higher than 30 per cent, while they have been a low 2–3 per cent for Indian banks. At about $900 billion, China's bad debts are thought to be six times the toxic loans which almost obliterated America's banks.) China's chief bank regulator warned that 'all sorts of risks have arisen'. Minxin Pei called it a 'potential tidal wave of future non-performing loans'. Predictably, the explosion of cheap credit created a bubble in asset prices. Nearly a fifth of the cash went into speculating on the stock market, where daily volumes reached three times the five-year average. Gaming revenues in Macau touched record highs, and property prices went back to pre-crisis levels. Even garlic prices jumped tenfold in big cities, inflated by speculative cash. *Newsweek* reported that an astonishing 60 per cent of the stimulus money could have gone into the stock and real estate markets.

Clearly, China is betting on its tried and tested model: 'we will invest massively and consumption growth will trickle down from that unprecedented expansion'. Classical textbook theory says that hyper-investment always ends in bubbles. But China has time and again repudiated academic wisdom, perhaps because nobody could fathom the sheer size and momentum of China's ambitions. Perhaps their drive and execution is on a scale that textbook writers could neither predict nor imagine, so they simply failed to write a theory that could account for this 'extraterrestrial' phenomenon. Perhaps the Chinese are writing a new theory of 'tidal wave investing', a model in which capital is spent on such a brutal scale that it ends up lifting the whole tide, where the sea level itself moves up to an entirely new plane. By building roads, railways, factories, ports, ships, power plants, universities, schools and hospitals at a pace and scale previously unknown to mankind, has China pitched its economic model outside traditional economics?

The jury will remain out as long as China continues to make unexpectedly smart moves, continues to think completely out of the box. Look, for instance, at its deep thrust inside Africa. The conventional wisdom is that China is commercially colonizing Africa for oil and minerals. But that's an obvious conclusion. Hardly anybody has caught on that China could be eyeing Africa's *consumer* markets. After all, if you look at all of Africa as one country, its economy is uncannily similar to India. Africa is growing at 6–7 per cent every year; its demographic profile and per capita income is equal to India. There are 150 million elite consumers, and another 500 million aspiring ones— again, a lot like India. And China is doing 'another America' to Africa: it is giving cheap loans and tax credits to woo Africa to buy its cars, bicycles, computers, chocolates and T-shirts. With one deft stroke, China could be filling its consumption deficit—with an economy of India's size. With one clever move, it could be answering critics who believe that China is doomed unless its citizens begin to consume. Unacknowledged by many, it may be tackling that problem on two tracks, one of which is in faraway Africa! As long as China is full of such surprises, the jury will have to remain out on whether China will falter, or whether economic textbooks will have to be rewritten.

There is also plenty of contrarian analysis which tries to prove that China may escape with a small-sized crisis and bubble. Only a quarter of the middle-class households have taken mortgages on their homes— and even there, the 'margin' of the loan is less than 50 per cent. So the ordinary Chinese is not terribly in debt; average household debt is only 35 per cent of income, as compared to 130 per cent in Japan in

1990. The other plus point could be China's relative poverty, which should keep its exports competitive even in the face of declining world demand. The argument runs somewhat as follows: Japan and Germany had peaked out at 10 per cent and 12 per cent of global exports in the 1980s; since China's income is much lower, and its population six times more than what Japan's or Germany's was in their peak-out phase, China could still increase its share of world exports from 9 to 15 per cent. According to the *Economist*, 'As factories in the rich coastal areas switch to more sophisticated goods, the production of textiles and shoes can move inland where costs are cheaper.' This argument gained some credibility when China overtook Germany to become the world's top exporting nation towards the end of 2009—because China's exports had fallen only 16 per cent while Germany's fell far more steeply. But there's a challenge here. To continue with export buoyancy, China may have to keep its currency devalued against the dollar by mirroring America's utterly cheap money policy; but that by itself could push the economy into a severe asset bubble. So China is between a rock and a hard place.

Finally, China could be grappling with an entirely new imponderable: the prospect of a protectionist face-off with the US. In earlier crises, the American consumer had remained strong. In a sense, America and China were on the same side as troubles erupted in other geographies. But now, the problem was in America's backyard, and its consumer was hunkering down to stop buying and start saving. This had a direct and dramatic impact on China, whose exports shrank by nearly a fifth in early 2009. As recession deepened in America, cries to save 'jobs being lost to China' got shriller and shriller. President Obama drew first blood when he slapped a 35 per cent import fee on tyres from China. The Chinese ambassador to America called it a 'very dangerous precedent'. A month later, China hit back with 36 per cent duties on America's nylon exports. A week later, America slapped anti-dumping penalties on Chinese-made steel pipes. Within twenty-four hours, China opened investigations into US-made passenger cars, accusing the Americans of evading customs duties by bringing parts into China for assembly. Whenever slogans begin to dominate public discourse in distraught times, partisan politics, and not sensible economics, usually wins the day. These preliminary trade wars could merely be the tip of a protectionist iceberg as politicians' posture and grandstand before worried voters.

If western protectionism is still an imponderable—because the world hopes that better economic sense will prevail—China nonetheless has got some genuine worries on the value of its US treasury holdings. As M/s Obama, Geithner and Bernanke print trillions of dollars to desperately try and revive a bankrupt credit economy, the US dollar could rapidly lose value, thereby seriously depleting China's $750 billion of US treasuries. This is a real conundrum for M/s Jintao, Jiabao and Xiaochuan—there are no quick fixes here. China sold a record $35 billion of US treasury bonds in December 2009. If it continues this dumping, it could jack up interest rates in America, stubbing out whatever little prospect there is of a recovery in consumer spending, and with it, whatever little prospect there is of a recovery in Chinese exports to America. But if the Chinese hold on to dollar assets, they could sharply deplete their national wealth. Lawrence Summers has called this the 'balance of financial terror'. Which way will the cookie crumble? It is a trillion dollar question whose answer could yet determine the fate of a post-Lehman earth.

But whichever way the cookie crumbles, one thing is certain. Both America and China have to re-learn some grandma's recipes to fix their wayward, hare-like economies. For far too long have the two hares scratched each other's backs in a credit-fueled cycle of 'prosperity'. Now, the American hare must slim down and stash away some savouries for a rainy day. And the Chinese hare must give up his addiction to state-injected steroids.

A Tortoise with New Muscles

A tiny economic milestone occurred in mid-2009. India exported more cars than China in the first half of that year—a good 20 per cent more! Ford Motors quickly followed through with an announcement that India would be the manufacturing hub for the global launch of its small car, Figo. Hyundai had already done that, exporting 300,000 India-made cars. The pièce de resistance was the launch of Tata Nano, an entirely home-grown 623 cc car that fulfilled all safety and emission norms, but was priced at $2,500—the cheapest ever made anywhere in the world. The *Economist* called it a 'product of impatience and chutzpah'; *Time* christened it the 'upstart econobox'. Carlos Ghosn of Renault/Nissan quickly announced plans for his ultra low-cost car, saying this could only be done in India. In tandem with all this frenetic activity in India's auto industry, a local outfit became the world's second largest auto forging manufacturer.

India had also overtaken China as the fastest growing mobile phone market in the world, not just in percentage terms, but also in absolute numbers. For several months on the trot, Indians bought 10–15 million cell connections every month, pushing the total number of users to over half a billion. Over half the new connections were being bought in rural India. Given India's large population, and the fact that China had maxed out, you could say this was entirely expected. But wait— India now exported 60 million mobile handsets to over sixty countries in the world. At 250 million units by 2012, it was 'poised to become the telecoms manufacturing hub of the world', gushed Nokia's India chief. Samsung, Motorola, LG, Sony Ericsson—everybody was scrambling to build more manufacturing capacity in India.

Again, something counter-intuitive was happening. Remember, China was the exporter–manufacturer of the world, with its cheap currency, land, labour, credit and low taxes. India had never been that obsessed about pushing car or handset exports. Indian interest rates and production taxes were incredibly high. Then how did this happen? Perhaps it was a triumph of cheap Indian skills, and high productivity caused by intensely competitive conditions in the economy.

Around the same time, India jolted bullion markets by buying 200 tons of gold from the IMF. Nobody even had a whiff of such a large deal. India did it in truly uncharacteristic style: bold, swift and decisive. There was a delicious amount of 'revenge' built into the transaction. Less than two decades ago, India was forced to pledge its gold with the IMF, since its foreign exchange reserves had plummeted to an alarming $1.3 billion. Now, India had picked up half the gold on offer in one fell swoop. A Bloomberg reporter called India 'hot game (which must have left) a few top officials in Beijing red-faced this week. "How on earth did India beat us to the punch?" policymakers must be asking.' Global markets, stunned at India's tiptoeing audacity, took gold prices to a new high. 'Barack Obama and Timothy Geithner must be as annoyed as they are bewildered. Didn't India get the memo? Developing countries are supposed to keep their excess cash in Treasuries. Gold?' continued the Bloomberg report. It's difficult to fathom what could have caused such excitement around the world. Was it because so much gold was bought in a single deal? Was it because this signalled a dramatic shift in sovereign reserves away from the US dollar into gold? Or was it because India was the most unlikely candidate to spring such an aggressive move on a huge world market? 'India really did display the savvy of a hedge fund here. It got what it wanted, surprised markets and could sit back and reap the benefits as gold rallies,' concluded Bloomberg.

India notched up another small milestone as the number of its students in the US crossed 100,000 for the very first time, with China in hot pursuit at the second place. India had stayed at the top of the charts for the eighth year in a row, according to the Open Doors 2009 survey.

An invisible proclivity for India has also been spreading through Fortune 50 boardrooms in America. Vikram Pandit was made CEO to pull Citibank out of its post-Lehman abyss. Earlier, Indra Nooyi had become the first woman Chairman and CEO of PepsiCo. Even before that, Rajat Gupta had done a highly successful stint as CEO of McKinsey. Vinod Khosla is among the top five venture capitalists in America, and Ajay Banga has made it to the top job at Mastercard. (As might be expected, no person born and brought up in China has scaled a similar peak in any mainstream American corporation. This has got little to do with the competence of Chinese leaders, who should be as good as people anywhere else. It's just that China has embraced the world and English language for less than a generation.) Pandit, Nooyi, Gupta, Khosla and Banga were all born and brought up in India. They may have lived all their working lives in America, but they had become adults in India. They had finished college here; their parents and family still live here. They visit 'home' almost every year. There are scores of other such 'native' Indians, born and taught in India, who are leading less visible, but equally influential, American institutions. Being honest professionals, these people would never act out of bias, or do any undue favours for India—and yet, their success has given the country of their birth a reflexive advantage. It's taken the fear of the unknown out of the equation.

Perhaps that's why Indra Nooyi had the confidence to get the global PepsiCo board to convene in Mumbai, only the second time that this mega-powerful clutch of American businessmen had met outside the US. Nooyi may have grown up believing in the entrepreneurial miracle of Mumbai's famous dabbawalas, who deliver 200,000 home-cooked lunch boxes with 99.99 per cent accuracy every single day. So she confidently put a bunch of semi-literate pavement entrepreneurs before eleven members of one of the strongest corporate boards in the world, including top honchos of Novartis AG and Colgate Palmolive. She knew her sophisticated board members would be riveted by the logistical skills of these rustic geniuses. That's exactly what happened: the board listened spellbound, first to the humble Mahadeo Havaji Bachche, followed by elite presentations on India's wonder car Nano, the technology revolution and fractiously efficient democracy. Indra Nooyi's 'India immersion programme' had hit home: her board had acquired a deep insight into her 'home' market, which had posted a 50 per cent volume growth in the preceding quarter, the highest anywhere in the world. If Indra Nooyi had not been an Indian, perhaps this meeting would have been a routine laptop-and-slide presentation in a Manhattan skyscraper. That's the unintended yet reflexive advantage India is reaping with several 'sons and daughters of its soil' making it big in the US. It's virtually impossible to put a number to this 'gain', and yet its magnitude is undeniable.

These 'gains' are not limited to the corporate sector alone. People of Indian origin, born and brought up in their native country, are hitting the top spots in media, policy think tanks and American civil society. Fareed Zakaria, a Bombay boy, is an editor at *Newsweek*. Raju Narisetti heads *Washington Post*, while Rajeev Chandrashekharan is the Iraq expert. Ashley Tellis has an authoritative voice among Washington's policy wonks. Three Indian Americans, including Venkatraman Ramakrishnan in 2009, have won the Nobel Prize in the sciences. Nitin Nohria is the first non-White (and tenth overall) dean of the 102-year-old Harvard Business School. He is one among twenty-five teachers of Indian origin in a total faculty strength of 200. People like Dipak Jain, Jagdish Bhagwati and Pankaj Ghemawat hold high professorial chairs in other business schools, as did the recently diseased C.K. Prahalad. Gita Gopinath was studying at a prestigious New Delhi college when

India embarked on major macroeconomic reforms in 1991; two decades later, she became the third woman ever and the first Indian after Amartya Sen to be named tenured professor of international macroeconomics at Harvard. Dr Sanjay Gupta, CNN's renowned health editor, declined his appointment as America's surgeon general. Bobby Jindal is the Governor of Louisiana, and is on the radar as somebody who could run for President. Preet Bharara was the New York prosecutor in the Galleon hedge fund scam (allegedly hatched by several Indian Americans too!). There are over three dozen Indian American politicians, springing out of a 3-million strong community which is the fastest growing, best educated and richest ethnic group in the US. Like the corporate CEOs, all these 'sons and daughters' of India are sworn to a fair and professional ethic; they would never do anything that is biased in favour of their home country. Yet their understanding of India's complex nuances helps in 'explaining' their motherland and making it more accessible to mainstream America.

The phrase 'Indian multinational' stopped being an oxymoron as Indian companies bought over 800 foreign firms between 2005 and 2009. The Tatas acquired giant western corporations like Jaguar Motors and Corus Steel. Today, over 65 per cent of the group's $70 billion comes from overseas operations, prompting its chief to say his successor could well be an expatriate.

The Indian space vehicle Chandrayaan-1 even found conclusive traces of water on the moon (confirmed by NASA's on-board M3). This was joyously endorsed by NASA at a worldwide press conference to celebrate the discovery. At $75 million, Chandrayaan-1 was a good 20 per cent cheaper than any other scientific mission to that part of the universe. On 14 November 2009, its 29-kg Moon Impact Probe detached from the main orbiter and crashlanded close to the Shackleton Crater in the south polar region of the moon. India became the sixth power to join the lunar club, along with the US, Russia, the European Space Agency, China and Japan.

But some of India's other 'wins' are a bit notorious too. As shopping malls have proliferated, Indians have acquired a rather unsavoury status as the world's top shoplifters! The Global Retail Theft Barometer 2009 puts Indians at the number one spot among forty-one countries. Now, what can you say except to claim that this is an ironic proxy for India's robust consumer revolution!

The Indian economy has always been likened to an elephant or tortoise. Both are nice, harmless, non-threatening animals. Not cuddly or pretty or spectacular, just dour and stable and always there in the background. That's largely how the world has seen India's economic story unfold. It's been good, not spectacular. It's got a B+ grade: it neither scorches the track, nor destabilizes it. Its leaders are gentle and avuncular, not aggressive and sexy salesmen. It's a good guy to have around the household, but you wouldn't bet on him. At least that's the way it was before Nine Fifteen.

Then the discourse changed. The gentle got suffixed with 'giant'. The dour got transformed into a 'sheet anchor'. The tortoise 'quickened' its pace. The elephant could 'dance'. Slowly but discernibly, quite like the subject country itself, the adjectives of the global discourse around India began to change. And as India bounced back from the 6 per cent 'China watermark', earlier and quicker (and many now say, in a more broadbased way) than the hare, diffidence gave way to admiration.

Some of India's delightful economic quirks jumped under the arc lights. India sells 1 million motorcycles every month. Car demand is rising by 30 per cent every year. For two-minute Maggi Noodles, demand is increasing by 25 per cent per annum. In 2008, India crossed the twin landmarks of a trillion dollar GDP and $1,000 per capita income. While it took sixty years after Independence to cross the first trillion dollars of GDP, the next trillion will come in seven to eight years, as the economy is likely to double to $2 trillion by 2015, and double again to $4 trillion by 2025.

India's growing economic might created ripples even in faraway China. Dao Shulin, a scholar at China's Institute of Contemporary International Relations, shrugged off a customary wariness to openly acknowledge that: 'With its territory stretching into the Indian Ocean, India has a total area of 2.97 million square km, out of which 43 per cent is plain area, allowing for its land resources to be utilized fully. Second, it is rich in human resources . . . especially in English language education, enabling India to communicate freely and conveniently with western countries such as America. Its scientific research level comes out on top in the world. India has not only maintained relations with traditionally friendly countries such as Russia, but improved relations with western countries represented by America.'

How did the tortoise get its new muscles? Once before, India had suffered perilously in the 1997 Asian meltdown. GDP had bottomed out at 4.5 per cent, but India's 'foreign exchange reserves were strained, interest rates went sky high, companies defaulted on loans and dragged down banks'. But a decade later, despite the post-Lehman panic, despite the fact that foreign investors pulled out $12 billion from the stock market and foreign credit vanished, reserves stubbornly refused to move below the quarter-trillion mark. Mercifully, Indian banks had much more capital on their balance sheets; their borrower corporations were also much less leveraged. Even companies like Tata Steel, Tata Motors and Hindalco—which, in a rush of blood, had taken huge debts to buy out global icons like Jaguar, Corus and Novelis—rode out the trouble without begging for relief.

Why did India suffer so little in the Great Recession of 2008? Easily the single most important factor was the robust financial system. Indian banks had shunned mortgage-backed securities and credit default swaps, those exotic but toxic financial instruments that had brought the western world to its knees. What's more, the 'services' orientation' of India's economy ended up saving the day for exports. While merchandise sales were down 30 per cent, information technology exports stayed steady. Even Indians living outside the country pitched in, remitting a breathtaking $46 billion to the motherland, up $3 billion from the previous year.

While skittish foreign buyers pulled out dollars from the stock markets, their strategic counterparts shovelled in more than twice that amount into Indian factories and assets. Finally, India's central bank (the Reserve Bank of India) stayed cool and calm. In 1997, it had panicked, hiking interest rates to 'savagely restrictive' levels. This time, it actually lowered interest rates, put more credit out, and allowed the rupee to drift down against the US dollar. The government cut taxes but spent more than it had budgeted. 'This combination of easy monetary and fiscal policies cushioned the shock,' says celebrated columnist Swaminathan Aiyar.

Jim Walker is unreserved in his praise for Y.V. Reddy, governor of the Reserve Bank of India through those turbulent days: 'He was the only governor of a major central bank who (a) paid any attention to money and credit growth, (b) understood that asset prices play a signalling role in the economy, and (c) applied differential risk-weighting to potentially troublesome sectors well in advance of serious overheating ... (not) a single Indian financial institution ran into solvency or liquidity problems.'

There is now a subdued acknowledgement of the superior quality of India's growth when compared to the quantity juggernaut unleashed by China. Both the countries are saving a massive 40 per cent or thereabouts of their GDPs. But the bulk of India's savings comes from households, which are more resilient through economic cycles. The majority of China's savings are done by corporations, many of whose accounting standards are questionable, and which, in any case, are far more susceptible to the vagaries of market ups and downs. India's growth is also far less debt-induced than China's; its loans are growing at half of China's pace, even as the nominal economy is growing much faster. Even the usually condemned rural sector is buzzing. Rural-to-rural migration is as strong as rural-to-urban movements, rural industry is growing faster than its urban counterpart, and rural tax payments are increasing rapidly. More encouragingly, Indian consumers and entrepreneurs are managing to buy and grow at much higher interest rates than in China, which simply means that every rupee spent or invested in India is generating a far higher return than a yuan in China. On top of this, India's consumption-to-GDP ratio, at over 55 per cent, is reminiscent of fast-growing western economies in their heydays. To foreign equity investors, that fact alone promises windfall returns in the future.

Finally, India's GDP is structurally stronger and greener. 'A much smaller industrial portion (28 per cent) than China (52 per cent) and a much larger services share (53 per cent) than China (34 per cent) is biased toward less pollution and energy-intensive growth,' says Stephen Roach.

All of this has convinced UBS that India's economy is entering 'a golden period'. Real GDP growth is likely to average 8–9 per cent for the next ten to twenty years. The youngest and highest saving/consuming population in the world, which is also among the least indebted, makes for an irresistible story. Throw in $2.5 trillion of infrastructure investments in the next fifteen years, and the cup of good news flows over.

But hanging over this optimism is the threat from a government which is getting deeper and deeper into debt. To say it straight, India's public finances are completely messed up. The budget deficit is 11 per cent and total public debt is 80 per cent of GDP—over three times the average for Asia (without Japan). Mercifully, India has managed to grow quite strongly despite such persistently high deficits. Perhaps because most of this debt is funded by domestic savings, external—or dollar-financed—debt is merely a tenth of total public debt, compared to 60 per cent for other Asian countries. Household savings cannot be freely converted into overseas capital, leaving them captive in the hands of the government. Even banks have to keep a quarter of their deposits in government bonds, giving the state another captive facility to finance its debt. Finally, the Indian government owns nearly half a trillion dollars of productive assets in the public sector, which mitigates the dangers from its debt overhang to an extent. Still, if there is one dark cloud hovering ominously over India's economy, it has to be the precariously high levels of public debt.

In fact, India is a curious study in contrasts: a feeble government, perhaps getting weaker by the day, and an energetic civil society whose aspirations and ambitions are soaring by the minute. The government must fix itself, or it runs the grave risk of converting aspirations into disappointments, and ambitions into anger.

That is the overriding challenge for India's newly muscular tortoise, as it tries to close the gap with China's adrenalin-pumping hare.

Rule *of* Law, Rule *by* Law

Group Danone SA is a Paris-based multinational food giant with operations across five continents. In 1996, it formed a 51:49 joint venture (JV) with China's much smaller Hangzhou Wahaha Group Co. Wahaha, founded by Zong Qinghou, had started life as a three-person operation selling bottled water to schoolchildren; at the time of forming the JV, it was China's largest bottled-water company. The Wahaha trademark was to be transferred to the JV; agreements were signed and filed with Chinese authorities, but perhaps not followed through vigorously. This oversight proved very costly for Danone.

The Danone–Wahaha JV flourished, clocking sales of $2 billion in

2006. But cracks had begun to appear. Danone got a whiff that Zong had established 'mirror' companies which were illegally using the Wahaha trademark—they were allegedly piggybacking on the JV's advertising and sales network to sell virtually identical products. Danone saw red over what it thought was an act of unjust enrichment and breach of agreement by its partner. After several unpleasant rounds of eyeball-to-eyeball negotiations, the parties reportedly settled on a deal in December 2006; Danone agreed to pay nearly half a billion dollars to integrate the 'mirror' companies into the JV. But Zong reneged saying he had been 'forced' to sign. He is thought to have asked for an extra $250 million to transfer the 'mirror' companies. Danone pulled out of the talks, and filed lawsuits in Los Angeles, requesting for arbitration in Stockholm. Zong pushed for arbitration in Hangzhou; his move succeeded, as the arbitration commission ruled the trademark had never been legally transferred to the JV. By implication, Zong continued to own the Wahaha trademark; he twisted the knife further, suing several Danone-nominated directors for breaching non-compete obligations by serving on the boards of other Chinese companies competing with Wahaha.

By now public sentiment had been roused. Media commentators and ordinary people were beginning to see the whole dispute through the prism of 'nationalism'. Fuel got added to fire when the state-controlled *China Daily* valued the Wahaha brand at $2.4 billion. Some argue Danone's PR efforts completely failed; be that as it may, the French company was painted as a 'foreign wolf' trying to corner consumers and victimize a homegrown outfit. Sentiment was divided—while sensible people wanted justice to be done, there was a stronger undercurrent which wanted exceptions to be made on such emotional issues. On balance, it would be fair to assert that Chinese sympathies were entirely with Wahaha. Ultimately, on 30 September 2009, Danone agreed to abort the JV and sell its 51 per cent stake at a quarter of the price it was originally asking for. The curtain came down on a messy affair in which twelve lawsuits were filed within China and six other jurisdictions; the issue had even escalated to Presidents Hu Jinao and Nicolas Sarkozy.

China's tainted milk scandal is another case that has grabbed the headlines. Sanlu Group Co was accused of mixing melamine with baby formula. Melamine, an industrial chemical known to cause renal failure and kidney stones, allowed the adulterated milk to pass the quality test for protein. At least six children died, and 300,000 took ill. After a hue and cry in the media, a Chinese court sentenced two men to death, and handed a life term to chairwoman Tian Wenhua. $160 million was awarded in compensation, but affected families alleged such a 'woefully inadequate' package was unilaterally decided without involving the victims at any stage. The victims' families were kept at least 100 yards away from the courthouse; a few parents were even detained as they tried to get closer to the proceedings.

We have already discussed the cases of Liu Xiaobo and Akmal Sheikh.

Two attributes of China's current legal ethos are evident. One, Chinese law is not a blindfolded, emotionless instrument based on cold principles of jurisprudence; it gets tempered by notions of 'patriotism' and 'nationalism'. Second, the Chinese state is comfortable treating laws as an instrument of policy (rule *by* law) as against western democracies, where the principles of law are inviolable forcing public policy to be implemented within the law (rule *of* law).

So how has modern Chinese law evolved? Let's take a quick peep into history. Ancient law in China evolved between two opposite philosophies. The predominant one was Confucianism, which believed that people were innately good—if the ruler set a high ethical standard, society would be fair and just. The opposite philosophy was Legalism; it mandated that people should be tightly controlled by a set of rules that are enforced with a heavy hand. Lord Macartney's 1792–94 mission to China resulted in the first western chronicle of China's legal system. Under the Qing dynasty, an independent judiciary did not exist; state officials played the roles of detective, judge and jury. There were no lawyers, the 'courts' only settled criminal cases, while civil ones were handled via mediation. There was general contempt for people who initiated legal action.

Foreigners began to meddle after Great Britain defeated China in the 1840s' Opium Wars. Unlike what they did in India, colonial powers did not supplant China's imperial laws with western ones. The bend in the river occurred here, a watershed period in the histories of China and India which slung them on utterly different trajectories.

Beginning with the Treaty of Nanking in 1842, each foreign power—
Great Britain, United States, Germany, France and Japan—forced a set
of 'unequal treaties' upon China. In almost every instance, Chinese
laws were not applicable on foreign nationals, who could not be taxed,
nor arrested, nor tried by Chinese authorities. Earlier, the 'brutal
violence and beastly intemperance' of British sailors would attract stiff
Chinese penalties; under the new treaties, ordinary citizens watched
helplessly. (Chastened by these experiences, later generations fell easy
prey to communist propaganda against western-style laws.)

The early decades of the twentieth century led to an even sharper
divide. Sun Yat-sen overthrew the Qing dynasty and formed a Chinese
republic modelled on the French presidential cabinet. A provisional
Constitution was adopted in 1912 which had a smattering of liberal
features, including equality before the law and enhanced rights for
women. Unfortunately, the early decades of the republic were full of
unrest; the decade from 1916 to 1927 was particularly stricken with
strife and wars. The Japanese invasion coincided with the Second
World War (1939–45), followed by a fierce civil outbreak between
Chiang Kai-shek's nationalists and Mao Zedong's communists. In
1949, Chiang's forces fled to modern-day Taiwan, and Mao took
control of mainland China.

Mao nullified every single law that existed in China; he repudiated
a written legal framework, pushing for loyalty and collective action.
Law enforcement passed into the hands of party cadres. Each official
became a political leader, magistrate, detective, judge and jury, rolled
into one. Since Mao was fascinated by Soviet socialism in the early
years, legal officials interpreted and implemented rules borrowed
from the Russians. But these edicts remained a set of loose rules; in
Mao's worldview, a legal system 'dams up the free flow of revolution'.
The justice ministry was closed in 1959, lawyers were banned, libraries
were destroyed, law schools were closed, and people practicing law
were branded 'counter-revolutionaries'. The number of lawyers
dwindled from 60,000 to 2,800. Mao wanted 'the rule of the individual,
not the rule of law'. According to Kenneth Lieberthal, 'As of 1977,
therefore, China was governed by decrees, bureaucratic regulations,
and the personal orders of various officials; it had no codes of law at
all. In addition, many decrees, regulations and so on were kept secret.'

Don King of Hong Kong University describes China's legal system under Mao as more 'administrative' than 'legislative'.

China made four attempts before a formal Constitution acquired some legal teeth. The earliest was in 1954, when a Constitution was adopted based largely on the Soviet document. It was soon ignored and rendered useless. The next one, promulgated in 1975, reflected the excesses of the Cultural Revolution. The Communist Party was made unquestioningly supreme, private property succession rights were abolished and several protections, like equality before the law, were made toothless. This Constitution, virtually stillborn, was replaced by another one just three years later. Within four years, this interim document was repealed too. China finally adopted a relatively robust Constitution in 1982 which reflected Deng's plan of economic reconstruction and modernization. While it may not have been a paragon of evolved statecraft, the 1982 document at least had the sinews of a reasonably modern state. Based on Deng's concept of 'four modernizations', it acknowledged the need for stability and continuity of laws, equality of all people, and a mechanism to ensure that laws would not be whimsically changed.

The Constitution somewhat aptly described China as a 'people's democratic dictatorship'. The National People's Conference, or NPC, was created as the supremely powerful body. It could amend the Constitution with a two-thirds majority, create new laws, sack officials, fix the national budget, and oversee national and state plans. A smaller organ, the Standing Committee, was carved out for day-to-day functioning. Practically, everybody took orders and instructions from the Communist Party of China.

India's Twice-born Constitution

A brilliant young English lawyer Thomas Babington Macaulay stood before his parliament in 1833. He made an impassioned appeal, saying the role of British colonizers was to 'give good government to a people to whom we cannot give a free government ... I believe that no country ever stood so much in need of a code of laws as India.' Earlier, Macaulay had warned that Europeans in India could become 'a new breed of Brahmins', urging that 'a privilege enjoyed by a few individuals in the midst of a vast population ought not to be called freedom. It is tyranny.' Later that year, he was asked to set sail to India, charged with the gigantic task of codifying the law of India; he described it colourfully, saying his job was to create 'one great and entire work symmetrical in all its parts and pervaded by one spirit'.

Macaulay's task was onerous. The British East India Company had begun trading in the subcontinent in the early seventeenth century. While its primary export, British broadcloth, failed to find too many buyers in India, the reverse trade—of Indian goods being sold in Great Britain—was extremely lucrative. The Company soon realized that it needed to wield political power to control the terms of trade with native Indians—and also oust its Portuguese competitors. Fortuitously for the British, India's mighty Mughals began declining after Emperor Aurangzeb's death in 1707. Over the next century, the loose federation of tiny monarchies built by the Mughals crumbled into a fractious bunch of local 'kingdoms'. The Company plucked several of these 'cherries', expanding its political fief over large tracts of India. Wherever Europeans settled or created factories, those settlements became an 'imaginative geography' governed by laws made by the British Crown and the East India Company.

That was the bleak legal landscape which greeted Thomas Macaulay, India's first law member and head of its first Law Commission, in 1833. He had the unenviable task of welding together conflicting laws and untrained officials—described by James Fitzjames Stephen as 'vices of vagueness'—into a system of justice. A new charter was created for the East India Company which completely transformed India's legal edifice. An all-India legislative council replaced regional legislatures. Law-making powers were taken away from the provincial governments in Bengal, Bombay and Madras Presidencies. One set of laws and courts were established for everybody.

Institutions of law and civil society made halting yet surefooted progress under the British rulers over the next century. These decades were scarred by the first war of independence in 1857 and violent reprisals against the political 'disobedience' movements led by the Indian National Congress. As the self-rule ideal gathered momentum, Gandhi recast the Congress into a 'parallel government like' structure. The central working committee began to function like the de facto 'national cabinet' and provincial Congress committees were reorganized along linguistic lines. The first attempt at setting up an 'Indian Constitution' was the Nehru Report of 1928 for Dominion rule. It spoke of common electorates with seats reserved for religious minorities. The people were given a set of fundamental rights. The British ignored the proposals, but these came in handy for the Congress when it agreed to contest elections under the Government of India Act of 1935. The country had its first brush with widespread electoral democracy, however fledgling and imperfect that may have been. Ultimately, these experiments in democracy led to India's independence just over a decade later.

Congress-led ministries had taken power in almost all the provinces after the end of the Second World War. Since India's independence was imminent, a Constituent Assembly was convened on 9 December 1946 to write the laws for the newborn country. The assembly was piloted by Dr B.R. Ambedkar who was the law minister in the interim government. Dr Sachidananda Sinha was its oldest member: he urged the assembly to follow the approach of America's founding fathers in Philadelphia. The assembly took three years to write the longest Constitution in the world. Inevitably, legal draftsmen copied large chunks of the existing Government of India Act of 1935. An earlier exercise to set up a genuinely federal country was virtually jettisoned, as the assembly developed a 'fear complex'—how would such a plural country survive under a 'weak' central government? So several extra powers were created for the centre; for instance, in an earlier draft, the Governor of a province was to be elected. In the final draft, he was made an appointed agent of the Central government (a provision which was to be abused several times before legislative curbs were imposed many decades later). The powers of the President were almost identical to the powers of the Governor General under the Act of 1935.

Thus it came about that the Constitution of independent India was genetically dominated by Westminster-style democracy. The British parliament passed the Indian Independence Act, 1947, and royal assent was granted to free India from colonial rule on 15 August 1947. Across the Himalayas, China's Communist Party emerged victorious in 1949, and Mao Zedong became its dictatorial leader. At this stage in the history of India and China, the bend in the river became a sharp fork, flinging these ancient civilizations irretrievably apart.

The Indian Constitution is the highest law of the land, supreme over all other laws passed by legislatures. A slew of fundamental rights were given to ordinary citizens (and several to aliens too), benchmarked against the United States Bill of Rights: among these were the rights to equality, freedom of speech and expression, freedom of religion, cultural and educational rights, and constitutional remedies. The principle enunciated in America's famous case of Marbury vs Madison—a government is one 'of laws and not of men'—resonated through the document. The Supreme Court was given the power to 'declare the law' and quash anything which violated these fundamental rights. Governance was made utterly secular, with the complete 'absence of a legal connection between the state and a particular religion'. These powers were amplified in the famous Kesavananda Bharati case, where the Supreme Court prohibited parliament from tinkering with the 'basic' structure of the Constitution, saying: 'No party in power could use its legislative majorities to abuse the constitutional processes to convert a republican India into a hereditary monarchy, a secular India into a theocratic state, a federal India into a unitary state, an India of citizens into an India consisting only of subjects.'

Early on, India's courts got trapped in litigation around the right to private property. Judges were accused of taking a narrow, legalistic stance; in a poor, feudal society deeply divided between the few haves and an overwhelming number of have-nots, courts were seen to 'favour' the rich and wealthy. Reforms aimed at redistributing land ran into judicial 'obstructions' like the right to appeal and natural justice. Indian courts continued to remain remote, exclusive islands, cut off from the common person, until the judicial system nearly died a sudden death in the middle of the 1970s.

On 12 June 1975, the Allahabad High Court disqualified India's sitting prime minister Indira Gandhi for 'corrupt electoral practices'. Unless the ruling was reversed, Indira Gandhi would have had to resign and remain barred from political activity for six years. Upon appeal, Justice Krishna Iyer granted a 'conditional stay' because the offences were of a minor nature, but although he ruled that she could continue as prime minister, she was not allowed to vote or draw a salary as a member of parliament. This was a pyrrhic victory for Indira Gandhi, whose moral authority was rapidly eroding. A fortnight later, a desperate prime minister proclaimed a state of emergency in the country; she invoked the Maintenance of Internal Security Act, the Defence of India Rules and other laws to arrest opposition leaders, gag the media, and suspend fundamental rights of citizens. Going by an extremely narrow interpretation of the letter of the law, the Supreme Court virtually decreed that citizens had lost their fundamental right to life and liberty. Mercifully, the emergency was lifted eighteen months later, and Indira Gandhi's Congress party was soundly thrashed in the elections that followed. The new rulers, who had been incarcerated during the emergency, brought in the historic 44th amendment to the Constitution; this undid several of the draconian laws promulgated during that dark period. Fundamental rights were put outside the pale of emergency provisions, and laws unconnected with the emergency could be challenged in a court of law even during a spell of emergency rule.

India's Constitution was born a second time; an elitist and 'legalistic' judiciary was jolted into activism on behalf of the 'common man'. The '80s and '90s saw India's courts pushing the limits of 'constitutionalism'. In the famous Bhagalpur blinding case, thirty-one alleged criminals were detained by the police in a small district in east India. A posse of policemen said they were going to bathe the detainees in gangajal (holy water) in order to cleanse them, and then poured acid into their eyes, blinding them permanently. It was a shocking case of law enforcers handing out vigilante justice (Bhagalpur's citizens, suffering under a rising crime graph, took out a procession in support of the police action). A crusade by journalists and other activists took the case all the way up to the Supreme Court; the case made criminal jurisprudence history by becoming the first in which compensation was ordered for violation of basic human rights. Similarly, the court awarded compensation to Rudul Shah for the loss of his limbs during fourteen years of traumatic police custody.

In 1981, the Bombay Municipal Council decided to evict all pavement dwellers from the city. Olga Tellis, a journalist, took up the evictees' plea that this violated their fundamental right to life, since it took away their livelihood. The court held that 'if there is an obligation

upon the State to secure to citizens an adequate means of livelihood
and the right to work, it would be sheer pedantry to exclude the right
of livelihood from the content of the right to life'. Among other relief,
the court ordered that slums in existence for twenty years or more
should not be removed unless the land was required for public
purposes. In several other cases, the court ordered that death row
prisoners were entitled to food, clothing and shelter on par with
ordinary prisoners—life behind bars should not mean a less than
human existence. Free legal services were made a 'processual piece of
criminal justice'. A court ordered the payment of minimum wages to
casual migrant labourers. In Mohini Jain's case, the court chided
private schools for charging exorbitant fees, articulating a socio-
economic right to education. Castigating a mental institution for the
abhorrent conditions in which inmates lived, the court went to the
extent of laying down the amount of money to be spent on meals and
medicines. The 'greening' of India's courts began with the closure of
limestone quarries for harming the Mussoorie hills. The principle of
'polluter pays' became an article of faith.

Today, India's Public Interest Litigation (PIL) movement must be
among the most activist in the world. Pioneered by Justice P.N.
Bhagwati, it brings legal aid to those who are 'unable to approach the
court for relief'. Bhagwati began pursuing cases of 'epistolary
jurisdiction', triggered by a few lines written on simple postcards
mailed to the court. Nilbati Behera was a hapless mother who wrote
a letter complaining about her son's death in police custody; the court
treated it like a writ petition, and proceeded against the Orissa state
government. When Sunil Batra, a jail inmate, wrote exposing how
another inmate was brutally assaulted by a police official, the court
converted the postcard into a habeas corpus petition. It was a simple
PIL which forced the government to investigate Prime Minister
Narasimha Rao's role in allegedly bribing members of parliament to
save his government.

But despite very good intentions, the story of judicial fair play in
India is riddled with instances of delay, exploitation and sheer apathy.
For every good outcome, there are perhaps a dozen examples where
the wheels of justice have miscarried. Shahnawaz Khan is a practicing
lawyer in Bhopal. Twenty-five years ago, his office was just across the

road from Union Carbide's pesticides and chemicals facility. His skin would itch and his eyes would burn from fumes emitted by the factory. In 1983, he sent the plant a notice asking them to clean up their act. The management came back hard at him, threatening to counter-sue. Tragically, just one year later, on the night of 3 December 1984, tank number 610 at the factory leaked 42 tons of lethal methyl isocyanate into the air. Thousands died immediately and hundreds of thousands were maimed for life; an entire generation was condemned to fatal illnesses, many of which are erupting ugly wounds in children born a quarter of a century later. It was the world's worst industrial disaster.

Warren Andersen, the worldwide chairman of the American parent, was arrested three days later in Bhopal, but was freed on bail within hours. A state plane took him back to New Delhi, from where he was allowed to flee the country (the whole act was rigged by the governments of America and India in connivance with Union Carbide, allege critics). Since then, Andersen has ignored arrest warrants and doggedly refused to return to India to face trial. Several cases are pending before the Bhopal Chief Judicial Magistrate, the Indian Supreme Court and the US District Court in Manhattan. Eight persons were convicted after twenty-five agonizing years in June 2010.

Back then, the government passed a special law assuming 'exclusive rights' to represent the victims in American courts, who individually may not have been able to get commensurate damages (ultimately the government lost the jurisdiction battle in American courts, which decreed that the case should be tried in India). Since the government had taken away individuals' rights by legal force, it had a moral obligation to indemnify them. But it did nothing of the sort; worse, in an astonishing surrender five years after the disaster, the Government of India entered into a controversial $470 million settlement with Union Carbide (in the same year, Exxon paid $860 million to just 38,000 victims affected by the Alaska oil spill). The figure was a demoralizing fraction of the original claim of $3.3 billion. The Bhopal figure was based on a count of 3,000 dead, and 105,000 injured—these were ad hoc numbers plucked out of thin air. The actual casualties turned out to be at least five times higher, but the settlement amount was not changed; at the exchange rate prevailing in 1989, it worked out to less than a $1000 per victim. At today's rate, it is less than $300 per victim—and that's relevant because a large amount of the compensation is yet to be paid out.

America's Dow Chemicals bought Union Carbide sixteen years after the Bhopal disaster, setting aside $2.2 billion for pending liabilities of the company it had taken over; not even a penny of this has come for Bhopal's ever-increasing list of victims. The horrible tragedy got compounded as poisonous chemicals dumped in the closed Bhopal plant are thought to have contaminated drinking water, heaping more misery and illness on almost 30,000 residents. An inspection in 1994 revealed 44,000 kg of toxic tarry residue and 35,000 kg of alpha-naphthol lying in open decaying gunny sacks and corroded drums. Eighteen thousand tons of effluents are buried, and 23,000 tons abandoned on the grounds of the 67-acre complex. Rains over several decades could have washed these poisonous chemicals into the soil. Legal petitions are flying around between the courts of several states, but men, women, children, goats, chicken and cattle continue to be assaulted by genetic defects caused by twenty-five-year-old methyl isocyanate and freshly contaminated drinking water.

China's Story of Virtual Justice

There is no word for 'rights' in classical Chinese—and that, in a quixotic sort of way, highlights China's uphill legal journey. Having chosen to rule *by* law, China condemned itself to a few mishaps in the early years. Deng wanted to quickly repair the vacuum created by three decades of legal annihilation; he wanted citizens to be on a tight political leash while enjoying marginal economic freedom. Nobody could challenge China's ultimate leaders. Such a political structure, which could loosely be defined as benevolent communism with a sprinkling of competitive capitalism, had no parallel in human history. It was an experiment prone to accidents and excesses in the early years.

The Carnegie Endowment sponsored a fascinating study on 'Judicial Reforms in China—Lessons from Shanghai' in April 2005. It was led by Veron Mei-ying Hung, an accomplished lawyer and scholar from Stanford University. She is a member of the New York bar and admitted as a barrister in England. While the study focussed on Shanghai, it showed up shortcomings across China's legal system.

At a mere 1.4 per cent, the study threw up an unnaturally low ratio of cases filed against local authorities; quite evidently, local party chiefs were able to arm-twist lower-court judges to reject cases filed against them. Fear could be the other deterrent: private business was simply too scared to sue government agencies with powers to stall almost any project. This fear was reflected in another ratio—cases involving industry and commerce were a negligible 2–3 per cent of the already negligible number of first-instance administrative cases. The final bit of statistical evidence was the unusually high withdrawal rate of 42 per cent. It was an ironic 'index of interference'—to begin with, hardly any case was filed against state agencies, and then, nearly half of these were withdrawn.

Lawyers, especially those who double up as human rights activists, are a targeted species in China. A UN report called China's criminal law the 'sword of Damocles which can be invoked to harass, intimidate and sanction lawyers'. Wei Jun's case made it to the UN in 2004, when his phones were tapped; the police asked the Judiciary Bureau to suspend his licence to practice law and sentence him to three years of forced labour reform. The story of Zheng Enchong has become a modern-day legend. He was first arrested in June 2003 for 'illegally providing state secrets outside the country', and released after serving a three-year sentence. More recently, he was detained the day after he spoke about corruption cases against a Shanghai tycoon in *Epoch Times* and thrashed by an unidentified person in the police station.

Guanxi or *renqing* are harmless Chinese words which may roughly be translated to mean 'contact' or 'enquiry', but they have acquired a sinister tone in legal folklore. They describe how local party officials try to influence judges regarding cases involving their 'friend or friend's friend'. In mature legal systems, this would amount to meddling with court procedures, often leading to a mistrial. 'Local protectionism' is another innocuous-sounding but troublesome phrase. It requires local judges, whose salaries are paid by local chieftains, to pass orders which are good or 'beneficial' for the locality. So local profiteering becomes an ideal—anything that helps the local economy prosper is more important than principles of judicial fairness.

A strange category, called 'major and complex' cases, is the most vulnerable. These terms are vaguely defined, and end up including all large cases, especially class action suits in labour and eviction disputes. Courts are morally cajoled, often instructed, to pass orders which promote the 'larger social good', even if legal principles are compromised. 'Major and complex' cases are decided by a special adjudication group under the CPC's politico-legal committee (which often includes the local police chief, nullifying the 'Chinese wall' that should exist between police and judiciary). In effect, the CPC's political line prevails; unsurprisingly, government authorities have seldom lost these cases.

Through all these ups and downs, China's legal system has grown in scale; it now handles over 7 million cases per year with over 200,000 judges and 160,000 lawyers. But China has shown an unusual unwillingness to pick up precedents or copy rules and principles from other legal systems. Foreign lawyers cannot interpret or practice Chinese law, nor represent clients in court. A fundamental weakness persists about the quality of judges and how they get paid. From two law schools in 1979, the number has swelled well beyond 200 now, yet a very small fraction of the judges hold Master's or doctoral degrees.

The early 2000s saw China take a few quick strides in legal reforms. From 1998 to 2004, about 8,000 judges and other court officials were punished for violating laws or discipline. In March 2003, a young man named Sun Zhiyang died in policy custody. Sun was a Wuhan University graduate and fashion designer, who had come to Guangzhou to work. He was accosted by policeman at an internet bar and asked to show his immigrant papers. He had not applied for his permit and forgotten the ID card at home. He was detained—an autopsy showed he was savagely beaten for seventy-two hours before he died. Sun's violent death enraged popular sentiment. Ultimately, under mounting public pressure, two of the guilty were sentenced to death and seventeen other accomplices imprisoned for different terms. Sun's family was given $53,000 in compensation by the state. Three legal scholars filed a petition challenging the 'custody and repatriation' system under which Sun was detained; shortly afterward, it was scrapped, creating a ripple of euphoria among activists that China was finally moving towards 'constitutionalism', or rule *of* law.

In another case in 2004, a state agency had failed to notify Zhang Chengyn about his right to participate in a review exercise; when Zhang sued, the Jiangsu High Court responded by enforcing the 'due process' principle, even though it was not embedded in the underlying law. Perhaps for the very first time in China, a universal legal principle, not explicitly in the rules, had been applied against a state authority.

Gao Yiming received a formal letter of appointment from Beijing Bide Development Telecommunications Technology in April 2007. But his mandatory health check revealed he was carrying the Hepatitis B virus. His appointment was terminated, in violation of the 2008 Employment Promotion Law, which specifically bans discrimination against people with infectious diseases. Gao sued the company and a Beijing district court awarded him nearly 20,000 yuan in compensation, the first time that such a case was successfully litigated in China.

All of this led to a surge in grassroots activism. Over forty petitions for constitutional and legislative review were filed. The media too pitched in with very rich—and free—debates around issues of 'constitutionalism', prompting ordinary citizens to join in with gusto on the internet. Such positive frenzy prompted the state to launch a second five-year reform programme in October 2005. It set fifty key goals for legal reform, but did not touch the holy cows of CPC supremacy and 'consultative adjudication', a euphemism, as we've seen, for ensuring political control over jurisprudence. Some reform was attempted in death penalty cases—while witnesses were earlier asked to submit only written statements, some are now appearing at trials and getting cross-examined. Another goal was to see that oral confessions, often obtained through torture, should not contaminate judgments. A formal effort was made to create 'guiding opinions' and 'guiding cases' for judges via recorded case laws.

But that's where most of it stopped, quickly turning activists' euphoria to a muted sense of betrayal. President Hu Jintao's speeches added to their pessimism; earlier, he would rather freely pitch the Constitution as 'a citizen's weapon' for protecting his or her rights, but now he consciously avoided using similar language. Instead, he gave more powers to the party's Central Political and Legal Affairs Commission (CPLAC), which controlled the police, prosecutors and courts. *Lessons from the Colour Revolutions* was a propaganda film produced by this commission. It highlighted the plight of Georgia, Ukraine and Kyrgyzstan after 'pro-West' forces seized power; policeman and court officials were made to watch the film and exhorted to 'combat various subversive activities of enemy forces'. The party appointed an ex-policeman and staunch loyalist as the new chief justice of the country; the official did not have any experience of being a lawyer, judge or prosecutor.

Constitutional activists have finally resigned themselves to a few realities: that rhetoric overwhelms real action, that the Communist Party resists any reform that even remotely challenges its power structure. Today, China's laws are perhaps best described as 'half done', trapped in a somewhat raw and semi-evolved state.

My Scam Is Better Than Your Scam

Rio Tinto, Australia's largest producer of iron ore, had two unfortunate run-ins with China. It refused to sell an 18 per cent equity stake to China Aluminum Corp; it also had a bare-knuckle confrontation with the state-backed China Iron and Steel Association, which wanted Rio Tinto to drop prices by 40–50 per cent. Rio Tinto stood its ground; shortly afterward, four of its employees were detained in Shanghai. They were accused of bribing Chinese steel officials to obtain sensitive information and were charged with commercial espionage under the law on guarding state secrets. They were also accused of accepting bribes from Chinese companies to allocate iron-ore. Government-controlled media jumped in with 'evidence' that computers seized from Rio Tinto's Shanghai office contained confidential data. The primary accused, Australian national Stern Hu, was denied access to counsel. Foreign publications like the *Economist* contended that the Rio Tinto case was one of a piece with other actions being taken against foreign companies, including a Citigroup subsidiary in Shenzen and property developers in Tianjin. The *China Press*, an overseas newspaper, retaliated that linking several events was 'conjecture', and 'conjecture cannot become a legal basis for judging a case'. It highlighted the example of an engineer of Chinese descent who was arrested in America for stealing commercial secrets—if the West never made a big fuss about those cases, then why was China being treated differently?

As the dispute escalated, it acquired an ugly nationalist tinge fuelled by media in Australia and China. The *Australian* said the case will 'completely ruin China's image in Australia'. *Sydney Morning Herald* asserted that 'China needs to understand that economic development does not stem from cannons and prisons'. On the flip side, a state-secrets watchdog in China alleged Rio Tinto extracted charges of $100 billion over six years; Phoenix Television accused Rio Tinto of 'sucking the blood' out of Chinese consumers and taxpayers. In colloquial Chinese, people may have been incensed to see 'their cooked duck fly away'.

But it's not been all fire and brimstone. Zhu Sibei of *Yangcheng Evening News* is one of the journalists who have offered constructive commentary. He believes the law on guarding state secrets does not clearly classify documents as 'secret' or 'public', allowing the state to 'determine what is secret without explaining what is secret'. Pheline Kline of *Financial Times* called for a revision of the law to avoid political meddling and unfair trials behind closed doors. *World Business Report* noted that industrialized countries have strong laws to prevent leaks, whereas China was 'completely chaotic': it urged China to pick up elements from the United States Spy Act of 1996 and promulgate a law against commercial bribery. Yet others have sought to turn the spotlight away from Rio Tinto, and focus instead on the scourge of local corruption: Why were so many Chinese steel officials willing to leak secrets? Why do multinationals regularly employ high-level government officials to facilitate their operations in China? *International Finance News* saw a problem in the state's excessive involvement in the economy, which tempts foreign companies to bribe officials. Such sober commentary in Chinese media augurs rather well for civil reforms there.

Eventually, China seemed to back off the amorphous accusations of 'bribing and stealing national secrets'; but it pressed ahead on charges that Stern Hu and his colleagues had accepted bribes from Chinese companies. For nearly six months, the four Rio Tinto officials were neither heard nor seen in public. Finally, they were produced in a Shanghai court in March 2010; unusually for China, foreign reporters were allowed to watch the proceedings live on closed-circuit television from a room on a different floor. The three-day trial began with the accused admitting to their guilt on a few charges, widely seen as a bargain for a lenient sentence (since the formal concept of 'plea bargaining' does not exist in Chinese law). But that was not to be. All four were sentenced to nearly ten years each in prison. Australia's foreign minister reacted by calling the punishment 'very harsh'; he went on to protest that 'there are serious unanswered questions which the international business community will want to pursue with China'. *Newsweek* reported that: 'Foreign businesses seem gloomy and resigned in the wake of Rio Tinto. As the president of the EU Chamber of Commerce wrote in the *Financial Times*, members' market sentiment has seldom been so "bleak or pessimistic" about playing by China's murky rules.' Although four Chinese companies were explicitly named as the bribe-givers, the court remained silent on any penalties or charges against them.

'Satyam', in several Indian languages, means 'the truth'. Unfortunately, on 7 January 2009, 'satyam' became synonymous with crooked conduct. On that day, India's biggest corporate scandal erupted in Satyam Computer Services Limited, a multi-billion dollar company spanning sixty-seven countries and six continents (it served over 650 global companies, 185 of which were Fortune 500 corporations). Its founder, Ramalinga Raju, faxed a shocking confession to the stock exchanges on that brisk Wednesday morning: 'It is with deep regret, and tremendous burden that I am carrying on my conscience, that I would like to bring the following facts to your notice. The Balance Sheet carries as of September 30, 2008 inflated (non-existent) cash and bank balances of over $1 billion. The gap in the Balance Sheet has arisen purely on account of inflated profits over a period of last several years. Every attempt made to eliminate the gap failed. It was like riding a tiger, not knowing when to get off without being eaten. I am now prepared to subject myself to the laws of the land and face the consequences thereof.'

All hell broke loose. The Satyam stock tanked 78 per cent and Indian markets fell over 7 per cent before the stock was swiftly removed from the Sensex, India's benchmark fifty-share index. Later that evening (India time), the New York stock exchange halted trading in Satyam stock. Broking firm CLSA called it 'India's Enron, an accounting fraud beyond imagination (and) an embarrassing and shocking episode in Indian corporate governance'.

To their immense credit, India's regulators moved with unusual alacrity. Ramalinga Raju was arrested within two days and charged with criminal conspiracy, breach of trust and forgery. The company's CFO was detained for questioning and arrested a day later. On the third day, India's Company Law Board used its exigent powers to sack the entire board of Satyam Computer Services; but unlike in the past, the government did not nationalize the company or take direct charge. 'The current board has failed to do what they are supposed to do. The credibility of India's IT sector should not be allowed to suffer,' saying this, the minister appointed a couple of private sector professionals with unimpeachable integrity and global credibility. The Securities and Exchange Board of India (SEBI) energetically jumped into the fray; its low-profile chief spoke incessantly to the media, trying to calm skittish markets. It also began enquiries across a spectrum of possible fraud, from special audits of fudged accounts to violation of insider trading rules. The Institute of Chartered Accountants issued a show cause notice to PriceWaterhouseCoopers, the globally acclaimed firm which had certified Satyam's false accounts. Police investigators told the court that nearly 13,000 out of the 53,000 employees of the company were fake—the founders were withdrawing nearly $5 million every month as salaries of these non-existent employees.

It was now critical to keep key customers and employees from fleeing Satyam. The board had the vision and intelligence to understand that it should not be digging in and running the company. Its job was to keep the ship steady in the first few weeks of the storm, and then navigate it over to a high-pedigree owner who would set it back on course. But the board ran into an unexpected regulatory glitch here. India's takeover rules were quite stiff: there were minimum equity pricing rules for new buyers. Shares could only be priced at a six-month average of previously quoted rates in large stock exchanges. But Satyam's shares had fallen from a high of Rs 544 to Rs 12, so the average six-month price was working out to nearly five times the current scandal-hit market price of the company. It was simply impossible to sell Satyam under those rigid pricing guidelines. Everybody implored the securities watchdog to relax the rules, but the regulator wanted to avoid the trap of one-time, ad hoc exemptions; 'We must have a mechanism to deal with abnormal cases,' said the

SEBI chief. The markets groaned in disappointment—it seemed India's regulators were getting bogged down in red tape. But to everybody's surprise, SEBI took less than five weeks to do the job; by mid-February 2009, new rules were notified.

Satyam's professional board now moved at breakneck speed to invite transparent bids for the company. Several blue chip suitors threw their hats into the ring. On 13 April 2009, just three months after that fateful 7th January, Satyam Computer Services was sold to a joint venture of British Telecom and India's Mahindra Group at Rs 58 per share. A stunned and excited world stood in standing ovation: India's solid, fair, but slow regulatory system had been transformed into a solid, fair and pro-active regime. The Satyam stock more than doubled after it was re-christened Mahindra Satyam.

*

There was much excitement in the animal kingdom. Everybody was getting ready for a television game show called Scales of Justice. The tortoise put on black overalls and a curly white wig, the kind that British judges wear in historical cinema. The hare had to cross-dress—his left side was clothed in a dull grey Mao suit, while the right was draped in the smart pleats of an army general. The game itself was simple—who could hold a scale steady between the weights of fairness and bias? If you managed to hold it still for sixty seconds, you won the game. The tortoise almost did it—but alas, the fairness scale dipped sharply in the 50th second. But the poor hare had to face rough weather, as the scales swung sharply up and down, up and down . . .

Two

GEO-POLITICS

The Re-arranging World of an Eagle, a Dragon and an Elephant

The desire to expand has always been at the root of a country's foreign policy and geo-political ambition. Over the centuries, this desire has taken many forms: to convert people to one's religion, to control more land, to garner greater influence on the affairs of another state, to harness more natural resources. Of all these desires, religious conversion and economic empire-building have been the most compelling.

China is a country almost indifferent to God and religion. Surveys routinely throw up an overwhelming majority of people—often as high as 70 per cent—who say that one need not believe in God to be moral. That's at sharp variance with countries like Britain, America, Saudi Arabia and Iran; since medieval times, when crusades were fought in the name of religion, Christianity and Islam have influenced their geo-political orientation. But the Chinese have never had an appetite to go to war or use diplomatic force to expand the influence of Confucianism.

India's response to religion is sharply different. One doesn't need surveys to assert that Hindus are deeply religious. And yet Hindus have never displayed the hunger to spread their religion to different shores. It's even debatable if the Hindu religion allows for conversions, since 'many Hindus continue to believe that Hinduism is an identity that can only be had from birth'. A supremely flexible and assimilative body of thought, Hinduism is often more a spiritual philosophy than a coded religion. It mandates strict rituals for believers, yet allows people to ignore all of them and still be good Hindus! The peculiar elasticity of Hinduism has ensured that India has *never* been expansionist in history.

Religion is clearly not driving the geo-political reflexes of China or India. But economic ambition is.

As the Dragon Makes Peace with the Eagle

It is rumoured that Chinese leaders have a fascination for Paul Kennedy's *The Rise and Fall of the Great Powers*. Kennedy, along with Joseph Stiglitz, Valery Giscard d'Estaing and Mahathir Mohamad, featured prominently in a twelve-part prime time documentary series on China Central Television in 2006. The idea was sold directly to the politburo by an elite team of Chinese historians. The documentary 'endorses the idea that China should study the experiences of nations and empires it once condemned as aggressors'. The rise of nine great powers, from Portugal, Spain, the Netherlands, the UK, France, Germany, Japan (yes, even Japan!), Russia and the US, was showcased. According to Fareed Zakaria, 'The basic message of the series is that a nation's path to greatness lies in its economic prowess and that militarism, empire and aggression lead to a dead-end.' If China has grand plans of geo-political expansion, then it has clearly deferred them for another day—'conceal brilliance, cultivate obscurity,' said Deng Xiaoping. So for now, China is using every conceivable platform to push public opinion in favour of the 'peace dividend' and build economic muscle.

Richard Nixon pulled China into the global mainstream with an extraordinary piece of diplomacy in 1972. Crafted by Secretary of State Henry Kissinger, he proclaimed the Shanghai Communiqué to a wide-eyed audience on the then-fledgling medium of global television. His words reverberated across newly launched satellites: 'The United

States acknowledges that all Chinese on either side of the Taiwan Strait maintain that there is but one China and that Taiwan is a part of China. The United States government does not challenge that position. It reaffirms its interest in a peaceful settlement of the Taiwan question by the Chinese themselves.'

The world changed on that day. Until then, the US did not even recognize China, reserving all its goodwill for Taiwan. With one stroke of the pen, Kissinger kicked off an arrangement which initially saw them 'through a period when security was a dominant concern'. Today, after the explosive emergence of China as an economic power, that limited initiative has become the bedrock of 'a trans-Pacific partnership lest the world may break up into regional units, whose competition, both economic and strategic, would have serious consequences'.

When Jimmy Carter became President, he 'found an eager and confident partner in Deng Xiaoping'. Carter invited Deng to Washington; to his surprise, Deng accepted, saying, 'I can come in two weeks.' He reached Washington on the first day of the Chinese New Year. This was during the most frozen period of the Cold War. Concerned that the Soviets would react to this 'ganging up' between America and China, Carter picked up the phone and called President Brezhnev. 'I explained that we had no intention of allying against his country.' Brezhnev was suspicious. 'He was inclined to cancel the planned negotiations on restricting nuclear weapon development, but he later decided to relent.' Carter's next call was to the Japanese, who too were feeling the heat from rapidly spreading Sino–US warmth.

With Ronald Reagan at the helm, the world expected the bonhomie to lessen. Reagan was rabidly anti-communist, and openly supported Taiwan. But the pro-China momentum took him along, especially since a giant economy was opening up to American business interests. All was well until 4 June 1989, when the excesses in Tiananmen caused a public outcry in the US. The relationship stalled a bit. In 1992, President George Bush Sr skirted an earlier understanding by selling 150 F-16 warplanes to Taiwan, only adding to China's growing irritation with a slight re-tilting of American foreign policy towards Taiwan.

When President Bill Clinton entered the Oval office, he was acutely aware that China's human rights record could not be allowed to blight

America's pursuit of trade and commerce. China's business potential was far too enormous to be linked with its unhappy record on civil society issues. But an aggressive Republican Congress pushed him into a confrontation with China. First he was nudged to upgrade the 'unofficial' protocol of Taiwanese diplomats. Next, the Clinton administration was forced to issue a visa to President Lee Tenghui of Taiwan to speak at his alma mater, Cornell University. China saw red. It accused the US of going back on its 'one China policy'. It took to missile brinkmanship, threatening Taiwan with swift retribution if that country ever declared its independence. The standoff escalated with Washington dispatching two carrier task forces to the area in an open act of counter-brinkmanship. That cooled tempers down a bit, and Clinton followed his blow-hot policy with a blow-cold statement that called for 'engagement not confrontation'. The rapprochement was sealed with the October 1997 Summit that committed America and China to 'build towards a strategic partnership in the twenty-first century'.

Small blow-ups continued to dog the relationship, but failed to erupt into anything major. In 1999, China was accused of stealing US nuclear and technological secrets, and making illegal campaign contributions in the presidential elections. There was an accidental NATO bombing of the Chinese embassy in Belgrade, which killed three people. But all of this was minor compared to Clinton's crowning achievement: he finally snared China into the World Trade Organization towards the end of his eight-year term.

On its part, China was happy with a rather anonymous foreign policy through the 1980s and '90s. Its singular focus was to attract foreign capital and grow its export–manufacturing economy. It needed America's unalloyed blessings for capital, technology and markets. It wasn't bashful about a pro-US stance at United Nations and other forums. According to Zakaria, 'For three decades, Chinese foreign policy has been geared towards satisfying the United States for a variety of practical reasons. First it was anti-Soviet strategy, then a desire for markets and reform, then rehabilitating the country after Tiananmen Square, membership in the World Trade Organization, and finally the Beijing Olympics.'

All through this period, China consciously downplayed friction with

Vietnam, claims on the South China Sea, and border disputes with Russia. Chinese leaders have also been shy about using 'strong' adjectives like its 'rise to global power'. At one stage, there was much debate on whether China should use 'peaceful rise' to describe its ascent on the global stage. 'Rise' was seen to be an aggressive phrase, meaning push or thrust. It was finally jettisoned, and after experimenting with 'renaissance', Chinese leaders settled in favour of the far more circumspect 'peaceful development'.

But China has displayed a calibrated belligerence on the prickly issue of Taiwan. According to Kishore Mahbubani, 'Taiwan, which was torn from China after its ignominious defeat by Japan in 1895, is the last remaining symbol of a century of Chinese humiliations. No Chinese leader can afford to be seen as the one who "lost" Taiwan in perpetuity. From time to time, Beijing makes it clear that it will declare war if Taiwan moves towards independence, regardless of the costs. And it would be dangerous to ignore this reality.' Washington fully appreciates this delicate balancing act. It also realizes that the China–Taiwan equation could be slowly mending on its own, as the two hostile siblings get 'intertwined economically'. Over $300 billion of investments have flown from Taiwan to China. Nine economic and trade agreements were signed in just the last few months. Kent E. Calder points out that '10 per cent of Taiwan's labour force now works in China, and four Taiwanese-owned firms are among the mainland's top ten exporters. Taiwan now trades substantially more with China than it does with the United States.' China has adroitly lowered tariffs on Taiwanese farm produce to woo its farmers. It has even lent priceless antiques to Taiwan's museums, despite the fact that China has historically resented the 2,972 crates of fine imperial treasures that Chiang Kai-shek had taken with him while fleeing to Taiwan. As an official put it shrewdly, China has found it 'cheaper to buy Taiwan than to attack it'. But this is instigating reprisal in Taiwan; in December 2009, thousands of people came out on the streets, protesting the 'secret, non-transparent' free trade negotiations between the two countries, fearing 'steep losses to Taiwan'. This could be giving a tailwind to the anti-China opposition Democratic Progressive party for the 2012 polls. What if the current pro-China regime in Taiwan loses those elections?

America now only occasionally tilts towards Taiwan—as we have seen in the case of the Cornell University visa or the sale of F-16s—more as a warning to China to remain restrained. It's America's way of rapping China on the knuckles, of showing who is boss. Having done that, it usually pulls back to more or less a pro-China stance. Often it has openly endorsed China's cause. In 2003, when the Taiwanese president asked for a referendum on the issue of independence, President George W. Bush chided him, saying 'the comments and actions made by the leader of Taiwan indicate that he may be willing to make decisions unilaterally to change the status quo, which we oppose'.

Until the turn of the twenty-first century, American policy towards China was running along its own track, unaffected by a rather gradual cozying up to India. But a qualitative change appeared during the reign of George W. Bush Jr, who always saw China more as a 'strategic competitor' than a 'strategic partner'. In his world view, India, the other emerging Asian power, and a democracy to boot, could be cultivated as a major bulwark against China's latent expansionism. That story follows now.

As the Dragon Slays the Elephant

India's foreign policy has not been that monolithic. It has danced to the ebb and flow of domestic political and economic events. The early decades were completely dominated by the intellectually romantic world view of Jawaharlal Nehru, India's first prime minister who was also his own foreign minister. One of his foreign secretaries, K.P.S. Menon, wrote: 'We had no precedents to fall back upon, because India had no foreign policy of its own until she became independent. We did not even have a section for historical research, until I created one ... Our policy therefore necessarily rested on the intuition of one man who was foreign minister, Jawaharlal Nehru.'

Nehru was an idealist, a pacifist, who chose to believe (his critics would say 'delude himself') that India gained by remaining non-aligned and against the Cold War. He had an enormous grasp over world history. He delighted in airing his views on the world stage. He would often call himself 'the last Englishman to rule India'. Even before India became independent, Nehru was appointed member for external affairs and Commonwealth relations in the interim government under the British. He declared that India would 'keep away from power politics of groups aligned against one another, which have led in the past to world wars and which may again lead to disasters on an even vaster scale'. Diplomats like Shashi Tharoor have argued that Nehru ignored an American overture to take over Taiwan's seat at the United Nations' Security Council; instead he offered it to China! Ironically, subsequent Indian governments have strenuously campaigned to get a permanent seat at the high table, with little to show for it.

Fareed Zakaria has captured the essence of Nehru's morality play: 'Nehru rooted India's foreign policy in abstract ideas rather than a strategic conception of national interests. He was disdainful towards alliances, pacts and treaties, seeing them as part of the old rules of realpolitik, and was uninterested in military matters ... A week into his new government, he walked over to the defence ministry and was furious to find military officers working there (as they do in every defence ministry in the world). Since then, all armed service personnel who work in New Delhi's South Block wear civilian clothes. For much of Nehru's tenure, his defence minister was a close political confidant, V.K. Krishna Menon, who was even less interested in military matters, much preferring long-winded ideological combat in parliament to strategic planning.'

Nehru was rudely awakened by the war with China in 1962. In his world view, China and India were going to be the 'friendly pillars' of an independent Asia. He was quick to recognize China as a sovereign nation after the 1949 Communist Revolution. He even conceded that China's claims over Tibet were largely legitimate. He refused to call China the aggressor in the Korean War, even as the US pushed for it. The India–China bonhomie of the mid-1950s was colloquially called *Hindi Chini Bhai Bhai* ('Indians and Chinese are peace brothers'). But the two countries practised this affection in qualitatively different ways. While India has been accused of 'emotional positivism', the Chinese were always more 'hard nosed and focussed on their territorial aspirations and strategic interests'. Almost inevitably, their sibling love soured when India gave political asylum to the Dalai Lama and his

Tibetan followers after they revolted against the Chinese government in 1959. A feverish Indian media and the 'liberal' sect of politicians denounced China as the 'unscrupulous aggressor' against Tibet. China, always a stranger to India's voluble free press, suspected the whole act had been orchestrated by Nehru's government. From that day onwards, Nehru became an 'imperial stooge' in Chinese eyes.

China hardened its position on the border dispute with India, another legacy of British colonial rule. China believes that a vast amount (120,000 sq. km) of its border land spread over three sectors—the western sector (Ladakh), the middle sector (Himalayan foothills) and the eastern sector that India calls Arunachal Pradesh and China calls South Tibet—'historically' belongs to China. It alleges that the British took advantage of the disunity and chaos in China to draw the boundary (called the McMahon Line) in 1914 between Tibet, China and British India. Although the agreement was initialed by the Chinese representative, it later refused to ratify the accord, claiming the British had used subterfuge to transfer land to India, favouring a country which was fully under British control (unlike China). India has always disputed this 'historical' claim, saying it is neither factual nor valid. Tawang, the current hotspot between India and China over the exiled Dalai Lama's visit to the Tibetan monastery there (the same monastery he had fled to from China in the '50s), lies just south of the McMahon Line, in the Indian state of Arunachal.

J.N. Dixit was a desk officer in charge of India's relations with China when the two countries went to war on 20 October 1962 (in later years, this bright young diplomat went on to become India's foreign secretary and national security advisor). The jury is somewhat out on who attacked whom. The popular view is, at least in India and several western capitals, that China attacked India. But some analysts—primary among them Neville Maxwell who wrote *India's China War*—also think that India instigated the war. Although Maxwell's views were pilloried in India, J.N. Dixit betrays some sympathy for his assessment. According to Dixit, Prime Minister Nehru made a grievous error of judgement in ordering 'an all-out general offensive against the Chinese forward posts and military positions all along the disputed border'. Perhaps a few top-ranking Indian military officials overestimated their own strength, or perhaps they underestimated the severity of China's response. Dixit believes a full-scale war could have been avoided if India's military posture had been 'selective, gradual and area-specific'.

Nehru rued his blunders later, admitting that 'military weakness was a temptation' he had succumbed to. Dixit points to other shortcomings. He believes that Nehru erred in not striking a quid pro quo earlier: 'We could have told the Chinese that, in return for our accepting their resumption of authority over Tibet, they should confirm the delineation of the Sino–Indian boundary as inherited by them and us from the British period.' In contrast, Pakistan proved to be far more agile. Prime Minister Zulfikar Ali Bhutto always had a 'certain competitive strategic vision about strengthening Pakistan vis-a-vis India, by forging connections with China'. Bhutto was quick to cede large tracts from Pakistan-occupied Kashmir to China, thereby sealing a political and military (and nuclear) axis against India.

With America and Britain jumping to India's rescue, the 1962 war ended, albeit with a major loss of national pride for India. For the next couple of decades, India got hyphenated with Pakistan. India–China skirmishes became a sub-text of India–Pakistan face-offs, with China using its open alliance with Pakistan to take potshots at India.

Nehru's daughter, who became prime minister in 1966, was not a chip off the old block. Indira Gandhi's foreign policy was much more practical, though she stuck to her father's rhetoric on non-alignment. In reality, she took a pro-Soviet stance in the Cold War, riled by America's tilt towards Pakistan. She shared a personal hostility with the Nixon/Kissinger team—Kissinger actually told his ambassador in India that 'the less I hear from you and the less I hear about India, the happier I will be'. She thumbed her nose at Uncle Sam and China when she sent her army across to East Pakistan and dismembered India's traditional enemy into two countries by liberating the territory now called Bangladesh. In 1974, she detonated India's first nuclear device, creating much euphoria at home, but paranoia in Washington 'that the world was on the edge of a rapid burst of nuclear proliferation'. But for all of Indira Gandhi's tough exterior and hard talk, India's weakening economy robbed the country of a meaningful role in world affairs. It also ended up on the losing side of the Cold War.

Foreign policy got bogged down in neighbourhood skirmishes with Pakistan, Bangladesh, Nepal and Sri Lanka, often over local terrorism.

Eight rounds of border talks with Chinese officials simply went through the motions, producing, in Deng Xiaoping's words, no more than 'a mound of stale rice buzzing over with flies'. All through those years of virtual non-engagement, China continued to embarrass India; in 1979, when Atal Bihari Vajpayee, the high-profile Indian foreign minister (who later became prime minister) was on an official mission, China invaded Vietnam. Thirteen years later, it repeated the snub by detonating several nuclear weapons when the Indian president was on a state visit to Beijing, later saying it was an 'error'.

It is perhaps no coincidence that the two Indian prime ministers who took early steps to open up India's economy also reached out to China. Rajiv Gandhi travelled to Beijing in December 1988, and boldly opened trade and commerce, de-linking those from the unsolved border problem. Later, P.V. Narasimha Rao signed a virtual 'no war' pact in 1993, when both countries agreed that 'neither side shall use or threaten to use force against the other by any means'; until the border row was resolved, 'the two sides shall strictly respect and observe the Line of Actual Control'. The two countries set up hot-lines for military officials to speak and verify how many troops were deployed on either side of the line. Despite such reconciliatory moves, India's policy towards China has always been ambivalent. Much later, Prime Minister Vajpayee would tell the world that he had imploded a hydrogen bomb 'in response to the threat posed by Chinese nuclear weapons'; his defence minister would describe China as India's 'potential enemy number one'. Not surprisingly, policy hawks have criticized India for its weak and reactive impulses against China. But there are Indian ministers like Jairam Ramesh who want it to create the 'intellectual capital to understand and deal with China more effectively. India's acquiring "big power" status on the world stage depends critically on this, apart from making peace with Pakistan—and the two are not unrelated.'

China, on the other hand, continues to have many issues to pick with India. It is convinced that India was unreasonably aggressive in causing the 1962 conflict. It grudges the fact that India has also not fully accepted China's rights over Tibet, despite recognizing the territory as an autonomous region of China. It thinks of India as a 'hegemonic' power in South Asia, which is trying to out-empire even the British, cutting out China's legitimate interests in that region. The Chinese also complain that India is a poor country, but its leaders nurture unrealistic military ambitions. It accuses India of deliberately using the myth of a Chinese threat to expand its arsenal of nuclear weapons. It damns India's policy of 'befriending the far, and attacking the near'. Finally, China does not get India's plural and complex democracy. It is suspicious about criticism hurled at China in India's free media, thinking of it as a plot hatched by the Indian government.

China retaliates typically with a series of pin-pricks that rile up India visibly. China tried to block an Asian Development Bank loan for a project in Arunachal (which China calls South Tibet), on the grounds that the project's geography was disputed. It protested when India's prime minister campaigned in Arunachal's elections. It truly nettled India by refusing to stamp visas on Indian passports held by Kashmir's citizens. India rejected 'separately stapled visa sheets' on these passports, forcing travellers with such documents to cancel their trips to China. The fact that many of these 'stapled visas' were given to political activists opposed to India's position on Kashmir just made the whole standoff that much more rancourous.

How important is the India–China equation for the rest of the world? A United Nations intelligence report titled *Mapping the Global Future by 2020* has 'likened the emergence of China and India in the early twenty-first century to the rise of Germany in the nineteenth and America in the twentieth, with impacts potentially as dramatic'. Chinese premier Wen Jiabao echoed this to his Indian counterpart: 'When we shake hands, the whole world will be watching.' John Garver calls them natural rivals with their 'decades-long, multilayered, and frequently sharp conflict over the lands and peoples lying around and between them'. Ashley Tellis calls it a structural conflict between two natural competitors who are seeking to increase their influence on the world. While it may not become a malignant rivalry, he believes that if the two countries continue to gather economic and military muscle at the current rate, 'there is a likelihood of this relationship turning into a dyadic rivalry'.

India and China also share a geographical water tower that feeds their rivers. The high-altitude glaciers of the Himalayas birth India's Ganga, Indus and Brahmaputra, and China's Mekong, Yellow and

Yangtze. Together, these rivers cradle nearly 3 billion people, or half the world's population. Alarmingly, a fifth of these glaciers have been destroyed in the last fifty years; the Intergovernmental Panel on Climate Change finds them 'receding faster than at any other place in the world'. *Time* calls it a global warming threat that 'can be seen in real time, with our own eyes'. The Earth Policy Institute calls 'the melting of these glaciers the most massive threat to food security that we have ever projected'. This has made China and India co-victims of a life-threatening ecological crisis. Will they cooperate to solve the problem, or go to war over food and water? Early signals are unclear. India is suspicious that China could be building dams to disrupt flows to downstream countries. Chinese researchers are not allowed to visit India's glaciers, and China is sensitive about allowing outsiders into Tibet. But if there's one area in which the two adversaries have sheathed their daggers, it's over the environment, witness their near-perfect understanding and bonhomie at Copenhagen, as they closed ranks against the developed countries.

The India–China love–hate equation spills over into bidding for energy assets around the globe. See the way China outwitted India in Myanmar's Shwe gas project. In 2004, India's gas authority won the bid; but China leaned hard on the military junta to change the parameters, and ultimately wrested the deal. But of late, both countries are seeing plenty of merit in cartelizing their purchases. China did not bid against India for Britain's Imperial Energy, and India returned the favour by staying away from Syria's Tanganyika Oil. Since China and India import 40 per cent and 70 per cent of their oil respectively, the next step could be to pool their bids to maximize bargaining clout. Both would also like to join hands to kill the extra charge of $1-2 per barrel of oil, called the 'Asian Premium'. India has dangled a $7 billion bait of power equipment buys from Chinese companies to meet its stretch generation targets. Yet these are slivers of cooperation in an otherwise strained engagement; despite low key promises of support, China is known to have thrown several last-minute spanners into India's exceptional civil nuclear treaty with America.

The two countries are also sparring in a somewhat bizarre manner over counterfeit products. In June 2009, Nigeria seized a large consignment of fake anti-malarial drugs. While these were marked

'Made in India', investigations proved they had come from China! The Chinese government apologized to Nigeria and arrested six traders who were ultimately sentenced to death after a quick trial. The Chinese ministry of commerce refused to give more details but kept insisting that India should also take some responsibility since Indian traders have been found to ship spurious drugs to Nigeria in other instances.

A new theatre of competition is opening up in East Asia. Just as China wants a piece of action in South Asia (with Afghanistan, Pakistan, Bangladesh and Myanmar), India is 'looking east' at the ASEAN +3 (i.e. Japan, China and South Korea) countries—it has already concluded free trade agreements with ASEAN and South Korea. India would like the grouping extended into East Asian Summit (EAS), made up of ASEAN +3, India, Australia and New Zealand; to balance China's influence, India would not mind including the US and Russia. China, of course, would like the ASEAN +3 group to retain its primacy. While it's early days to see how this alphabet soup of emerging Asia–Pacific alignments will play out, it's just one more face-off that China and India have to deal with.

Perhaps the most perceptive commentary has come from Stephen Cohen. According to him, 'India–China relations are greatly affected by China's generally dismissive views of India.' China regards India as a soft power which can be made to fall in line, if not totally dominated. China is convinced that 'its civilization is older and greater than India's'. It believes that Churchill's description of his rival—'he is a modest man with much to be modest about'—applies equally here. India, with its 'modest accomplishments should behave in a suitably modest fashion; Indian assertiveness, the Chinese believe, does not seem to be justified; given New Delhi's feeble economic and strategic record.' Indians respond to this with 'intrigue and fright'. The perceptions at both ends are 'mired in stereotypes', and awareness about each other is 'abysmal'. Many Indians suffer from a siege mentality, believing that China is out to encircle it by building alliances with Pakistan and Nepal. India is also hopelessly outflanked in the arms race—India's $30 billion defence budget is puny compared to China's official allocation of $70 billion (Rand Corp estimates China's actual spend at about $200 billion). At 2.1 million in active duty, China has the world's largest standing army. India has the third largest, after the US, with about 1.2 million officers and soldiers. While China's stockpile is likely to go up to 1,500-2,000 nuclear warheads soon, India's is estimated at only ninety.

Quite naturally, India's suspicion of the Chinese has survived over generations.

As the Elephant Makes a Nest with the Eagle

Indian diplomacy stayed largely faceless from the 1980s to the end of the twentieth century. The country's energies were consumed in first dealing with the national bankruptcy of the early '90s, and then in reinventing its inefficient, insular economy. However, India re-emerged on the world stage when its GDP began accelerating by 7–9 per cent every year. The commercial world was now eager to embrace India and its China-like potential. But India was still a nuclear renegade in the shadowy world of geo-political power play.

The Nuclear Non-Proliferation Treaty had been in force since 1968. America, Britain, France, Russia and China, the existing nuclear powers, declared that only they had the right to hold nuclear weapons. India chafed at that exclusion, and rejected the treaty. What's more, it exploded a nuclear device in the Rajasthan desert in 1974, sealing its fate as a nuclear outlaw. For a quarter of a century, it weathered hostility and sanctions, but stubbornly refused to cap or open up its weapons programme to international inspection.

Then, in 1998, it exploded another nuclear device, under the newly elected right wing, pro-US, nationalist government of Prime Minister Vajpayee. World powers erupted in fury, imposed harsher sanctions, but again India held its nerve. Slowly, it began to dawn on America that an adamant India was unlikely to concede—but equally, it had to be roped back into the nuclear mainstream. India was already the world's second fastest growing economy, and the only bulwark against China in Asia. In March 2000, after decades of virtual non-engagement, Bill Clinton became the first US president to visit India in more than twenty-two years. But his visit was high on atmospherics and somewhat short on substance.

But Clinton's successor, George W. Bush Jr., was most determined to reach out to India. His government's National Security strategy document of September 2002 pushed for a 'strong relationship with India'. The US National Intelligence Council report, which mapped the world in 2020, concluded that 'the arriviste powers—China, India and perhaps others such as Brazil and Indonesia—have the potential to render obsolete the old categories of East and West, North and South, aligned and non-aligned, developed and developing'. Bush kicked off his 'engage India' campaign in typical cowboy style: he 'dropped in' unannounced at a meeting between the Indian external affairs minister and Condoleeza Rice. Bush took the Indian minister for a stroll in the Rose Garden, and then led him by the arm into the Oval office. That changed the game for India and America. Later that year, India did the politically unthinkable when it offered military bases to US troops preparing to strike Afghanistan after 9/11. India wanted to equate its battles against Pakistan-supported terrorism in Kashmir with America's war against the Taliban and al-Qaeda. While America declined that offer, the bonhomie between President Bush and Prime Minister Vajpayee was palpable in the months that followed.

Bush and Vajpayee got talking about a US–India nuclear treaty to lasso India back into the mainstream. But before the deal could be done, Vajpayee's government suffered a shock election defeat in 2004, and Prime Minister Manmohan Singh's weak, left-leaning coalition government took over. It seemed the end of the road for the nuke deal. Not only was Manmohan critically dependent on the communists, but his own Congress party and other political allies had traditionally panned a 'subversive US hand' for almost all past ills.

Manmohan Singh is not a career politician. He lost the only election he ever fought in his life; in fact, he holds the dubious record of being the only prime minister of India who was not directly elected to parliament, but joined the government as a member of the upper house. He is a shy and withdrawing kind of person, that rare politician who happily admits that he does not have the charisma and debating abilities of his rivals. It's a strange twist of destiny that his self-effacing candour and earnest demeanour have struck a chord with India's middle classes. He is the only prime minister since Nehru to have been re-elected after completing a full term in office.

Singh's apparent shortcomings are perhaps also his strength. He does not carry a blinkered vision of history. He does not suffer from the Indian politician's curse of short-term, reactive decision-making. He has the intellectual apparatus to understand how the world is changing with the rise of Asia, the diminution of Europe, the remodelling of America, the relentless momentum of China and the emerging continents of Africa and Latin America, and how this can be harnessed by a freshly thinking, non-doctrinaire India.

As India's economic clout grew, Manmohan Singh's foreign policy ambitions reignited. After all, as the finance minister in the early 1990s, he had unleashed the country's animal spirits; now as prime minister he was crafting a brand new foreign policy for a country surging in confidence. He perhaps remembered the words of T.N. Kaul, India's celebrated ambassador to the US, who was convinced that America would 'respect India when India does not go with a begging bowl, asking for charity and so-called aid'. Singh made a few deft moves early in his tenure to woo America—upgrading patent laws in 2004, removing an Indian company's right to veto its foreign counterpart's foreign investment, 'opening the skies' to American airlines, and placing a $7 billion order for fifty Boeing aircraft. Having softened America with his economic hardsell, Manmohan bet his job on the nuke deal. His quest was sharp: to convert India from a renegade to a legitimate 'equal' on the world nuclear stage.

Prime Minister Manmohan Singh struck an unusual friendship with President George W. Bush. One was widely criticized as 'India's weakest PM'; the other seemed to love the epithet of 'America's war-mongering president'. There was even a personal twist in their relationship, which ought to have made Bush wary of Singh. The Indian prime minister's daughter was a vociferous, New York based human rights lawyer, forever in the forefront of anti-Bush campaigns. But both men put aside personal issues. Bush visited India in March 2006, the first visit to India by a Republican president. More significantly, this was the second visit by an American president within six years.

Bounding down the aircraft's stepladder, Bush's body language was effusive with Manmohan, who broke protocol to receive him at Delhi's Indira Gandhi International Airport late at night. Turning to Condoleeza Rice, Bush was overheard saying: 'I want this deal done.' Over the next few days, both men made visible displays of bonhomie, laughing, chatting, putting arms around each other's shoulders. (On a later visit to Washington, when President Bush's popularity had nosedived and he was getting ready to quit the White House, Manmohan actually told him, in full media glare, that 'all of India loves you'. He was politically castigated back home for that misplaced exuberance.)

President Bush concluded his 2006 visit with a nationally televised address from New Delhi's historic Old Fort. Framed against the imposing ramparts of history, Bush delivered a stellar eulogy to India and its rising potential in world affairs: 'For many years, the United States and India were kept apart by the rivalries that divided the world. That is changed. The United States and India, separated by half the globe, are closer than ever before, and the partnership between our free nations has the power to transform the world.'

Away from the feel-good rhetoric, India and America were locked in fierce negotiations over the nuke deal. To Prime Minister Manmohan Singh's credit, he did not succumb to any blandishments or tough posturing. He had drawn his 'thick red lines' on the deal, committing to India's parliament that 'no part of this process would affect or compromise our strategic programme . . . to inflict unacceptable damage on an adversary indulging in a nuclear first strike. We will offer to place under safeguards only those facilities that can be identified as civilian without damaging our deterrence potential.' He simply could not have dared to compromise India's weapons programme, or open it up for inspection.

Ultimately, he got much of his way. India was allowed to keep its weapons' reactors outside international gaze. Its civilian nuclear plants were put in the custody of the International Atomic Energy Agency (IAEA). India was now free to import uranium from the nuclear suppliers' group for its power plants. China and Pakistan protested vehemently at what they saw as an 'unusually favourable', pampered treatment of India's nuclear ambitions. But the deal was done. (Much later, President Bush visited India on a speaking trip in 2009. A private citizen now, Bush went to have lunch with his 'old pal' Manmohan Singh. He thanked people for coming to meet a 'retired guy'. When asked about the nuke deal, he quipped, in typical Bush style, 'Yeah, we got it done even though we had to break a bit of China.' Bound by protocol, the Indian prime minister is understood to have smiled, rather out of politeness.)

A beaming Manmohan was all primed to receive bouquets from his home constituency. To his immense shock—and chagrin—he ran into a volley of brickbats. Ideologically rebuked, the communists withdrew support to the government. Its politburo chief, Prakash Karat, launched an intemperate personal attack on the prime minister. Manmohan was banking on Vajpayee's right wing Bhartiya Janata Party (BJP), the original authors of the nuke deal, to back him. The BJP reneged on its ideology and opposed the deal, hoping to replace the Congress in government. The Congress party and its allies took refuge in timid ambivalence. A big chunk of India's intellectual elite, comfortable with the status quo, out of step with the throbbing aspirations of a young, confident, upwardly mobile nation, chose to see the issue in extinct Cold War terms. 'Why are the Americans being so nice to us? There must be a hidden agenda!'—that became the refrain of an endemically suspicious and under-confident segment. It was an unthinkable congruence of political interests; China, Pakistan, India's BJP and communists, and left intellectuals, they were all were on the same side in opposing the nuke deal. Fareed Zakaria has this to say about such commentators in *The Post-American World*: 'Many Indian elites have continued to view the world through a Nehruvian prism—India as a poor, virtuous third world country, whose foreign policy was neutral and detached (and, one might add, unsuccessful). They understand how to operate in that world, whom to beg from and whom to be belligerent with. But a world in which India is a great power and moves confidently across the global stage, setting rules and not merely being shaped by them, and in which it is a partner of the most powerful country in history—that is a new and altogether unsettling proposition.' India's politicians and left-tilting policy wonks seemed to be completely out of synch with ordinary citizens; the latest Pew survey shows that 76 per cent of Indians surveyed (higher than even Israel's 71 per cent) carry a favourable image of America, up from 66 per cent in 2008.

Ultimately, Manmohan won the day. He gambled his government on a precarious vote of confidence on the nuke deal in parliament. If he had lost the vote, he would have had to quit, and the deal would have been irretrievably lost. But he carried the floor with a 275 to 256 victory. He got surprisingly strong support from Rahul Gandhi, the

young scion of India's ruling family, widely seen as the next prime
minister. In a rare, and shy, speech in parliament, Rahul exhorted the
country that: 'Fear should not be our guide, as we need to act with
courage. The difference between a powerful country and others is that
a powerful country does not think about how others impact it but how
it can impact the rest of the world.'

Manmohan Singh had become a hero in victory. His hitherto diffident
allies hailed him as a 'polite man of steel'. 'Beware the fury of the
patient man,' they thumped their tables in ecstasy. It may be entirely
unrelated, but this triumph in parliament was followed by a resounding
victory for the Congress party in the general elections that followed a
few months later.

As the Dragon Also Makes a Nest with the Eagle

China spent over $55 billion on the 2010 Shanghai World Expo to
remind the world that it had not lost its dazzle through the great
recession of 2008. It reached out to Arturo DiModica, the Italian–
American artist who had created Wall Street's famous mascot, 'Charging
Bull'. *Newsweek* reported that the 'Shanghai beast will weigh almost
twice its New York brother's 7,000 pounds'. The article quoted a
Chinese official claiming their bull will be 'younger and more energetic,
symbolizing the energy of Shanghai's economy. Its head will look up,
while the Wall Street bull looks down.'

Clearly, America is now staring at a fast re-arranging world, with
many of the pieces outside its grasp. Foreign policy analysts call it a
'multipolar' world, which has been radically rearranged from the
bipolar one that existed during the Cold War. Then it used to be a
simple, straight fight between the American alliance and the Soviet
bloc. America knew how to deal with that world of intrigue, force,
power and naked military play. Today that black-and-white edifice
has crumbled. The bad guys have gone, and the Soviet Union is no
more.

Today's equations are far more complex, and still evolving. By far
the most important equation is the one being crafted between America
and China. 'Our future history will be more determined by our
position on the Pacific facing China than by our position on the

Atlantic facing Europe,' said Theodore Roosevelt, almost a century
ago. Somewhat later than he may have expected, the prediction is
finally ringing true. Niall Ferguson calls it Chimerica, a new 'nation'
that was born after the end of the Cold War. 'For a time it seemed like
a marriage made in heaven,' Ferguson writes in *The Ascent of Money*.
'The East Chimericans did the saving, the West Chimericans did the
spending.' China grew furiously, and Americans gorged on low interest
rates and inflation. It is perhaps this reality of 'you scratch my back,
and I will scratch yours' that has forced normally combative Americans
to be indulgent towards China. People like former national security
adviser Zbigniew Brzezinski believe that China will exercise its powers
in a 'patient, prudent and peaceful fashion, unlike some contrary
manifestations on the part of Russia, also a revisionist power, but a
much more truculent one'. Brzezinski is an advocate of G2, where
America and China coexist peacefully by accommodating each other's
spheres of influence.

Secretary of state Hillary Clinton wants to use 'smart power'—a
clever potion of military might, economic clout and cultural influence,
a mix of the traditional strategies of hard and soft power—to deal with
China. She believes the twenty-first century should be a multi-partner,
not a multipolar world. Other advisers in President Obama's
administration would like to replace the earlier 'engage and hedge'
approach with one that 'maximizes opportunity but also manages
risk'. The phrase in vogue is 'strategic reassurance'. Whichever words
are used to dress it up, the strategy has to be a twenty-first century
variant of the 'carrot and stick'.

Happily for now, an asymmetric dynamic drives the relationship
between China and America. China exported over $350 billion worth
of goods to the US, and lent $800 billion by buying American treasuries
in 2009. Just as China needs America's markets, the US needs Chinese
debt. Even a slight wobble in this equilibrium could throw millions of
Chinese workers out of jobs, and push American interest rates
uncomfortably high. Lawrence Summers has called it the 'balance of
financial terror'. But Americans can take comfort in their unquestionable
military superiority over China. The economic might of the two
countries may be converging, but the military equation is loaded in
America's favour. Even as China frenetically spends 10 per cent of its

GDP on arms, that is still a tenth of the Pentagon's humongous appetite for weapons. The US has twelve nuclear-powered aircraft carriers, while China is still building its first. America has thousands of sophisticated nuclear warheads and missiles, against the dozen plus that China can put together to threaten it. The America–China comparison, at best, is about hugely asymmetric superpowers.

Yet China is a difficult country to fathom, and that troubles many Americans. Very little is known about China's nuclear alert systems, or how close it is to mounting its America-range nuclear missiles on submarines. The Pentagon has not been able to persuade the Chinese to send their chief of strategic nuclear forces to Washington; indeed, no American official has been allowed into the headquarters of the Chinese armed forces, an underground facility in Fragrant Hills, west of Beijing. The sophisticated Chinese war machine on display at the sixtieth anniversary parade created disquiet in the western world. It was mentally contrasted with the Soviet Union of yore, which was a weak economic power that tried to sustain a disproportionately large army, and eventually lost the plot. China, on the other hand, is first building a strong and modern economy. It's building a robust balance sheet, with trillions of dollars in surpluses and reserves. Today it is in China's interest to show a benign face to America. After 9/11, it opened up its intelligence on al-Qaeda and radical Islamic groups in Asia. Even as it opposed America's invasion of Iraq, it chose to stay quiet at the United Nations. China's silence was a key factor in swinging the Security Council's endorsement, in the teeth of opposition from countries like France.

America has often leaned on China to play the good cop in North Korea. Since China supplies Pyongyang with almost all its oil, it enjoys some persuasive powers over Kim Jong-il. America has often called in those favours, and China has obliged; in 2003, it even cut off fuel supplies to North Korea for a few days. One can cite example after example where China has played a constructive role, keen to be seen as 'the good guy'.

Ordinarily, China's non-threatening, conformist record of the past few decades should be good enough to allay fears. But somehow, the sceptics and doubters are not fully convinced. 'We need to urge China to become a responsible stakeholder' so that it will 'work with us to sustain the international system that has enabled its success'—almost every US diplomat uses these words when talking with, at or about China. American policymakers dread the day that China is forced to 'go it alone and create international organizations that fundamentally clash with US interests ... which could make the future very uncomfortable for the United States'. They speculate on what would happen after China's economy has become larger than America's. Once its military might is comparable, will China continue to be a good guy? Will China's ambitions change once it has put a man on the moon (targeted for 2020), and mounted several America-range nuclear missiles on submarines lurking in the Pacific? Will a century-old history of humiliations and suffering under western powers uncoil into a primeval desire for retribution and dominance? Will China remain happy playing second fiddle to America, or will it carve its own spheres of influence, at least as an equal?

When a country of China's size 'develops'—nay, *doubles* its economy every eight years—it scorches the earth for resources. With a fifth of the world's population, China now consumes half its cement, a third of its steel, and over a quarter of its aluminum, creating a tectonic shift in raw material markets. China's outbound FDI was over $50 billion in 2008, doubling from the previous year. Its creeping economic hegemony over Sudan, Zimbabwe and other African territories is awesome. China–Africa trade scaled over $73 billion in 2007; Africa has become China's second largest contractual project market and third largest investment destination. China controls two of the largest oil companies in Sudan, and consumes two-thirds of its oil exports. It helped build Merowe Dam on the Nile, Sudan's most prestigious project. It gifted Guinea-Bissau a marble parliament building. It buys platinum and iron ore from Zimbabwe. It colonizes vast tracts of agricultural land in outright commercial deals. Joshua Ramo, a former *Time* magazine foreign affairs editor and Goldman Sachs China advisor, has coined the term 'Beijing consensus' to define how China has overtaken the 'Washington consensus' in investments, aid and trade to Africa: 'it does not impose onerous conditions on African states' policies, and is more active than the West in promoting industrialism in the global South'.

Inevitably, there is a darker side to this 'Beijing consensus', as Chinese arms and reconnaissance devices have found their way into the hands of the ruling juntas. In Namibia, a Chinese state-owned manufacturer of security scanners has been charged with bribing local officials to win a $55 million contract (until 2008, President Hu Jintao's son was the head of this company, although he has not been implicated in this case). China has also gained some collateral diplomatic advantage by spreading its tentacles in Africa. Historically, African countries have supported Taiwan. Over the last decade, six of them, including South Africa, have switched allegiance. A grateful China has canceled 150 items of maturing government debt owed to it by thirty-two African countries. Such a friendly credit policy also fits in with China's designs on Africa's consumer markets. Taken as one, the African continent virtually mimics India's mass consumer market. There are 150 million elite consumers, and 500 million aspiring ones. China is 'doing an America' to Africa, hoping to swap tax and loan credits with Chinese cars, chocolate, electronics and T-shirts. With a single smart stroke, China could have filled its consumption deficit by adding an India-sized market to its kitty.

But the thrust inside Africa has been so deep, uncompromising and wide that local people are pushing back. Take China Metallurgical's $1.4 billion investment into nickel mines in Papua New Guinea. An assistant labour secretary told *Time*, 'What I don't understand is why they (the Chinese) are so stubborn to not respect our local culture. We are a democracy. They have to play by our rules or we will rise up.' The locals panic about losing their land, and are miffed by rumours that China will use their nickel for a secret weapons programme. On the other hand, expatriate Chinese engineers call the natives 'completely uncivilized and running around almost naked'. China compounds this attitude by shipping armies of labourers to overseas construction sites, often on illegal visas; an estimated 740,000 Chinese labourers were working on projects from Angola to Indonesia in 2008, up 58 per cent from the previous year. These aliens bring along everything with them, 'from packs of dehydrated noodles to the tell-tale pink-hued Chinese toilet paper'. Such an isolated 'bubble world' has been compared to American military bases in the Middle East. Within a few years, petty Chinese traders follow, setting up shop and threatening native entrepreneurs. Unsurprisingly, anti-Chinese riots have become common, 'from the Solomon Islands and Zambia to Tongo and Lesotho'.

After all is said and done, China has reserved its friendliest face for Asia, its primary sphere of influence. For a country which did not have diplomatic relations with key Asian states in the 1980s, it now commands a loyal affinity with much of East Asia. It used the 1997 financial crisis skilfully to make friends with South Korea, Indonesia, Singapore and Thailand. In 2007, it even held joint military exercises with ASEAN countries. On New Year's Day in 2010, China inaugurated the world's third largest free trade area (behind European Economic Area and NAFTA) with ten South-East Asian nations. Tariffs on 90 per cent of traded goods will be removed in a market of 1.9 billion people. But China's artificially low yuan is now hurting ASEAN exports. Vietnam devalued its currency 5 per cent to keep it competitive; there is unease over the invasion of Chinese labour into power plants and mining projects. In an unusual occurrence for this authoritarian state, a lawyer has sued the prime minister for approving a Chinese bauxite mining project. At another level, Indonesia is having second thoughts about a free trade pact with China—it is planning to ask for a delay in removing tariffs on some items like steel, textiles and electronics. Its once-bustling nail industry is on the verge of closure, unable to compete with China's over-capacity-deflated steel prices, hugely discounted iron ore purchases and exceptionally cheap currency. Indonesia has invoked WTO rules on unfair trade, but this is likely to have little effect.

In South Asia, China's FDI in Pakistan is about to scale $15 billion in projects ranging from heavy engineering to telecommunications. It has invested $3.5 billion in Aynak copper mines in the heart of Taliban territory in Afghanistan, even as it dreads a radical Islamic influence on its restive Uighur minority. It can count Australia, whose commodities find a big market in China, among its buddies. Baosteel Group already owns 15 per cent of Australia's Aquila Resources. China's FDI in Australia is galloping, having topped $13 billion in 2009. Of late, some strains have appeared, as Australia granted a visa to the rebel leader of China's Muslim Uighurs. China also summarily arrested officials of Rio Tinto (the Australian mining giant) for 'spying'; many believe China is retaliating against Rio Tinto's refusal to sell equity to China Aluminum Corp.

Over in Latin America, China and Argentina have swapped $10 billion of their currencies to bypass the US dollar. There are over 4,000 Chinese supermarkets in Argentina, besides the unquenchable search for oil. China Investment Corporation recently picked up a 17 per cent stake in Canadian miner Teck Resources. The Industrial and Commercial Bank of China bought 20 per cent of South Africa's Standard Bank for over $5 billion. The Chinese are even building the Pearl River housing project in St Petersburg.

The Chinese sweep across the world is simply awe-inspiring. Its eve-expanding circle of friends—it's too early to call it a sphere of influence, but circles do grow into spheres!—has got the sceptics within America's foreign policy establishment truly worried. According to Immanuel Wallerstein of Yale University, 'As of the 1970s, the United States was a declining power. The foreign policy of all US presidents from Nixon to Clinton, including Reagan, was basically identical. The chief objective was to slow down the decline by means of soft multilateralism.' America stuck alliances with Japan and western Europe to keep them tied to its leadership. It launched a campaign to whittle down weapons of mass destruction so it could maintain its own lead. And it forced countries to open their economies so it could perpetuate its financial dominance.

Uncannily, China could have become an unintended beneficiary of this policy of 'soft multilateralism'; will it now challenge America's dominance, perhaps closer to the middle of the twenty-first century? Half the respondents in a survey conducted by Lowy Institute and MacArthur Foundation in China thought America posed a security threat. Seventy per cent opposed the idea of the US government buying a controlling stake in a major Chinese company. The bestselling *China Is Not Happy* chafes at China's overdependence on America. Was President Obama's first China visit a sneak preview of things to come?

Barack Obama is styled as America's first Asia-Pacific president—his coming-out party was a nine-day trip to Asia, with three days in Beijing in November 2009. The haunting image of that visit is a lonely Obama framed against a serpentine Great Wall stretching behind him. The president was roundly criticized for allowing China to control his diary. Where he went, who he met, how his visits were shown on television or internet—the CPC seemed to have choreographed each step. American hardliners nostalgically recalled President Clinton's flamboyant breeze-through in 1998, when he gave a live television interview, interacted openly with Chinese students and addressed a free-for-all press conference with President Jiang Zemin. As against this, President Obama's Beijing trip was uncomfortably thin on atmospherics. Hu Jintao firmly disallowed any questions at their joint press conference; Obama silently acquiesced. Later, a top editor of *Southern Weekend* was demoted for an Obama interview that was more candid than authorized. The Council's president emeritus, Lelie Gelb, wrote a scathing article calling it the 'amateur hour at the White House'. But commentators like Joe Klein were more willing to give their president the benefit of the doubt: 'A foreign policy based on bluster—railing against an 'axis of evil'—is easier to sell than a foreign policy based on nuance.' Others called it a 'high risk, low profile' strategy: President Obama giving up 'quick wins' in favour of a long-drawn engagement with China, without upstaging or threatening it.

Barack Obama extolled the virtues of free speech at a 'town hall' with 500 carefully selected members of the Communist Youth League in Shanghai, but the speech was broadcast only locally in the city, and the internet feed was suspiciously slow. China refused to give way on the yuan, forcing America to delete the words 'exchange rates based on the economy'; it audibly castigated America for the global economic crisis, asking it to take 'a serious look at its root causes'. To be fair, on Tibet, Obama did manage an adroit 'draw', saying it is part of China, but also asking China to resume talks with the Dalai Lama. There was hardly any mention about sanctions on Iran and North Korea, although Obama fans say he extracted a promise of 'significant diplomatic cooperation' on North Korea, Afghanistan and Pakistan. Was Obama unable, or did he not try hard enough, to bring America's unquestionable military, industrial and technological superiority to bear in his dealings with China? Whatever the explanation, the visit left America with a grim foreboding of divided world supremacy.

What riled India was an overt invitation to China to step into South Asia and help 'promote peace, stability and development in that region'. India's phalanx of America-baiters saw it as China leaning on a 'submissive' America to give it a larger role in 'India's domain'. Even the usually soft-speaking Indian prime minister reacted sharply, saying he 'failed to understand' China's new found 'assertiveness'. Even as

America and China scrambled to clarify that neither had a role to play in the 'bilateral' India–Pakistan equation, a lingering doubt remained that America may have ceded a bit of South Asia to China.

A bare five days later, President Obama got the chance to deftly equalize any perceived China–India imbalance when he greeted Manmohan Singh as his first visiting head of state. *Time* reported an atmosphere of 'easy conviviality, surrounded by a bubbly case of celebrities and power brokers who toasted the bonds between the world's largest democracies'. Clearly, the Indian visit had the celebratory veneer of an equity partnership: perhaps not an equal-stakes one, but yet the bonhomie of an equity equation. The economist prime minister buoyed Uncle Sam's spirits by saying he saw America's woes as a 'temporary aberration' which would not topple the dollar from its perch as the world's reserve currency. As against this, Barack Obama's China visit seemed like a tense creditor–debtor engagement, in which the lender (China) was subtly extracting a price for bailing out the borrower (America) with an $800 billion lifeline.

Four weeks later, at the Copenhagen Climate Summit, the Americans were given another grim reminder of Chinese belligerence when President Obama broke into a side-meeting between the group of 'hold-out leaders' from China, India, Brazil and South Africa. Obama was keen to do a deal—he conceded that the carbon cuts be 'non-binding', but wanted China to list their climate targets in an international registry. According to the *Washington Post*, a Chinese negotiator by the name of Xie Zhenhua 'launched into a tirade, pointing his finger at the US president'. Wen Jiabao, the Chinese premier, asked his translator to ignore those remarks, but 'when Xie erupted again, Wen, who was chairing the meeting, ignored him'. Was Wen helpless, or was it an orchestrated Chinese version of a 'good cop, bad cop' negotiating strategy on display there?

Just weeks after the 'finger-wagging' incident at Copenhagen, China got into a terrible scrap with Google which had detected a 'highly sophisticated and targeted attack' on its computers 'originating from China'. China hit back, saying Google had engineered the whole thing to cut losses, since it was badly trailing Baidu, the local Chinese search engine. Amidst this standoff, China test-fired a land-based missile-defence system, becoming the second country (after America) to use a missile to destroy another one in space. Going against usual diplomatic practice, China failed to inform the Pentagon in advance about the test. This was widely seen as an angry rebuke to America's decision to sell Patriot missiles to Taiwan.

Is China jettisoning Deng Xiaoping's foreign policy doctrine of 'conceal brilliance, cultivate obscurity'? *The China Dream*, an authoritative book by a senior professor at China's National Defence University, exhorts the country to 'aim for long-term military dominance so that America does not try to neutralize its power'. Having built enormous economic clout and independent spheres of influence in Asia and Africa, is China deliberately getting muscular with the United States of America?

As the Eagle, Dragon and Elephant Crowd the Same Nest

So as the American eagle, the Chinese dragon and the Indian elephant rearrange the world's nest, what will be the power points of a twenty-first century globe? Will the world be scythed by the axis alignments of the twentieth century—a somewhat predictable US–Japan–India 'axis' to 'contain' China—or will a new geo-political axiom emerge to supplant the axis politics of the Cold War era? Will America, China and India have the good sense to create a benign matrix of (competitive) alignments, as against the rattling sabres of the axis years? After all, isn't China just a rival, not an adversary, of the US? Hasn't America chosen engagement, not containment, as its primary strategy with China? While America avoided trade and economic ties with Moscow during the Cold War, hasn't China emerged as America's largest trading partner? Hasn't America invested heavily in both the Chinese and Indian economies? Why has there never been any major conflict between America and India, even as the two countries have held very different world views in the past? Therefore, aren't all the signs propitious for what Hillary Clinton has called the multi-partner, not multipolar, world? Doesn't everything point towards a mutually beneficial, albeit competitive, matrix of alignments, as opposed to the lacerating axis alignments of the Cold War years?

The answers to these key questions lie in another series of questions. Will the American economy recover its strength, or will it bleed from the post-Lehman gashes for decades to come? Will America get so consumed in solving its internal economic mess that it begins to cede space around the globe? Did President Hu Jintao come across more assertive than usual in dealing with a somewhat defensive President Obama in Beijing? Will the Chinese economy continue to defy laws of gravity and financial prudence, or will it level off, perhaps even down-glide a bit? Will India's leaders give up their happy-trailing-China mindset to make a determined bid for decades of double digit growth? Will increasing protectionism push China and America into trade wars? Will China get adventurous with the idea of trying to replace the dollar with the yuan as the world's reserve currency (of course, it will have to make its currency convertible on the capital account to do that, with consequences which could be quite unpredictable)? Did China buy $50 billion of IMF bonds to bolster its influence on the world's economic architecture? What if China dumps American treasury bonds, pushing up interest rates and wounding the two economies somewhat irretrievably? Will India's leaders have the gumption to step into the void and harvest the flow of dollar investments this could trigger?

Is there an 'India card' that America can play against China? Is there an 'America card' that India can play against China? And is China getting increasingly wary about these chimerical cards that India and America can play around with? After all, an opinion scan of over eighty American and Indian military officials in Jane's Foreign Report suggested that 'China represents the most significant threat to both countries' security in the future as an economic and military competitor'. A US officer went to the extent of saying that 'we want a friend in 2020 that will be capable of assisting the US militarily to deal with a Chinese threat'.

Is this kind of war talk an overreaction? Is this bit about 'cards' just discredited poker talk from a bygone era in world politics? Isn't it much more about hard-nosed economic bargaining, about self-interest-driven diplomacy in which each country wants to maximize its own gains rather than become obsessed about inflicting maximum damage on the other? Doesn't America need China today as much as it may need India tomorrow? Doesn't India stand to lose much economic clout if it allows America to dominate its China policy? And doesn't

China need to have peace on its long borders with India if China's economic juggernaut is to continue rolling? Wouldn't America want both China and India to remain within US-led governance structures rather than operate outside of them? In short, isn't it all about a matrix of (competitive) alignments, in the twenty-first century?

If economic interests are driving America, China and India into a nest of peaceful cohabitation (or matrix of alignments!), what about their political flash points, which could, in unguarded moments, trump the benign forces of trade and commerce? For instance, how will the countries deal with Iran? America's Hyde Act enjoins it to 'secure India's full and active participation in United States' efforts to dissuade, isolate, and, if necessary, sanction and contain Iran for its efforts to acquire weapons of mass destruction'. But India's powerful domestic pro-Muslim lobbies will never allow this to happen. What's more, China has been known to wink at Iran's weapons programme in order to secure Iranian supplies of oil and gas. Both China and India are vying to pick up a piece of Iran's cross-country oil pipeline. This is anathema to a deeply resentful America.

Then there is the nuclear-armed, Taliban-threatened Pakistan, the intractable fourth corner of the America–China–India triangle. The latest Pew survey throws up an unexpected shift in the way America is perceived in India and Pakistan. While 76 per cent of Indians view America favourably, almost 64 per cent of Pakistanis view it as an 'enemy', a fallout of the US war in Afghanistan. South Asia's shifting sands make it a theatre of explosive instability. America clearly needs Pakistan for its offensive against the Taliban and al-Qaeda. So, much to India's chagrin, America continues to arm Pakistan and tolerate its subversive activities against India. America could even use Pakistan as a 'Taiwan-like' card to keep India on a leash. For China, a proactive axis with Pakistan has supreme utility—it keeps India's military occupied on the western front, and gives China a vocal anti-India proxy to play with.

Then there is Afghanistan, emerging as the extended fourth corner of an India–China–America–Pakistan quadrangle. America would like to quickly neutralize the Taliban and get the hell out of Afghanistan, but that's far easier said than done. Pakistan is leaning on America to give it a 'grand bargain' in Afghanistan, as quid pro quo for allowing

American drones to bomb Taliban strongholds from Pakistan territory. China too would like Afghanistan to become a 'satellite state' for Pakistan—to limit India's influence, protect China's economic interests in the Aykan copper mines and keep Taliban out of its Uighur problem. And India is doing all it can to enhance its clout in Afghanistan—it has invested $1.2 billion, double of what it had done in 2006. A third of this money is being used to build canals and hydro-power dams; this alarms Pakistan, as India could gain control over Afghan rivers that are crucial for downstream waters entering Pakistan. What's more, India enjoys a friendly equation with President Karzai and opposition leaders like Abdulla Abdulla (both have studied and stayed in India during their student and exile days). So the competitive turf in South Asia just got extended beyond Kashmir and Tibet.

Another visible ace for China is the influence it exercises over a nuclear-armed North Korea; by encouraging North Korea's covert operations, or frowning upon them, China can increase or relax a subtle pressure on America. Using its North Korean and Pakistan equations, China can always keep America and India from getting too cozy with Tibet's Dalai Lama. And then there is Japan, which is caught in an interesting twist of history. Its new government is sidestepping a century of brutal conflict to flirt with China, especially in regional trade groups like ASEAN +3. There is a straw in the wind about a free trade agreement between the world's second and third largest economies. In December 2009, 143 members of Japan's parliament and 500 other influential people led by Ichiro Ozawa, the new ruling party chief, flew in five planes for a special visit to China; a history of hostility seemed to disappear at a warm meeting with President Hu, who agreed to get himself photographed, one at a time, with each guest.

Just two weeks later, Prime Minister Yukio Hatoyama became the first Japanese premier to visit India in twenty-five years. There was visible excitement around his meetings with Indian industrialists and politicians, including his promise to link the yen and rupee to boost investments. There was a near closure of billions of dollars of Japanese investments in the ambitious Mumbai–Delhi freight corridor. The usually friendly ties between Japan and India seemed a lot cozier; as against this, Japan's tensions with China over the oil and gas fields in the East China Sea are always lurking near ignition point. It's also worth remembering that Japan has cut its defence spending to less than 1 per cent of GDP, making it ever more militarily dependent on the US. Any excessive overture by America towards Japan, or eager thrusts by Japanese investors to create massive economic assets in India, could excite Chinese suspicions of an emerging America–Japan–India axis of 'evil', given the scars of history.

Finally, there are the imponderables, the questions with less tangible answers. The political chemistry of the world could change in 2012. America will have a presidential election, the Communist Party of China will appoint successors to Hu Jintao and Wen Jiabao, and Taiwan will go to the polls. Will a younger generation of Chinese leaders, the aggressive 'princelings' who take power in 2012, be more acquisitive and impatient? Could they use the heavy hand if the current friendly regime in Taiwan is defeated in the 2012 elections? And how will the new American president react to all these developments?

Will China be the only major twenty-first century power to remain outside the pale of democracy? Will it be tempted to expand its footprint in spaces over which American radars may have weakened? Will trillions of dollars in the bank—and sophisticated self-made DF-31 Intercontinental Missiles and J-10 fighters in the arsenal—excite adventurism? Or will China display Confucian faith in its asymmetric strategy, patiently growing its circle of friends and relationships around the world, without rocking the boat? What if America begins to feel threatened by such a calm expansion of Chinese influence all around itself? Will it react by belligerently asking China to back off? Will it try and rebuild the military axes of the twentieth century, adding India to its list of twenty-first century allies? Will India, long smouldering under its pathetic defeat in the 1962 war, shed its characteristic pacifism?

Or are all these questions merely a kind of intellectual war game being played by analysts—and in reality, China will never forget that it has become a superpower precisely because it has chosen the path of 'peaceful development'? Even more philosophically, have human beings become infallible enough to shun greed and power? Has a history of ambition and plunder by the powerful got so blunted by rising prosperity that it will never repeat itself?

The answers, my friends, will be blowing through and creating the winds of the twenty-first century.

Three

ENTREPRENEURS, CONSUMERS AND ENGLISH SPEAKERS

A Tale of Two Demographies

By 2050, there will be around 9.1 billion human beings on our planet, up from 6.5 billion today. India will stabilize at a population of 1.6 billion and China at 1.4 billion.

Our world will grow older: by 2050, the number of sixty-five-year-olds would increase from 560 million to over 1.5 billion. Over 300 million will be in China.

By 2050, China could have 90 million people in the eighty-five-year-plus bracket. While the western world has taken a couple of centuries to grow old, China would have aged within a few decades.

In 2050, India would still be a 'young' country.

*

In the 1970s, China's and India's large populations, growing unsustainably, were seen as a threat to the world. Both countries were poor, and once their resources were divided by their large populations, the per capita numbers foretold a frightening tale of deprivation and impending disaster.

These prophesies of doom rang sharply for two leaders, forty years apart in age and eons apart in political wisdom. India's Sanjay Gandhi was in his twenties, the brash, wannabe car-entrepreneur son of Prime Minister Indira Gandhi. He was feared and hated, but people dared not tell anybody that. He demanded, and got, fierce loyalty from his cohorts of young, indisciplined political followers. China's Deng Xiaoping was a seventy-year-old communist revolutionary who succeeded Mao Zedong in 1978. He had lived through decades of political and military struggle, seen decades of success and failure.

Sanjay Gandhi had been thrust on India's people by an indulgent mother who allowed him to run roughshod over the country's political institutions—an impatient, dictatorial, unelected young man who had little respect for India's democracy. On the other hand, Deng was virtually brought out of exile to repair China, a country almost annihilated by Mao's Cultural Revolution.

Deng Xiaoping and Sanjay Gandhi may have barely heard of each other in the mid-'70s, even as they began controlling the destinies of the two largest countries on earth. Both chose to focus on population control in their early days in power. Both used coercive methods to achieve quick and visible success. China's political system sanctioned the use of force; even India's democracy was temporarily paused, allowing Sanjay Gandhi to use fear and compulsion. China's system responded to force, and its population began to slow down. But India's democracy got its revenge on the ruling family, sweeping them out of power in the 1977 elections; 'family-planning' became a bad word and India's numbers continued to swell. China's communist system 'succeeded', India's democratic state 'failed'. Ironically, decades later, China's success would become a 'constraint' and India's failure would be hailed as a 'demographic dividend' (perhaps it's more correct to call it a 'democracy dividend'!).

Here hangs a wonderful tale, an accident of history which was impossible to predict.

China's population had increased by a sharp 25 per cent in the '60s; it came as no surprise, therefore, that the 'one child norm' was among the first policy measures that Deng took up vigorously. The propaganda lines on posters were catchy—'Mother Earth is too tired to sustain more children' or 'One more baby means one more tomb'. The first assault was on China's state-owned enterprises (SOEs), followed by equally aggressive moves in rural areas. It was a tried-and-tested carrot-and-stick approach. Those who had only one child got a special stipend. The single child also got free education and was preferred for state jobs when he or she grew up (later, some of these spoilt, notoriously chubby single children were nicknamed 'little emperors'). Those who violated the rule by having a second child were forced to pay a 'social fostering charge', often as high as a family's annual wage. Employers of 'rule-breaking parents' were encouraged to take stiff action, especially in SOEs. In the early years, 'stiff' action often became quite harsh—and thereby effective. Only a few exceptions were made; for instance, you could have a second child if your first-born was permanently disabled, or the parent of a single child had remarried, or a biological child became possible after an adoption and a long period of infertility. Some stringency was later relaxed, when a rural family was allowed to have a second child if the first one was a daughter.

Local governments pitched in with free contraceptives, medical consultations and abortions. Officials were given attractive cash and career incentives to meet targeted birth rates in their areas. One estimate suggests that 300 million potential births were curbed by the 'one child' campaign. In the twenty-five years between 1979 and 2004, China's annual population growth slumped, from 2.01 per cent to 1.16 per cent. By 2005, it had slowed to 0.65 per cent, about half the world average.

Sanjay Gandhi was born into India's first political family: he was the grandson of Jawaharlal Nehru, India's first prime minister, and the younger son of Jawaharlal's daughter Indira Gandhi, prime minister in the 1970s. Sanjay shared little with his illustrious grandfather: while Nehru was a lawyer and Cambridge scholar of world repute, Sanjay barely managed to complete his formal education. But he had his mother's gumption and a stubborn dream to build India's first private car company, Maruti Ltd. The mother indulged her son's entrepreneurial fantasy, but took political flak for granting him out-of-turn favours. As things turned out, the car factory stalled in mid-track, and the project was virtually abandoned (it was later sold to Japan's Suzuki, and is currently the market leader in India).

Sanjay's entrepreneurial fantasy was soon replaced by political ambition when his mother appointed him to the top job in the Congress party's youth wing; he was now officially part of the de-facto power centre. Sanjay hit upon a five-point programme to mobilize his youth party workers. A series of political mishaps had pushed India into a state of 'emergency' in 1975. Democratic rights of ordinary citizens were suspended and opposition politicians were put behind bars; India experienced the kind fear and censorship that prevails in totalitarian states. Several excesses were committed by officials drunk on unbridled, unaccountable power. One among those was the indiscriminate sterilization of poor people, often to meet unrealistic 'targets'; as in Deng's China these came with cash and political incentives. Over 1.7 million vasectomies were performed in September 1977 alone, equal to the annual average of the previous ten years. Mercifully, this anarchy continued for less than two years. Indira Gandhi lost the 1977 elections, and among the first things the new government did was to annul the sterilization programme. Subsequent governments did not want to flirt with the delicate issue of 'family planning' and India's population continued on its growth trend of over 2 per cent per annum.

And so it came about that as China's population growth slowed down, India's continued to gallop. Conventional wisdom through the '80s celebrated China's 'success' and berated India's 'failure'. China had warded off the threat of uncontrollably large numbers while India was seen to be sinking into the abyss of overpopulation.

But the accidents of history did not stop here; this fascinating tale had a few more twists left to it.

The world turned again in a hugely unpredictable manner. Computers and communication technologies shrank it in ways that were unimaginable in the '70s and early '80s. Trade boomed, capital whizzed around the globe in real time, satellite technology delivered live images, jobs got outsourced to low-wage countries, and big corporations expanded to Asia, South America, Africa and the Middle East in search of cheap labour and large markets. India remained a fortress economy, cut off from a fast-changing world; on the other hand, China was the principal beneficiary of this global rush for capital, land, jobs and markets.

Will China Grow Old Before Getting Rich?

Today, propelled by Deng's 'one child' policy of the 1970s, China is growing old very fast. Two forces are at work. One is making people live longer, creating more old people in the population; but at the same time, the one-child norm is reducing the number of young people in the country. As fewer young people come into the productive age group of 15–65, and more get pushed into the post-retirement old-age group, China's demographic tailwind could rapidly become a headwind. The growth of China's labour force could end by 2030, beginning a decline of the kind seen in today's slower western economies. The demographic bonus could vanish.

The problem is that such a rapid ageing is usually seen in mature, urbanized, industrialized economies that have grown over centuries. By the time these countries had grown old, they had also grown rich, like the US and Japan. BRICs estimates suggest that by 2030, China's best case would be a per capita income of $22,000 against the US's $61,000, Japan's $60,000 and Germany's $51,000.

Demographers point to a country's dependency ratio and per capita income as key variables to track. The dependency ratio is simply the fraction of people who are either under-15, or over-65—that is people who cannot earn a living for themselves and are dependent on the 15–65-year-olds. Japan has already hit a dependency ratio of 50 per cent, while Korea could get there in 2026, but the per capita income for both countries will be higher than $30,000 at that point. As against this, China could hit 50 per cent at a per capita income level of only $11,000. By 2050, China's dependency ratio could reach 70 per cent, implying that seven people will depend on ten in the working age—again, at a far lower level of per person income.

But all is not lost yet; there are interesting counter-cyclical trends which could blunt China's population deficit. For one, the quality of China's workforce could be superior, as parents lavish all their love, affection and resources on a single child. The 'education quotient' per child is also likely to be much higher than earlier averages, as the 'one child' generation goes through China's high quality schools and colleges. So on a 'quality adjusted labour supply' basis, China may not face shortages of the kind that a pure mathematical model may throw up.

To cap it all, China is looking to ease its one-child norm, which could swivel the current dynamic in a positive direction. In July 2009, Shanghai became the first city to launch an aggressive campaign to encourage more births. But the initial response, especially from urban areas, has been lukewarm. Only about five couples are applying for a second child every day in 115,000-strong Huinan. According to the *Washington Post*, a common refrain seems to be: 'We were at the centre of our families and used to everyone taking care of us. We are not used to taking care of and don't really want to take care of others.' Some complain that 'you have to remodel your apartment', or 'you have to have a resumé ready by the time the child is nine months old for the best preschools'. Others go as far as saying that 'ours is the first generation with higher living standards, we do not want to make too many sacrifices'. It could be tougher than anticipated to reset the population clock.

Finally, there are many economic sectors that actually benefit from an ageing population. Insurance, pharmaceuticals, biotech, health foods, pension and wealth-enhancing financial services, vacation homes, nursing homes—there are many businesses that will grow as relatively wealthy Chinese grow old!

There were 238 million Indians in 1900. This number remained virtually unchanged for half a century. Even the age structure of this population remained static. But after Independence, infants and older people began to live longer. From thirty-seven years in 1947, the average life expectancy has gone up into the sixties now. Population leapt to 360 million in 1961, and has nearly trebled in the next half century.

Since half a billion of its people are under twenty-five, India still has a few decades to go before an ageing crisis hits the country. By 2020, the US could be short of 17 million people of working age, China 10 million, Japan 9 million and Russia 6 million, but India will have a surplus of 47 million people in the working age. If India can harness this population dividend by giving better health and education to its people, it could become the job exchange of the world. But if it fails to do that, India could become a job graveyard.

From Communists to Crony Entrepreneurs

China has nearly 2,000 listed companies; over 80 per cent of these are state owned. India has over 6,000 listed companies, over 95 per cent of which are privately owned.

There are ninety-one Chinese companies in the Forbes 2000 list for 2009—four out of every five are state owned. In contrast, there are forty-seven Indian firms in that list, nearly half of which are in private hands.

India has not launched a single new public sector company in the last two decades.

An Asian Corporate Governance Association ranking put India in the third place and China ninth among eleven countries.

*

George Soros came to India in December 2006. His visit created a predictable amount of media stir. Soros was on a book promotion tour, but he seemed more interested in patting India on the back. India's economy and markets were booming. India is a much stronger bet than China, Soros said. The headlines screamed, as if on cue; a nation labouring under a 'China complex' was thrilled.

I interviewed Soros for CNBC-TV18, the country's leading business news channel that I had founded in 2000. After the recording was done, I asked him, 'George, you've seen China and India at very close quarters. What is the *one* thing, that single fact, which in your opinion gives India the edge over China?'

Soros thought for a while. He then looked me straight in the eye, and simply said one word, 'Entrepreneurship.' After a pause, he added, 'Your entrepreneurs have built world-class companies. I simply don't see that in China.'

There hangs yet another tale: when it comes to harvesting entrepreneurial energy, India may have got it set up better than China. Mao's Cultural Revolution, unfortunately, cut off the oxygen to China's entrepreneurial lungs. Tarun Khanna, an Indian professor at Harvard Business School who has done outstanding work in studying entrepreneurship in China and India, says: 'China wiped its slate clean in the Cultural Revolution. Literally and metaphorically, it got rid of intellectuals, human capital, private enterprise, everything.'

Until 1978, private ownership of any kind was banned in China. But today, Chinese citizens can own property, businesses and shares. Land-lease titles have been made long-term, inheritable and transferable, but have stopped short of full ownership. There were 40 million private enterprises (now down by 2 million in the recession) which had been growing at 30 per cent every year until 2008. On the surface, this looks like a trouble-free crossover from communism to capitalism. Its genesis, unfortunately, is rather turbulent and corrupt.

Thousands of state-owned companies were sold quite frenetically in the early years. While theoretically they ended up in 'private' hands, in reality most were cornered by party officials or state governments via thinly concealed indirect structures. This created an illusion of entrepreneurship in China; the number of 'non-state' enterprises grew from 244,000 to a mind-boggling 7.87 million in 1996. But nine out of ten were owned by local party officials or indirectly by state-owned enterprises. An IFC survey found that stakes of insiders increased from an average of 5 per cent in 1996 to 32 per cent in 2002. Clearly, most entities ended up ultimately owned and controlled by communist cadres. Such a 'privatization' was quite unfair; unlike genuine entrepreneurs, these cadres took no risk, which devolved on tax-paying town residents. But now that these businesses were classified as 'private', they were free of all obligations towards the state. Bank credit was as easy as transferring cash from one pocket to another, since the same bunch of officials who now controlled the enterprise also ran the local bank. Predictably, many went on the rampage, stripping assets, siphoning profits, inflating losses and generally inflicting all the evils of unregulated capitalism. Minxin Pei has called this the 'decentralized predatory state', one where the exploitative actions of a market economy are layered over the excesses of state control.

Feng Chen discovered many instances of crony communism in a field study of three firms in central China: 'Privatization in China has been carried out in opaque ways, with little regard to the principles of fairness and justice. The government has never made it an official national policy and no national legislation exists to dictate the process. There are only a few government guidelines, which are far from clear and whose enforcement is highly problematic . . . In this process, SOE managers typically establish their own companies into which they siphon state assets through various dubious means . . . The transaction is often arbitrary and poorly regulated, involving complicity among SOE managers, private buyers and local officials in carving up benefits at the expense of the workers.'

As was perhaps to be expected, a flawed beginning ensured that bottom-up entrepreneurship never took early roots in China; instead, most economic activity sprung from a largely top-down model. Today, there are four models of Chinese entrepreneurship: the state-owned enterprise (SOE); its derivative, the listed joint stock SOE with the state retaining some shares; the foreign invested enterprise (FIE); and the small, private, market-oriented local company. It's possibly the most accomplished model of 'state capitalism' in the modern world; even where the state is a minority shareholder, it often ends up controlling the board. A study of 154 listed firms showed how individual shareholders had less than 0.3 per cent—as against 50 per cent held by the state—of the total board seats. Kaushik Basu, a professor at Cornell University (and currently the Chief Economic Advisor to the Indian government) believes that 'despite major moves to liberalize the economy since 1978, China remains one of the most state-owned economies of the world'. The influence of politics is all-pervasive, with half the entrepreneurs being members of the Communist Party, the so called 'red capitalists'. A survey found that 90 per cent of all the wealthy people (with personal assets of more than $14 million) were children of high-ranking party officials.

But if all this is true—if Chinese entrepreneurship is fake or illusory—then what explains the fact that Chinese goods have taken quality-conscious western markets by storm? Is that possible, without genuine entrepreneurs leading the charge? Where is the dichotomy?

To understand this phenomenon, you have to take a closer look at 'Made in China' goods strewn about in American malls. You should engage the friendly shop girl in conversation and ask her to explain: 'How come these Chinese goods are so good?' She will promptly say, 'Sir, most of these products may be made in China, but they are manufactured in factories owned by *our* companies.' That's it—the factories are geographically located in China and the labour is Chinese, but the owners are foreign. At one stage, Wal-Mart alone accounted for 10 per cent of all Chinese exports to the US. Most other foreign investors also put money into consumer goods—textiles, apparel and footwear, toys and electronics. That's the striking 'dualism' of China's economy, a thriving export sector dominated by multinational corporations which are productive, efficient and quality conscious. Their top-notch output, which is almost a third of China's GDP, has been on steroids for over two decades. It has historically grown at 25 per cent every year, double the average for the rest of the economy (until the export crash of 2008–09). A worker in a foreign-owned enterprise is nine times more productive than another in what is euphemistically called the 'non FIE sub-economy'. Among the top twenty-five major exporting companies, just four are Chinese, while the rest are American or European. So this is not native Chinese enterprise—it is expatriate entrepreneurship!

To put it a bit more starkly, China offered labour arbitrage to foreign capital—it opened the floodgates, offered foreign companies an unlimited supply of very cheap labour, and 'on-shored' what was in reality just a western manufacturing facility.

An obvious fallout of this 'outsourced' workshop model is that China has become a giant sub-contractor, but is yet to make its mark in the world of ideas and brands. Most of the top 100 exporters make electronic goods for foreign buyers. Take the biggest one. It's a Taiwanese owned company called Shenzen Hongfuin Precision Industry Co., popularly known as Foxconn. It's owned by Terry Gou and was among the earliest entrants in 1988; since Chinese labour was far cheaper, it made sense to set up there. It is the largest producer of electronics and computer components worldwide, on contract from companies like Apple, Intel, Dell, Hewlett-Packard and others.

In fact, of the top ten exporters, only one, Huawei Technologies, is a Chinese company that sells Chinese brands. But its entrepreneurial credentials are suspect. It was founded in 1988 by a former People's Liberation Army officer, Ren Zhengfei. Today, with $18 billion in sales, it's the second largest telecom hardware maker in the world, behind Ericsson but ahead of Alcatel–Lucent and Nokia. Global leaders like Norway's Telenor have chosen to replace their Ericsson technology with Huawei's ultra-fast Long Term Evolution or LTE. It is on *BusinessWeek*'s list of ten 'most influential companies'—one in six people on the planet could be using its hardware—but the chances are that you've never heard of it. Like many Chinese giants, its operations are opaque. Its founder has never spoken to the foreign media. Its website suppresses the fact that Zhengfei is a member of the Communist Party. The US government banned it from bidding for 3Com, calling it a potential security threat. Earlier, the British government had forced it out of the Marconi deal. Even the Indian government views it with suspicion; several floors of its R&D facility at Bengaluru are thought to be shrouded in secrecy and completely out of bounds for Indian employees.

Lenovo, perhaps the best-known Chinese brand, is also not quite home-built. It acquired a global brand presence for its computers by buying out IBM's product line. Yet it has struggled to expand overseas, switching focus to protecting market share at home. Haier, the only recognized Chinese maker of home appliances, is weighed down by the lowbrow image of its products. This brand vacuum is now worrying China's top leadership. No less a person than Prime Minister Wen Jiabao has been exhorting entrepreneurs to create 'brand name export products'.

There is one area in which many American-educated Chinese entrepreneurs have excelled—that's in launching internet and technology start-ups. For instance, Baidu is China's Google, Dangdang is its Amazon, Taot is its eBay, and Alibaba.com is a hugely successful business-to-business marketplace. Baidu is China's largest search engine with over 60 per cent market share, a rare company which has given Google a 'bloody nose'. It was the first Chinese company to be included in the Nasdaq-100 index (the first Indian company to be included was Infosys Technologies, an icon of corporate governance). But many believe that Baidu's raging success is because it allows users to download music illegally. 'If the courts were to rule that Baidu should pay maximum statutory damages for all the infringing tracks available through its service, it would have to pay many billions of dollars in compensation,' fumes the music industry watchdog. Baidu is also accused of actively abetting the Chinese government's internet censorship campaign and tampering with search results to favour large advertisers.

Robert Crompton is a film-maker, entrepreneur and venture capitalist whose documentary *Win in China* tries to undo the 'myth' that China lacks entrepreneurship. He, in fact, goes to the other extreme. 'China is winning the global race to create the most entrepreneurial economy on the planet. Their investments in entrepreneurial infrastructure dwarf India's, America's and the European Union's,' he claims grandly. By way of evidence, Crompton talks about the research park at Zhongguancun that creates a new company every 4.6 days—'it already has 21,000 companies employing nearly one million people'. His documentary is named after a popular Chinese television show in which 120,000 budding entrepreneurs vie for a $5 million booty. Crompton is rather proud of Zhou Yu, or 'the Wolf', who won the television show: 'He implemented questionable business ethics and bent the rules for his advantages. The Wolf does personify China's entrepreneurial ideals—(he) really did make people uncomfortable. Yet he captures the spirit of today's Chinese business people.' The show's website calls it an 'astounding display of individualism and monetary greed in a proclaimed communist state'.

I haven't seen the show, but I can quite imagine it to be somewhat like the WWF of beefy, shadowy entrepreneurs. Crompton reserves his choicest sneers for India; according to him, while Chinese entrepreneurs are 'flamboyant', he did not see 'a single Porsche on the streets of Bangalore. Indian achievers are too humble.' This is the most unusual definition I've ever heard of entrepreneurial success—you've got to be the arrogant owner of a Porsche! I usually hate to preach, but if I ever meet Mr Crompton, I will give him my definition of an entrepreneur— just as a genius is '1 per cent inspiration and 99 per cent perspiration', an entrepreneur, in my humble book, is '1 per cent capital and 99 per cent persistence, focus and humility' (ever heard of Warren Buffett?). I am not too surprised that the Chinese government allowed Crompton to use archival footage from the '40s onwards, something that is usually denied to any independent media professional. Without meaning too much disrespect, I must admit *Win in China* seems to be walking a rather thin line between independent journalism and PR.

In direct contrast to *Win in China* is *guojin mintui*, a Chinese phrase catching rapid currency—it means 'the state advances and private sector retreats'. There has always been plenty of evidence of China discriminating against private entrepreneurial talent in favour of large state- or foreign-owned enterprises. An IFC study in the late '90s pointed out how private local investments were banned in more than two dozen industries, including such high-potential ones as telecom, banking, highways and railroads. There were several instances of private firms trapped in title disputes whose assets were seized. Sun Dawu had taken Dawu Farm Group from scratch to a 1,600-employee, $13 million enterprise. But he was arrested and thrown in jail for three years. What was his crime? Unable to raise loans from state banks, he had borrowed money from his employees at high interest rates. He was accused of 'disturbing the financial order'; his operation shrunk to half its size, and hundreds of employees were laid off.

Today, the Chinese media is full of stories about the 'second wave of nationalization', as stimulus-cash-fattened state enterprises gobble up fast-expanding private companies. Rizhao, the largest private steel company, was forced to sell majority equity to Shandong Iron and Steel. Food giant COFCO extracted a 20 per cent stake in Mengniu Dairy. The travails of Lian Zuqian, a young coal mine owner, are making headlines; two years ago, he had invested $37 million in buying a 300,000 ton operation in Linfen. But he was being coerced to sell to a state-owned buyer for $16 million. Over 1,500 coal mine owners in Shanxi are battling a similar threat, putting nearly $7.5 billion of private investments in jeopardy. 'I think some will commit suicide because they cannot return money to their friends,' Lian told *Forbes* magazine.

Ming Huang, a finance professor at Beijing's Cheung Kong business school told *Newsweek*: 'Blurry rules and corruption fosters short-term thinking here. Entrepreneurs don't feel safe—there are many examples of the government taking over private businesses or changing the legal landscape so they can take their profits as quickly as they can.' The average size of a private operation has been static at thirty employees for nearly two decades, 'due mainly to their difficulties in raising capital', *Newsweek* concluded.

Marshall Meyer in *Knowledge@Wharton* believes that the 'government will always remain in control of the 100 largest firms in China', giving it direct ownership of nearly 50 per cent of GDP. Another large chunk will be invisibly controlled via board majority on several private corporations. Eight out of ten of the largest listed companies in China are state-owned; among the other two, one is owned by a long-time member of the CPC, while the other is controlled by the government via overlapping management. In India, nearly half of the ten largest listed companies are in private hands; among the government-owned companies, each and every one is a decades-old monopoly in oil and energy. India has not launched a single new public sector company in the last two decades. In fact, a few among the older public sector companies have been privatized, while the government is reducing its stake in all others.

So China has created huge, state-owned monopolies, while India is unraveling knotty socialist behemoths.

Death, Consolidation, Rebirth

Entrepreneurship is embedded in Indian genes, goes a popular folklore, especially for the Sikhs of Punjab, and traders from Gujarat and Marwar. There could be a poetic exaggeration here. Yet it can't be denied that India's political and social structures have preserved entrepreneurs, if not exactly cut them loose. India's politicians have always stoutly defended the institution of private property. Even as the state invested in big-ticket capital assets in the early decades after Independence, land continued to stay in private hands. India's sprawling rural economy has always been entirely 'capitalist' in its orientation. Even the urban economy allowed private enterprise to grow under a somewhat draconian regime of licences and approvals. India's legal system, antiquated and dogged by delays, has nonetheless conducted itself according to the finest principles of English Common Law. So justice may be delayed in India, but is rarely denied to people who can hire good lawyers. The Bombay Stock Exchange is among the oldest in Asia. Capital and credit have always been available, albeit for a 'price', for private enterprise. What's more, India nurtured the English language, and made it the medium of conducting business.

Even as Mao's Cultural Revolution was wiping out entrepreneurs in the '60s and '70s, India was building a curiously 'mixed up' economy. The government shovelled capital into what it called the 'commanding heights'—that's how the state came to own giant infrastructure projects, large factories, and even some consumer industries like hotels and electronics. But private companies were allowed to co-exist: they were just tied up in licences and entry barriers. Even as private industry expanded in size, it remained slow-growing, uncompetitive and oligarchic. Tangentially, a vibrant services economy took wing, since the government had left it completely free. What's more, some internationally benchmarked educational institutions sprung up in engineering, management, accountancy and design. These charged ridiculously low fees, churning out an army of well-trained, hungry, middle-class professionals. Even in those stultifying times, Indian advertisers, publishers, designers, researchers, managers, copy-writers, film-makers, architects and technicians could match global peers in style and precision. Cutting-edge technology companies like Infosys, HCL and Wipro were born around this time; mercifully, or perhaps out of ignorance, the state did not strangle these outliers who were left to do as they pleased. Within two decades, these technology companies would scorch the West with their exploits and unleash entrepreneurial energies across young India.

In the '70s and '80s, local entrepreneurs in consumer facing businesses also understood the critical need to build brands. Private hotel chains like the Taj and Oberoi could stand up to any international property in providing luxury and hospitality. Textile brands like Raymonds and Vimal could take on anything that Europe had on offer. Godrej soaps were as fresh and tingling as Unilever's Lux. Ranbaxy and Cipla were selling branded drugs in competition with Pfizer. Videocon, Kelvinator and Onida were producing consumer durables of rather acceptable quality. Tata Motors, Mahindras, Eicher and Ashok Leyland were making trucks and tractors that could match any western product.

But equally, products and services were woefully primitive in some industries, principally those where private enterprise was banned or controlled. For instance, only three companies were licensed to produce cars—of World War II vintage. Only a state corporation was allowed to fly—private airlines were banned. Most of the utilities were state-controlled, although some like Tata Power continued to be private. All banks were nationalized, except for a few branches of tightly-controlled foreign players like Citibank and Grindlays. While the publications business was completely free, radio and television broadcasting was a state monopoly.

Whichever way you looked, Indian entrepreneurs were coiled up like a spring, ready to burst forth as soon as the government let go. Adding to the tailwinds was an exciting constituency of Indians who had migrated overseas (called non-resident Indians, NRIs). These people had built enviable businesses and professional track records in America and Europe. They had capital, skills, talent, relationships and a yearning to 'do something for the motherland'. A Molotov cocktail (pardon the Russian analogy, but the Soviet yoke had truly held back Indian enterprise through the 'wasted decades' of '60s, '70s and '80s) of entrepreneurship was waiting to explode in the '90s.

Early years of competition were tough for sheltered Indian business families, whose cozy monopolies were blown away by foreign competition and venture capital-financed first-generation Indian entrepreneurs. The world's fiercest companies descended on India. Microsoft, Oracle, GE, Hyatt, Samsung, News Corp, GM, Ford, Hyundai, Honda, Suzuki, Reid & Taylor, McDonalds, Prudential, Vodafone, Sony, ABB, HSBC, Standard Chartered—you name it, and it was in there, trying to wrest leadership from incumbents. Many old-world Indian business families quickly capitulated, but others regrouped, re-hauled and got ready for battle. Several first-generation entrepreneurs jumped in with venture money to grab early stakes in newly opened sectors. Today, almost every segment is witnessing a hand-to-hand combat for leadership between homegrown companies and multinationals—unlike in China, local Indian brands are giving it back as good as they get.

While the easy entry of foreign capital created enclaves of entrepreneurship in China, the exact opposite has happened in India, which has been somewhat less welcoming of investment dollars. India has encouraged quasi-protectionist policies, creating intangible entry barriers, favouring domestic capital and ownership in several industries. Ironically, this could have given a great fillip to domestic entrepreneurs. In market after market, homegrown brands are fighting for leadership, not merely making an effort to stay in the game. Airtel, Reliance and Idea are ahead of Vodafone in cellphones; Zee TV has bounced back against Rupert Murdoch's News Corp and Sony Entertainment in broadcasting; Videocon is punching back at Samsung in consumer electronics; Tata's Indica and Nano are jostling for road space against

Suzuki, Hyundai, GM and Ford; Coca-Cola continues to trail Thums Up, a local brand it bought from an Indian entrepreneur; ICICI, HDFC and Axis Bank are pummelling global financial giants like Citibank, ABN Amro and Bank of America; VIP suitcases stack up against Samsonite; Haldiram's is not allowing McDonalds or Pizza Hut to turn Indians into burger or pizza freaks; Zodiac's formal shirts are as crisp as Marks & Spencer's; Bajaj's two-wheelers are holding their own against Honda. Unquestionably, it's an equal tussle between local and foreign brands, and the intensity of combat is furiously fueling Indian entrepreneurship.

The competitive intensity in India is startling; perhaps no other market of the world is as crowded with start-up brands as India is. Take, for instance, media brands; at the last count, there are over a dozen Hindi and six English news channels, four English and two Hindi business news channels, over a dozen Hindi general entertainment channels, eight children's channels, nearly a dozen music channels—and once you go into the regional markets, the numbers increase exponentially. Today, India has over 400 television channels, created in less than two decades! Now look at the competitive intensity in the media distribution business; where else in the world do you have six direct-to-home broadcast brands and 70,000 mom-and-pop last-mile cable operators?

The telecoms industry is equally bewildering; opened to private competition just about fifteen years ago, it is today the fastest growing in the world. Over 15 million new buyers are being added every month to the existing base of over half a billion subscribers. Services reach 8,000 towns and cities and 500,000 villages. Perhaps nowhere in the world is entry into this business as easy as it is in India, with the result that intense competition among nearly half a dozen players has created the lowest tariff regime anywhere in the world. Some very sensible people are now crying out for a few entry curbs, since Indian telecom could become a victim of hyper-competition. But that's not a debate to be entered into here; the point is that such breathless growth has spawned a cottage industry of telecom entrepreneurs in retail, repairs, re-sales (and perhaps even in the grey market of stolen and smuggled handsets!).

Private companies are also executing big projects, laying pipelines, building airports and ports, paving roads, constructing ships, rigging up offshore exploration wells; all of this is happening in partnership with or in competition against multinational giants. Foreign capital has now become astonishingly mobile across India's borders. If the Japanese Daichi Sankyo and American Abbott Laboratories could scoop up the local Ranbaxy Laboratories and Piramal Healthcare's formulations division in two multi-billion dollar buyouts, then homegrown oil behemoth Reliance Industries bought shale gas assets in North America, even eyeing petrochemical giant Lyondel–Bassell in an aborted $15 billion deal. Bharti Airtel proved second time lucky with an audacious $10 billion all-cash buyout of Africa's Zain Telecoms. The Tatas, having acquired Jaguar Auto and Corus Steel, already get two-thirds of their revenues from overseas businesses.

While consumer-facing businesses give attractive, visible stories, there is a massive amount of activity happening in the trenches too. The US FDA has certified more companies in India than in any country outside the US—Microsoft's largest research facility outside Seattle is in Bangalore—perhaps a testimony to India's rule of law, innovation, and free markets.

*

Suddenly the lanes shifted, putting the tortoise ahead by a couple of laps. The hare was taken aback at this unexpected change of tracks. He tried to take a couple of quick leaps, but failed. Two of his hind legs were strangely tied to the Emperor's throne. He tried to plead with His Majesty, but to no avail. The Emperor was not going to cut the hare loose, even if it meant losing one race in a big relay; His Royal Highness just turned his face away. Meanwhile, the tortoise kept his cool, gathering steady speed. He knew his Master had left the track, vowing never to return. Several little tortoises, some from faraway lands called America and Europe, were lined up next to the track. They were giving him water, wiping the sweat off his brow, egging him on to move faster. The tortoise was a bit sanguine; this little lap could be in the bag. But it was still a very long race . . .

The Story of Two Stock Markets

Harshad Mehta was only in his late thirties when he pulled off a stock market scam in India which would have put Bernie Madoff to shame. The year was 1992 and there was much excitement around a freshly minted, rapidly privatizing economy. It was easy to spin get-rich-quick stories in an unregulated casino. For a man who had barely scraped through his accounting studies at college, Harshad Mehta was a deadly combination—a legendary crook and a master storyteller. He siphoned off a billion dollars from several Indian banks to rig the stock prices of ninety blue chips. Stocks doubled, trebled, quadrupled, and Mehta became the cult deity of wealth. But once the price bubble was pricked, his house of cards collapsed. He died in custody on the last day of 2001 as India's biggest defaulter, owing nearly $170 million to several banks. He also left behind an unsolved mystery of 2.7 million missing shares and seventy-two cases of conspiracy, cheating and fraud.

Harshad Mehta's scam was a shock therapy for India's stock markets. Although over a century old—it was set up under a banyan tree in 1875—the Bombay Stock Exchange (BSE) was little more than a privileged brokers' club in the early '90s. It traded for barely a couple of hours every day on the outcry method. Shares were held in physical form, and trades were squared off once in fifteen days. Upcountry brokers were forced to transact on a rickety phone network. Companies could cancel share transfers on the flimsiest of excuses, like signatures not matching or papers lost in transit. Not surprisingly, the system was prone to delay, abuse, price fixing, insider trading and frequent breakdowns. Total stock market capitalization was a poor 10 per cent of GDP.

But the scam jolted an eager government into action. A tough securities regulator was set up, but wealthy brokers continued to defy it. Then the authorities hit a brainwave; they instructed government financial institutions to put up equity for a truly modern, digitally savvy exchange christened the National Stock Exchange (NSE), which proved to be a game changer. NSE began trading in 1994; it was a unique structure that allowed the same equity instrument to be traded on both exchanges in the same city and across similar trading hours. Shares were dematerialized and electronic depositories were set up;

over ten thousand terminals in over 400 cities gave instant trading access to members. In eleven months flat, the new exchange logged up higher trading volumes that its 120-year-old competitor. The transaction settlement period dropped from fifteen to two days. To survive, BSE had to set up its own electronic system.

Today, the Indian stock market is among the largest in the world, next only to NYSE in terms of the number of shares listed, deals transacted and the size of retail investor participation. Around the time that Google was launching its record-breaking float, the *Financial Times* wrote that 'the world's biggest democracy can show Google how to conduct an online IPO . . . The Indian system is a refreshing example of a transparent IPO market, but it is also a rare one, especially in the insider-friendly Asian markets'. In May 2004, when a left-influenced change of government spooked investors and the stock indices fell 25 per cent in two days, Indian markets came through unscathed—not a single broker failed or defaulted or even took recourse to the trade guarantee fund. Today, foreign institutions can invest freely in India and the rupee is fully convertible on stock market transactions.

In yet another 'twin point' of history, China's stock exchanges took birth at exactly the same time that India's were reborn. The Shanghai Stock Exchange (SHSE) was set up in December 1990, and the Shenzen Stock Exchange (SZSE) in April 1991. The almost singular motive was to sell shares of State Owned Enterprises (SOEs), but an inexperienced China opted for a very complex system. The same company could not list on both exchanges—it had to choose one. Each company could issue five different types of shares: A-shares, which could be sold in local Chinese currency to local individuals; B-shares, which were sold in either US or Hong Kong dollars to foreign investors; C-shares, issued to Chinese state institutions or departments, which could not be traded on the main exchanges, but only 'over the counter' in institution-to-institution sales; H-shares, which was equity issued by mainland companies on the Hong Kong stock exchange; and finally, N-shares, which were issued on NYSE. A sixth—and the strangest—category was 'non-tradable' shares held by the government or its agencies. So the majority of shares in early listed companies were *not* floated; only the shares sold to the general public were tradable, making for very thin volumes and huge price volatility.

Since China likes to keep a tight control on its currency and foreign capital flows, it was forced to create these silos to isolate each currency, geography and class of investor. The early years were wracked by a dizzy gyration in stock prices. Before 1992, only eight companies were listed on SHSE with transferable shares worth less than 80 million yuan. On 21 May that year, the government lifted all daily price controls triggering a blow-out rally as the index leapt 94 per cent in one day. But in less than five months, the same index plummeted to less than half of where it was before the blow-out. Later, in 1996, both SHSE and SZSE put on 125 and 350 per cent over nine months, expecting a positive impact from Hong Kong's transfer to China. Contributing to the messy situation was a 'quota system' for selecting SOEs to float their shares; each province was given a fixed quota of companies they could bring to the market. Inevitably, the shadow of politics fell over the quality of paper floated. Unsurprisingly, no initial float has ever failed in China; and no publicly listed company has ever been de-listed. The unseen hand of political patronage is rather apparent here.

But such a fragmented structure created frictions at each margin, besides creating a playground for 'grey' transactions that illegally moved capital across prohibited boundaries to profit from price differences. A company with A, B and H shares today has three wholly different valuations; often, A-shares have traded at three times the value of B-shares or H-shares, puzzling investors. Common sense dictates that B-shares should command a premium, as foreign investors have superior access to information and analytical skills. But that's not the case, perhaps pointing to a speculative frenzy in China's domestic stock market that has taken A-shares to 'bubble' levels. Morgan Stanley pointed out that a third of reported corporate earnings in China in 2007 came from speculative gains in stock markets. For instance, the apparel company Youngor had earned nearly 99 per cent of its profits from subscribing to shares of China Life, Bank of Ningbo and Citic Securities. Although some norms have been tightened, banks in China have lent freely at very low rates to help companies build up their investment portfolios. (In India, banks are virtually banned from lending money to subscribe to shares.)

It is true that wherever there is a stock market, there will be a scam.

Even the tightly regulated American markets saw the astonishing Madoff and Galleon scandals in 2009. After Harshad Mehta's scam in the early '90s, Indian markets have weathered five crises: in 1995, the BSE was closed for three days after payment problems on a company which had crashed; in 1997, a mutual fund closed shop after defrauding investors; in 1998, the president of the BSE was sacked for allowing prices of three companies to be manipulated; in 2001, another price-rigging scandal by another ambitious broker was busted; and finally, in 2005, thousands of fake accounts were unearthed, that were getting illegal allotments of newly floated shares under the quota reserved for individual investors. But no major scandal has erupted in India's stock markets since 2005.

China, however, is still in the throes of a learning curve, grappling with frequent scams in its still maturing stock markets. Among the latest to bruise investors was the November 2009 arrest of thirty-nine-year-old Huang Guangyu (also known as Wong Kwong Yu in Hong Kong), the chairman of Gome Electrical Appliances, the country's biggest electronics retailer. *Forbes* had listed Huang as China's second wealthiest individual, estimating his worth at $2.7 billion. *Caijing* reported that Huang was detained for an alleged stock manipulation case involving a company controlled by his elder brother. He was eventually fined $120 million and handed a fourteen-year jail term.

China's 2-Trillion-Dollar Trickle Through

The buck stops—and also starts—with the consumer. When a Chinese or Indian family packs its kids into a European or Japanese compact, drives across the new toll bridge to the shopping mall, picks up a pizza and flashes its credit card to buy a plastic toy for the toddler, it's triggering demand for a mind-boggling array of industries—from steel to petroleum to cement to milk to maize to pigments to satellite bandwidth to telecommunication links to God knows what all.

But too many people—even Chinese leaders—concede that China invests too much but consumes too little. Today China invests nearly half its GDP, which is more than any country has ever done at any time in history. On the other hand, China's household income and consumption have *fallen* by 16 and 11 percentage points over the last decade; at 35 per cent of GDP, consumption expenditure is the lowest that any robust economy of comparable size has ever experienced (most healthy economies consume more than half their GDP). It's truly an unprecedented situation, unknown and unfathomed by mankind. Conventional theory says 'get ready for a bust'; even common sense would dictate that if you continue to pile up factories and bridges without people using them at the same pace, those factories and bridges are bound to shut or waste away .

But it must be equally conceded that China has successfully repudiated all prophesies of doom. For one, while it is low in percentage terms, consumer expenditure is sprinting to soon touch a hefty $2 trillion—nobody can sneeze at that number. For another, China could be scripting a new economic logic by investing on a scale hitherto untested. Traditional theory says that investment should be 'sustainable', that is, it should be 'matched' by rising consumption. But what if you pump so much capital into your economy—similar to putting extra fuel into a rocket—that you 'escape' the gravitational pull of low thresholds? Especially if the bulk of your capital is spent on infrastructure (roads, railways, schools, hospitals, ports), as against factories which produce toys and televisions? What happens when you launch the world's fastest train that cuts travel time between two cities from eleven to five hours (with very high fares of 700 yuan for first and 500 yuan for second class)? Is it possible that the saved time improves potential income so much that the extra yuan are not wasteful?

Perhaps unnecessarily large factories do create waste, but big infrastructure, especially life-enhancing social assets, could actually end up empowering people. By rapidly educating its workforce, by brilliantly executing immensely large projects, by importing expertise and dollars in a shrinking world, could a country create a 'shower of wealth and productivity' that 'trickles through' into the consumption 'bubble'?

This is China's 2-trillion-dollar riddle.

India's economy suffers from no such conundrum. It's classically— almost boringly—balanced, with nearly 58 per cent of GDP getting consumed by ordinary Indians. So which system is better? It's difficult, and quite unnecessary, to adjudicate on the word 'better'; but there's also no question that India's large consumption base gives the economy a far more stable foundation.

Size, though, is one facet, while psychology and evolution of consumer habits is just as important. These behavioural quirks often give more clues on how robust each country's consumer story is. Inevitably again, these clues are buried in the first eight decades of the twentieth century; the bend in history occurs at each country's colonial experience followed by their totally different politics after becoming free. From the early 1900s to 1949, China was convulsed by wars and civil strife. Later, Mao's Cultural Revolution obliterated even a vestige of consumerism in Chinese society. As against this, democratic India swerved towards socialism. All the 'commanding heights' of the economy, from steel to power to airlines and hotels, were amassed within the state. Mercifully, private enterprise was only muzzled, not effaced. It continued to coexist, suppressed by taxes and licences. Through all this, private property remained an 'inalienable right'. So a genuinely 'mixed up' economy emerged, where multinational brands like Lux soaps, Cadbury chocolates, Coca-Cola beverages and Intercontinental hotels survived. Even more ironically, a starving consumer economy managed to nurture some world-class business practices in advertising and brand building.

That's how the two countries were poised at the beginning of their economic renaissance. The Chinese consumer was trapped in a long grey tunnel of abstinence, while the Indian consumer was half-trapped, half-free, one hand tied behind his back, the other reaching out to touch and feel some ten-years-out-of-vogue products and brands. Except that even ten-year-old western goodies were pretty stand-out compared to China's consumer moonscape.

So quite the predictable explosion of pent-up desires occurred when Deng Xiaoping threw China open to gleaming western brands. A tidal wave of newly rich Chinese migrated to high-income coastal enclaves. Imagine a trainload of these people hurtling through a dull monochrome tunnel for thirty years, then suddenly bursting forth into the dazzling neon lights of a giant mall full of western cars, air-conditioners, vacuum cleaners, perfumes, chocolates, jeans, hand bags, designer linen etc. etc. What sweetened the splurge was the cash stuffed into the passengers' wallets as per capita incomes in the coastal enclaves soared.

Today the South China Mall in the Pearl River delta is sprawled over 9.6 million square feet, and there are seven more malls in China that are larger than Minneapolis's 4.2 million square feet Mall of America, the largest in that country. These giant Chinese malls are like a mini Las Vegas, with teletubbies theme parks, hotels, pyramids, Imax theatres and replicas of the Champs Elysee and Arc de Triomphe.

The behavioural graph of urban Chinese consumers is a textbook spike of rapidly gratifying desires. To begin with, there are a large number of these consumers; nearly 600 million live in urban areas, out of a total population of 1.3 billion. As China allowed private ownership, a humongous amount of state-owned housing stock was transferred into individual hands. That was the first wave of household wealth creation; as property prices increased sharply, the 'wealth effect' multiplied. Proud—and now richer—first-time house owners wanted to fill them with 'all the good things money could buy'.

There are about 30 million middle-class households in China, of which 8 million would be affluent; half of these are in Beijing, Shanghai and Guangzhou. By 2016, there could be 100 million middle-class households. In 2007, China's consumer economy was the size of Italy's, but by 2009, it is adding an Italy every year. Now consider that an average Italian spends over $11,500 on consumer goods each year versus only about $1,000 for the average Chinese; imagine the upsurge when the average Chinese begins to spend even a third of what the Italian does! But today, wealth is highly concentrated, with 1 per cent of the households owning nearly 60 per cent of the country's personal wealth. The rich are *really* rich—little wonder that more Bentleys are selling in China than in any other country!

Foreign investment rules were radically liberalized in 2004 when China joined the WTO, adding fuel to the consumer revolution. Foreign retailers could now own 100 per cent of their Chinese subsidiaries, operate in any geographical location, open an unlimited number of stores of any size, source merchandise locally and straddle the entire distribution chain from transportation and wholesaling to retailing. Foreign labels and specialty chain stores mushroomed. Professional, well-heeled Chinese took to European luxury brands and Japanese pop styles with aplomb. Louis Vuitton opened several new stores and Armani was the number one clothing brand, even in second-tier cities!

But urban Chinese consumers betray an uneven attitude towards brands to this day. They are willing to splurge on luxury products which can conspicuously be 'shown off' to peers and neighbours. However, for household items which cannot be 'shown off', or which have a 'commodity-like' appeal, brands are ignored. In the early flush of consumerism, foreign brands were preferred, but later on, local brands got in the game, provided their quality and snob value was visible. As we will see later on, Chinese and Indian consumers diverge rather sharply in their hunger for image-creating brands.

In 2009, nudged by rebates, subsidies and heavy bank lending, China outsold America in almost every category from cars to refrigerators to washing machines, even desktop computers. But that was in number of units, not in value; since American unit prices were much higher the consumer there spent more cash even as he bought fewer pieces. For instance, China bought 12.8 million cars and light trucks against America's 10.3 million, but Americans still spent nearly 70 per cent more in dollar terms than the Chinese. Similarly in other products: manufacturers would have sold 185 million refrigerators, washing machines and other pieces of kitchen and laundry equipment in China, compared with 137 million in America, but here again, Americans would have paid nearly 33 per cent more dollars for their purchases. According to the *New York Times*: 'In some sectors, Chinese buyers are already proving more lavish than Americans. The average flat-panel television sold in China is bigger than in the United States.' The article goes on to claim that 'at Nissan, sales of cars with larger engines that do not qualify for the sales tax reduction are growing even faster than sales of small-engine cars'.

Credit card spending rose 40 per cent in 2009, although China has only one credit card for every eight people. Credit cards were allowed as late as 2001, when home mortgages and auto loans were introduced. Despite a default rate of 30–50 per cent in auto loans in the early years, consumer credit is becoming robust—the proportion of car sales financed with loans doubled to nearly 25 per cent. But the *New York Times* reported fears that 'some of this year's loans could become bad debts in the next several years, as happened with the mortgage lending spree in the United States'.

A fascinating, emerging sub-category of consumers is 'the modern woman' and 'double-income, no-kids families' or DINKs. There are over 30 million 'modern women' in China who are college-educated, professionally employed, city-based, and single or married. The number of DINK households is small, at about 600,000, since DINKs are under tremendous pressure, from two sets of parents and four sets of grandparents, to have a child. They are high-earning, fast-living, twenty- to forty-year-old, city-bred and conspicuously consuming couples. Eighty-six per cent of modern women own property, as against an average 77 per cent for urban middle-class households. They are voracious readers of fashion and literary magazines; even current affairs, business and general entertainment magazines find a huge readership in this constituency. Nearly a third of 'modern women' and DINKs shop online twice or thrice every six months; they are ambitious and 'getting promoted at work' is the single most important aspiration for them.

China has already overtaken Japan as the world's second largest diamond market in sales; it has also pushed India to the second spot in consuming gold. The urban Chinese have also taken wing with a vengeance. Food consumption is dictated almost entirely by cultural habits. The Chinese, like Indians, prefer to cook fresh food every day, which means they make frequent trips to neighbourhood stores and buy in small quantities. Wal-Mart estimates that an average customer comes in 3.5 times every week, much higher than in the US. The non-working women in the family, either wives or mothers or grandmothers, do the daily cooking. Of late, in large cities, eating out has become the done thing—DINKs frequent speciality restaurants and western fast food chains that have reconfigured their standard American fare to cater to local tastes. The urban middle class dines out 1.7 times a week as against the three times for 'modern women' and DINKs. The small store-front restaurant trade that was among the first to be privatized is fiercely competitive. The consumption of high-calorie foods like milk and meat has increased. The average Chinese is becoming bigger and heavier. In several ways, Chinese and Indian consumers are perfect clones of each other when it comes to food habits.

Now the challenge before China is to pull its consumer revolution up by several notches. The problems are known and so are the solutions. China needs to change the structure of its economy. It has done a wonderful job in taking investments and exports to astronomical levels; it should now make services more attractive than manufacturing, by jacking up prices of energy, water, electricity, land and capital. More businesses should be privatized (unfortunately, the exact opposite is happening). The *hukou* system should be relaxed, allowing rural migrants to take their families to permanently settle in cities—but the government has only pledged to 'study' the problem and 'push for urbanization in an active and steady manner'.

China urgently needs to create confidence among its consumers to spend. Not willing to take risks, Chinese consumers have stashed nearly $4 trillion dollars in bank deposits. The state has to create a massive social security net which will convince Chinese consumers that they will be looked after in illness and old age. Today, they are covered for just $100 every year in lifetime pension. Earlier, pensions would lapse if a worker migrated to another province, but this unusually restrictive rule was finally changed on 1 January 2010. Health and unemployment insurance continue to be virtually next to nonexistent.

That's China's consumer story—straight, uncomplicated, big and game-changing for the world. The Chinese consumer is emerging from decades of denial, and his or her choices are following a predictable trajectory. India's consumer story, in contrast, is extremely complex and non-linear. But it's not small, or insignificant, or disappointing— in fact, it's large, exciting, and pregnant with huge potential. It's just terribly complex and nuanced.

Two Drunken Steps Forward, Two Sideways, One Back

A gear-shift happened in 1991, as the Indian economy was thrown open to private capital and global influences. If India continues to grow at current rates, income levels will treble, and the country will become the fifth largest consumer market, ahead of Germany, by 2025 (currently it is the twelfth). Again, as we've seen with China, an average Indian will be spending only a tenth of what the average German consumer would be spending. Just imagine the potential upsurge when the average Indian begins to spend even a third of what the typical German does. By 2025, nearly 300 million people will get out of poverty to become low-grade consumers with a decent lifestyle, while the middle class could swell to over 600 million. By 2025, nearly 23 million Indians, or an entire Australia, will be wealthy. India's rural areas are also in the game; nearly 40 per cent of current and future consumption will come from there. Even among urban areas, almost two-third of the market will exist in second-tier towns.

Even if he or she is eccentric and complex as an individual, the Indian consumer's category shifts are entirely predictable. Today, he spends nearly 40 per cent of his disposable income on food, beverages and tobacco. This will plummet to 25 per cent by 2025. His spending on transport, health, education, recreation and communications will leap to consume nearly half the budget. The macro picture, then, is not fuzzy at all; but why are we still raising a 'caution notice'? What's so amorphous and unfathomable about the Indian consumer?

The defining DNA of a typical Indian consumer is 'continuity with change'. He or she will adopt, experiment and flirt with new ideas and products, but slowly, with due deliberation, almost hesitantly at the beginning. An Indian prime minister once famously remarked that 'there are no U turns in India'—Indians simply don't switch tracks suddenly, shift gears rapidly and change habits quickly. It's not as if they are dogmatic or stuck in the past or trapped in a time warp. No, it's quite the opposite. They are modern-minded, willing to try new things, but gingerly, steadily, without letting anything sweep them off their feet. Dr S.L. Rao, an eminent economist, puts it most colourfully: 'It's like the walk of a drunken man. You know he will get home eventually, but it will be two steps forward, two steps sideways, one step backwards.' Another colloquialism too sums it up quite pithily: Indians are *like that only*!

India's consumption machine is being powered by three engines. The most stand-out among these is the generation of 'liberalization's children'—that's 250 million fifteen–to–twenty-five-year-olds, who have grown up in the cradle of an open and global economy. While their parents were starved on a diet of dull, state-owned television, they have grown up flipping between MTV, CNN, Discovery and dozens of local entertainment channels. Their parents lived with rations and controls; these kids are engaging with a bewildering array of consumer products, confident about their choices, nurtured in an environment which celebrates enterprise and wealth-creation. The second engine is feminine: the young, educated, modern Indian woman, running an office or household. Finally, the third engine is India's burgeoning rural economy, often painted in quaint colours, but one that could be more 'in the mainstream' than may be obvious on the surface.

Let's look at each engine, one by one.

Half a billion people in India are less than twenty-five years old. This single statistic is enough to take one's breath away. Six out of ten Indian families have a 'liberalization's child' who is the change-agent. But it's not a monolith generation. It's not even the conventional, rebellious, West-influenced youth that 'hang around' several Asian countries, from the Philippines to Korea and even urban China. Going by the invasion of American brands and youth symbols, one would have imagined this generation of young Indians to be Levi's-loving, MTV-worshipping, chewing gum-popping, Coke-consuming and Hollywood-struck—it's a bit of all this, but not swept off its feet. In fact, India's youth seek family approval more than rebellion. Of course they are much more non-conforming than their parents' generation, yet they are happy to subordinate their individual desires to what is 'good for their families'. They may stretch boundaries in private spaces, but within a family collective, they are usually happy to go along with their elders' mandate.

A slow contrast seems to be emerging between Indian and Chinese youth. While Indian youngsters are happy about a sense of 'belonging' to extended families and siblings, young Chinese are growing up more isolated in one-child, smaller, fewer sibling families. China's youth are showing early signs of moving from family affiliation towards individualism.

More than half of India's 'liberalization's children' are rural and poor, and beyond the sweep of consumer markets. At the other end of the spectrum are about a million youngsters who are 'super-rich brats'. They are the ones who have always flaunted designer, ultra-expensive western brands. Earlier, they would buy their stuff in London or New York. Now they can indulge their fancies in premium local malls. Another 2 million youngsters come from 'upper middle class' families; they are neither super-rich, nor brats, but could have a sneaking envy for both. They are the next-in-line consumers of high-end western brands. Then there are about 5 million 'big-city, well-off' kids who aspire to be rich and famous. They may buy the odd ultra-priced designer brand, often as a one-off craving, but for the most part they are happy with broader-appeal, mainstream fashion labels. Next is the 'stretch category' of 12 million youngsters who flirt with fashion brands in shop windows and occasionally succumb to the temptation of buying one. These are the potential converts, those who could get rich one day, and become regular buyers. Finally, there is the bulge category of 45 million youngsters who simply cannot afford to buy at malls. Yet they have eyes and desires. They watch the same movies and television shows as the kids from the other segments. They scoop up 'I ♥ NY' t-shirts from pavement markets, buy cheap clones of major denim brands, pick up pirated cds, and turn to unorganized markets for every other consumer aspiration.

Nearly 7 per cent of these youth have a college degree, but more than twice that number is comfortable speaking in English. Two out of every three twenty–to–twenty-five-year-old is already married. Most prefer Indian brands, environment and value systems for their toddlers. They believe that local personal care products are better than imported ones. The majority prefer to take a job in India and be close to their families. 'Mixing the best of East and West' is a cliché that fits them to a tee. Experts have called this a 'pressure cooked generation'. They have to weather unbelievable amounts of competition. There are 10 million claimants for 3 million college seats. The dash for jobs is even more intense. It's a quest that unites the whole family, as parents, aunts, uncles and cousins pitch in with resources, space and encouragement; such a concerted family effort to 'get the boy a good job' only fosters a stronger family bond.

The second, or 'feminine', engine of consumer growth shows charming similarity with some of the patterns thrown up by 'liberalization's children'. The Indian woman has acquired a centrifugal force in 60 per cent of households which are now nuclear, both in urban and rural areas. While only a quarter of urban women are formally employed in jobs, most have acquired the 'mindset of a working woman'. Nearly three out of four urban women have had some form of schooling; a fifth of the educated ones are college graduates. Consumer marketing expert Rama Bijapurkar calls it the advent of 'womanism, which is a gentler and less individualistic form of feminism. They want their opinion to count, value their own time, and look after their own interests. They do not see any glory in self-denial. It marks a change in the mindset of women rather than in behaviour.' Many have become 'do-it-yourself' entrepreneurs, starting cottage businesses and small vocations from home, although they still get categorized as 'homemakers' (or as they are more popularly called in India, 'housewifes').

This woman continues to be conservative in the way she runs her household, but is far more adventurous outside the house, with friends, or while chaperoning her kids to sports, tuition or skill-enhancing classes. In fact, she fancies herself as the 'chief executive of the household and the primary coach of children, ensuring their success in this ultra-competitive world'. She still likes to cook, or at least control the kitchen. But she is happy to switch out of cleaning and daily shopping, which is left to the household help. Instead, she is taking on what Bijapurkar calls 'outdoor work', like handling the family's bank finances, or dealing with local municipal offices, depositing bills, getting household malfunctions fixed, and attending parent–teacher meetings at kids' schools. This has added to her 'womanism'. Like India's youth, the urban Indian woman has little desire to ape 'western modernity'. Her modernizing instincts are calibrated; she is largely content with her higher self-worth at home, happy to give much of herself to her kids, honing newer aspirations for them, especially her girl child. She also watches a lot of television soap operas, which are stories about women somewhat like her, or hugely unlike her—but nonetheless, all centred on women. Such a high-voltage daily exposure adds to her aspirations and world view. She is most proud to contribute to the 'family EMI' (as middle-class Indians increase consumer purchases on credit, the EMI or Equated Monthly Installment to be repaid to the bank has acquired a folk legend of its own).

The third consumer engine in India is the rural one; it grew 25 per cent in 2008, even as urban markets bore the brunt of the slowdown. By 2011, nearly 750 million consumers are likely to be spending over $425 billion there. Quick intellect may tempt one to call it a mere 'adjunct' to urban markets. That would simply be erroneous. India's rural markets are formidable: they have 70 per cent of the population,

56 per cent of income, 64 per cent of expenditure, and 33 per cent of savings. Rural India buys 30–60 per cent of the consumer goods and durables sold in the country. For instance, Adidas and Reebok saw rural sales grow by 50 per cent once they reduced prices. LG's customized TV to pick up low density signals sold 100,000 pieces in villages in the first year. Road and phone connectivity have improved phenomenally. Contrary to popular belief, nearly half of all rural incomes are non-agricultural, which are more resilient than agricultural incomes that are thinly spread over tiny land holdings. Another myth is that rural and urban markets are chalk and cheese in their consumer proclivities. In fact, the rural rich and the urban middle classes show a remarkable similarity in their choices. If anything, the rural rich are caught in an upward spiral of aspiration buying. Even the village woman is beginning to defy stereotypes. Sprouting green shoots of 'womanism', she is displaying a mind and opinion of her own, often insisting that her young daughter attends school, perhaps against the wishes of the father. She has also been politically empowered, since many states have compulsorily reserved offices for her at village panchayats or local municipal bodies. Finally, there is the ubiquitous television soap opera, enhancing her fledgling 'womanism'.

The two categories that are flung outside this 'broad rural–urban consuming continuum' are the rural poor and urban super-rich. The impact of both these outliers is somewhat negligible, one because of almost zero purchasing power, and the other because of conspicuously miniscule numbers. The rural–urban continuum is even more visible in regions with good road connectivity and progressive governments, where these apparently distinct markets are fusing into a giant buyers' wave.

That then was the story of China and India, the two mega emerging consumer markets on earth. There is no winner or loser here: both hold enormous promise. If China has got a larger size to boast of, India has got a broader base. If Chinese consumers are black and white and predictable, Indian consumers are grey, complex but rooted. If the Chinese consumer is letting go on pent-up hunger, the Indian consumer is building steadily on an existing base.

*

The hare was wearing Niké shoes, Li Ning shorts and Cardin tees; the tortoise was in more modest Color Plus shorts, Bata shoes and Benetton tees. Both breasted the tape together!

Ni Hui Shuo Ying Yu Ma?
(That's 'Do You Speak English?' in Chinese)

English today is no longer 'synonymous with Englishmen'. It is the language of global commerce, political dialogue, science, technology and the internet. It has half a million words, more than thrice the number of any other tongue. At 1.5 billion users, there are three non-native English speakers for every native one. As a wag put it, Bill Gates and Microsoft have done more to popularize English in two decades than other proselytizers over several centuries. An Arab, Chinese, German, Australian, Russian and Indian are able to communicate with each other because of English. People who know English have a higher per capita income than those who speak other languages. With satellite technology and instant worldwide communication, almost entirely in digital English, the intellectual architecture of the world has been colonized. Ironically, eighteenth-century colonialism has put India on the right side of this twenty-first-century imperialism.

Thomas Macaulay was a member of the British Governor General's Council in early nineteenth century India. His assertion, whose authenticity is disputed by some people, shows his belief in the richness of English—'I never found one among (the Orientalists) who could deny that a single shelf of a good European library was worth the whole native literature of India and Arabia'. English had come to India as a 'peripheral trade language', competing with Portuguese, more than two centuries before Macaulay. As the British East India Company expanded its political influence, annexing territories and small princely states, English became the language of power. In 1774, English replaced Persian as the official language of the Supreme Court. Yet it was confined to the occupying British elite and a few English schools in Calcutta, Bombay and Madras.

But Macaulay's famous Minute on Education (1835) brought English out of its imperial closet; with one stroke of his powerful pen, he made

English the official language of India and the medium of instruction in all educational institutions. His objective was to create 'interpreters between us and the millions whom we govern, a class of persons, Indian in blood and colour, but English in taste, in opinions, in morals and intellect'. It was a plan designed to create a cadre of modestly paid Indian clerks, or 'babus', who would serve their British masters faithfully. Macaulay and Governor General Bentinck withdrew financial support from the teaching of Oriental languages, and funneled all the cash into the teaching of English language and European sciences. In 1844, Lord Hardinge ordered that preference should be given to employing those natives who knew English. By 1882, over 60 per cent of the primary schools were teaching the Queen's language. The Indian National Congress conducted all its pre-Independence sessions in English. Mahatma Gandhi edited *Harijan* and *Young India* in the same language. Several other publications sprung to fill the need of a swelling readership.

English was called the 'milk of the tigress', creating a new energy and opportunity for the natives. Unwittingly, Macaulay had inaugurated the largest English-speaking ethnic community in the world, and less than two centuries later, that race of native Indians would use this felicity with English to gain a decisive advantage in a rapidly globalizing world.

In 1947, when India became free, about 6 million people knew and used some form of English. The Government of India acknowledged its primacy, giving it the status of an 'associate official language' of the Indian Union. But there was a catch: English was to be phased out by 1965, to be replaced by Hindi, which was the 'majority language' spoken by the maximum number of people in the politically dominant provinces of north India. Unfortunately, it was an ill-conceived law, doomed to fail. It ignored the reality that several Indian languages— Tamil, Telugu, Malayalam, Marathi, Bengali, Gujarati, Oriya, Punjabi, Assamese, to name just a few—were not piffling dialects which could be easily erased by a legal mandate. These so-called 'minority languages' were full-fledged institutions, spoken by tens of millions of people and embellished by centuries of rich literature. In fact, if a world ranking of languages was done, many of them would qualify to be in the top rung, going by the number of people who spoke, used or wrote in them. It wasn't just politically imprudent, but also historically impossible, to stamp them out and replace them with Hindi in such a heavy-handed manner. Inevitably then, violent language—or anti-Hindi—riots broke out in 1965, and a chastened government was forced to amend the law, allowing English to continue as the associate official language 'indefinitely'.

Another misadventure was attempted in 1967, when the government 'accepted in principle that Indian languages should now be adopted as the media of education at all stages and in all subjects, including agriculture, engineering, law, medicine and technology'. There were howls of protest; the country's foreign minister quit in disgust. A round table of scientists in the capital resolved that 'English should continue as the medium of instruction in universities for specialized and higher studies in science as all the source materials at present were mostly in English'. The medical council also rejected the government order, saying it needed to 'fully utilize the world literature in teaching, patient care and research'. The council of engineers said pretty much the same thing, and, as is their wont, the lawyers were more vocal, deprecating the 'proposal to switch over to the compulsory use of regional languages in High Courts and in universities, and (calling) attention to some of the disastrous consequences of a hasty switchover'.

The decades following the '60s obliterated any vestige of the 'anti-English, pro-Hindi' sentiment. Hardly anybody talks about it any more. Instead, English is happily embraced as the 'language of vertical mobility' in the country—according to linguist E. Annamalai, 'the powerless believe that they can attain a position of power using the power of English'. From the poor peasant who does an extra job in the village foundry and the village untouchable who has become a pavement-squatting immigrant in a major metropolis, to the blue-collar worker who saves on rent by choosing a smaller accommodation and the Hindi teacher in a suburban government school—all of them dream of sending their children to an 'English medium' school, because that will guarantee them a better job and status in life. When a state government abolished English in government schools in the '80s, it was forced, by unremitting parental pressure, to restore it from the first standard onwards. Nearly 99 per cent of respondents in a Ford Foundation survey in 1983 said that if their children had to learn only one language, they would like it to be English.

Today, with over 350 million Indians displaying a reasonable proficiency in the language, India could claim to the world's largest English-using country in the world. Indians also score the highest average band of 6.9 out of 9 on the International English Language Testing System of Cambridge University. India might have over a million English teachers in over 300 universities, about 25,000 colleges and 250,000 schools. Eighty per cent of India's 2 million college graduates are English-speaking. India is among the three largest publishers of English books in the world, next to the US and UK. Salman Rushdie, Vikram Seth, Arundhati Roy, Kiran Desai, Amitav Ghosh—the list of world-renowned Indian writers in English is getting more illustrious with every passing year. Young tech-savvy Indians almost entirely use English in their e-mails and cellphone texts. English is the preferred language of commerce, law, advertising, mass communication, signage, airport and railway station announcements— and pretty much every other activity of daily life. There are scores of newspapers, magazines, TV channels and websites which publish only in English. Dozens of Hindi films have entirely English titles, such as *London Dreams, Luck, Wake Up Sid* and *Wanted*—these are Hindi films, but English is freely used to spawn a very young, urbanized and colloquially popular 'Hinglish'. '*Yeh dil maange more*' ('my heart desires more') became a blockbuster ad line for Pepsi in India.

In 2008, India could have earned $140 billion from its computer and English skills. Over 20,000 children in California are being e-tutored in mathematics and sciences by English-speaking tutors based in India. Whether in call centres, help desks, credit card services or higher quality research, India's BPO (business process outsourcing) companies are becoming the back-offices of America, Britain and the western world. Experts now hail India as a country with the 'intellectual infrastructure of a developed nation in English'.

English was once called a barbaric language in China. The dominant language in China is Putonghua, or Beijing Mandarin. There are seven minority languages: Kazak, Korean, Mongolian, Tibetan, Uygur, Yi and Zhuangand. Although China's official language policy is bilingualism, in practice the minority languages suffer a subtle and planned 'de-emphasis'. According to June Teufel Dreyer, 'China's language planners have also argued that if China is to modernize quickly, it needs to make rapid advances in science and technology; therefore, the second language taught in schools should be English or Japanese.'

Two events occurred at the turn of the century to decisively settle the language debate in China. Beijing won the rights to the 2008 Olympics, and China entered the World Trade Organization. China understood the need to quickly catch up with other English-speaking nations if it wanted to dazzle the world with its economic prowess. A series of foreign language campaigns were launched. Booths were set up for people to register, either as learners or English teaching volunteers. Road names, signs and restaurant menus were redone in English and local languages. English learning materials were provided free, especially for police forces, restaurant staff and taxi drivers. The language was seen more as a necessary skill, on par with driving and computer literacy. The Court in Beijing began training Judges on the 10th of every month. English was made compulsory in the third grade (until then, most students would get their first English lesson only in the seventh grade). China adopted American English, as against India's natural and historical affinity for British English.

Today, China has the largest English-learning population in the world, estimated at 200 million children and 13 million young people at university. 'Bilingual kindergartens' are becoming the first choice of Chinese parents, where kids learn to speak Putonghua and English. Some Guangzhou schools have begun giving math, physics and chemistry courses in English. State universities are asking Chinese professors to compile teaching materials in English for a tenth of the courses. Teachers who flunk an English language test are usually rejected for promotion to the next level. University students are required to pass the College English Test (CET) Band 4, while English majors must pass the Test for English Majors (TEM) Band 4 before graduating.

The British Council website in Beijing offers free tests, vocabulary and business English courses to over 2 million students. There are over 50,000 private language schools, from mom-and-pop shops to chains like English First, Wall Street English and New Oriental, enrolling millions of students. Some parents are willing to spend half their household incomes in sending their children to these private institutions. Universities of Illinois, Maryland and Nottingham have set up business-

English classes at their campuses. Critics of this headlong rush to learn English argue that Chinese languages could be reduced to 'a dialect'.

Over thirty years, 1.4 million Chinese students had been given visas to study overseas; only about 400,000 had returned. These returnees are called *hai gui* (or sea turtles) meaning 'returned from overseas'. Now China is making a special effort through the 'thousand talents programme' to lure people back with generous pay and perks. A staff scientist was given $875,000 to do stem cell research in China; another scientist got nearly half a million dollars to head a company specializing in human genome sciences. There are twenty-three America-returned scientists at the National Institute of Biological Sciences. Naturally, these 'sea turtles' boost the quality and culture of English usage in the country.

But even as the state pushes to increase English learning, it remains highly suspicious of unregulated foreign content. Foreigners cannot publish directly in China—all foreign chains need a Chinese partner and must have teaching materials approved. Foreign English teachers were banned until a few years ago. According to the *Economist*, 'China's Communist Party is reluctant because along with English textbooks and teachers come western ways of learning and thinking— ways that may one day threaten the party's authority.'

*

A confident tortoise, humming a popular English tune rather loudly, breezed past a somewhat disarrayed hare, who couldn't figure out the lyrics of the song that wafted across to him. The tortoise looked back, winked, and cheerily said, 'So long, take care,' leaving the hare even more confused. Was the tortoise wishing him well, or making fun of him? 'Ah, if only my English was as good as his,' the hare muttered under his breath.

Four

URBANIZATION AND INFRASTRUCTURE

A Rich Dragon's Glorious Head ... Not Slushy Paws

While campaigning for his first term in 2004, future prime minister Manmohan Singh urged people to vote his Congress party to power to 'transform Mumbai in the next five years so that people will forget about Shanghai and Mumbai will become a talking point'. He wanted to do 'something big for Mumbai that would capture the imagination of the country'. People delivered him their mandate, but the prime minister hasn't.

On 26 July 2005 Mumbai received 944 mm of rain. It was the highest recorded anywhere in the country and nearly half the amount that Mumbai gets in a year. The city collapsed in a dangerous slush. Suburban trains stopped, the airport was shut down, cellphone networks failed, power supply was cut and millions of people were stranded. A 150-year-old drainage system had not been upgraded; unbridled construction and heaps of plastic had choked the city river, causing uncontrolled flooding. Many people suffocated in marooned cars; more than 400 people died in the city.

Mumbai suffers from a handicap; it is the capital of a large, politically fractious state, as against India's capital city Delhi, which is a cohesive city–state. Delhi has done marginally better under its matronly chief minister Sheila Dikshit. Under her watch, the city has implemented a metro rail system. She has privatized electric supply despite protests from employee unions. Scores of flyovers have eased the traffic flow. The public transport system runs on compressed natural gas, not dirty diesel. Voters have rewarded her with a rare third term in office.

The 2010 Commonwealth Games were an opportunity to transform Delhi into a world-class city (and perhaps bid for the Olympics, another ambition that Prime Minister Singh had articulated). But that remains only an aspiration, despite the huge amount of money already spent. The city's alphabet soup of agencies looking after land, municipal services, public works and electricity—DDA, MCD, PWD, DUAC, NDMC, DJB etc.—have often worked at cross purposes. The games' international committee feared that facilities would not be ready; it even posted an international observer to monitor daily progress. The sports minister virtually threw in the towel, declaring that India must not bid for the Olympics; he took such a defeatist stance knowing full well that China has successfully hosted one and Brazil is next in line.

Now turn to what China did with Shanghai—it was a display of national resolve seldom seen in India. While Manhattan's skyline evolved over more than a century, Shanghai's was transformed in a decade. It has over 4,000 skyscrapers, twice as many as New York. For fifteen years it has grown at an annual clip of over 9 per cent, faster than the mother country. Its per capita income has grown fourfold even as its population has more than doubled. McKinsey calls it China's 'only truly modernizing city'. Shanghai now attracts a quarter of China's investment and has as big a share of its trade. Its stock exchange does 87 per cent of the country's trading. The services sector employs 60 per cent of its workers and supplies half its output—short of Tokyo's 83 per cent and New York's 92 per cent, but pretty spectacular for China's non-services economy. It is set to emerge as a global financial and shipping centre—its Yangshan deepwater port will be the world number one.

Shanghai has ridden the crest and trough of history. The Yangtse, at the confluence of internal and overseas trade, had made it a rising trading town by the thirteenth century. It came under European domination in the nineteenth. It was truly the Paris of the East—

thriving, cosmopolitan and culturally vibrant—when the Japanese overran it in the 1930s. It also suffered greatly under Mao Zedong who preferred dispersed urban settlements. Shanghai earned $40 billion in revenue for the central government, but got a mere tenth in return for essential infrastructure. It endured the ravages of the Cultural Revolution when intellectuals and urban elite were sent to the countryside. Soon after Mao's death, its mayor, a member of the infamous Gang of Four, was tried for treason.

Deng Xiaoping too ignored Shanghai in the early years; he thought Shenzen and Guangzhou could rival Hong Kong's clout because of their proximity. But greatness cannot be thrust upon cities—Deng later admitted that he had erred. In 1992, during his tour of South China when he made his famous 'to be rich is glorious' speech, he declared that Shanghai would be the 'dragon's head' of the Chinese economy.

By then official sanction had been given to develop Pudong to the east of the Huangpu river ('dong' means 'east of river'), as Shanghai's 522 sq. km extension. Within a decade an expanse of rice paddies, marshes, low-tech industries and staff housing estates morphed into a financial centre, a high-tech park, an industrial enclave, a tax-free territory and an export-processing zone. The development of Pudong New Area coincided with the Tiananmen crackdown, when western nations clamped down economic restrictions on China in anger. Pudong served the collateral purpose of attracting foreign investments, and the Chinese economy continued to hum.

Shanghai was given a number of freedoms that were not available even in special economic zones. It could waive or reduce customs duties. It could give a tax rebate of 10 per cent or more to foreign investors, who were allowed to set up banks, deal in local currency and enter into land development contracts. A stock exchange was set up. Beijing gave an annual low-interest loan of $200 million in addition to an existing commitment of $100 million. The city could issue bonds and stocks, and retain a share of the revenue. To encourage real estate development a special residency permit (blue-stamp *hukou*) was given to property buyers, convertible into permanent stay in five years.

It is the council-manager system that runs the great cities of the world. New York reminds us of Robert Guiliani and Michael Bloomberg. Shanghai had 'One Chop Zhu' who acquired that nickname for his zeal in cutting red tape when Pudong was being developed. Shanghai is also a launch pad for national politics. Shanghai's mayors in the 1980s, Jiang Zemin and Zhu Rongji, went on to become president and premier. It is a virtuous loop: once at the centre, they showered blessings on the city.

While Chinese mayors may be accused of overreach, Indian municipal leaders lack ambition. When Shanghai's fortunes were rising, Mumbai's were in decline. McKinsey reported that between 1998 and 2002, the city's annual economic growth (2.4 per cent) had slipped to half the national average (5.4 per cent) and well below Shanghai's (8.2 per cent). In quality of life it was a poor 163rd among 218 cities that *Forbes* surveyed. Nothing better could be expected in a city that paid $10 billion in yearly taxes but got back less than $0.3 billion as infrastructure investment.

To rev up to Shanghai's pace, McKinsey wanted India's premier island city to build more bridges to the mainland to allow quicker movement. It wanted Mumbai to build more than a million flats for the poor. A $350 million annual infrastructure fund could become a multiplier for private investment. Key departments like water supply and garbage disposal should be made into companies for better service. Twenty 'quick-win' projects would generate the momentum for change. The chief minister should double up as the minister for Mumbai, with all city departments under his direct charge.

Great cities need great leadership, but Indian cities have none. Their management is a colonial import, led by a commissioner who reports to a council of elected members, often a bunch of petty local politicians. Divisive politics complicates the equation. Mumbai is ruled by a communal local party, while the Indian National Congress has ruled the state for decades. In 1992, the Constitution was amended to confer power on city governments, making India's administration a three-tiered structure. States saw it as an attempt to bypass them; few have devolved their powers to tax property, vehicles and consumption to city governments. Responsibility continues to be scattered among various agencies. For instance, land in the capital is owned by the Central government, not by the city–state. 'The world over, land is the biggest source of revenue for a city government. Ours is a unique setup where we provide the services that make the land livable but

DDA (the central government agency) gets the money,' says Delhi's finance minister. As against this, Beijing expanded nearly threefold by acquiring farmland and selling it for industrial, commercial and residential purposes. About a third of its revenue came from land sales.

Stifled Voices, Hopeful Slums

Urbanization in China wavered with Mao's whims, the Cultural Revolution and the Great Famine; by 2000, the urban share of population had jumped to 30 per cent in just one decade. It is 46 per cent now but China believes its urbanization level is lagging behind its stage of industrialization (developed countries usually hit 60 per cent plus).

Though some Chinese cities have a long cultural history, most of them came up after reforms. During Mao's time industries were scattered, springing several towns. In 1958 the *hukou* or internal passport system was introduced. It tied people down to their places of birth. They could travel outside, but not work or get food coupons, schooling or medical care. Peasants got a raw deal; their income was 40 per cent lower, and consumption 23 per cent leaner, than urban residents. Most of them did not enjoy schooling, health and social security benefits that city folk did.

In the initial years of reform, urbanization was driven by the state. It would designate a city or a cluster as a special economic zone. Shenzen, the first, was a town of 94,000 people in 1980. Now it is a noisy trading and shipping centre of 9 million. The mid-1990s were a period of experimentation. About 20,000 towns and 360 cities came up in just five years (to 2000). Many of them ended up as ghosts.

Chinese city governments are now in the driver's seat of urbanization. City polices vary—local officials sit with state-owned enterprises and private players on how to provide backbone services like water, power supply, roads, bridges and telecommunications. For Pudong, Shanghai's municipal government opened up to the best in the world. Top architects were roped in to design iconic buildings. Lending agencies like ADB and World Bank financed water supply, sewage treatment plants, power distribution and transportation. They introduced new tendering systems and trained officials in project management. Deng

Xiaoping egged them on: 'Someone who takes the first step will fail. That is not important. What is important is that the Shanghainese will become more open-minded and bolder and develop faster.' The French government, with which Shanghai had colonial ties, assisted in marketing city properties to speculative investors in Hong Kong and Singapore. Land lease rights were sold to pay for expansion.

'I have a dream,' a former mayor and party secretary would say echoing the American civil rights leader Martin Luther King. One of his dreams was to build an artificial beach. The 'hai' in Shanghai means 'ocean' but the city did not have a beach; so 128,000 tons of sand was brought from Southern China to simulate one in the suburbs. A $290 million world-class tennis complex was another monument to the mayor's passion for the game. The Formula One circuit got a $300 million racetrack. A magnetic levitation train brought visitors from the airport to the World Expo venue in just seven minutes at a speed of over 400 km per hour. But then the mayor overplayed his hand; protests erupted when he wanted to spend $4.5 billion to extend the Maglev to the neighbouring city of Hangzhou. Middle-class people on either side of the proposed route feared damage from radiation. The mayor got caught on the wrong side of politics—he was said to be part of a rival Shanghai clique. He was accused of diverting $400 million of social security money into real estate. Finally, he was expelled from the party and jailed.

The Shanghai miracle displaced people on a massive scale. Between 1991 and 2000, the city government demolished 26 million sq. metres and relocated over 650,000 households. Overall, about a tenth of the population has been displaced since reforms began. More than a million farmers lost their farmland (but gained urban residency). Poor inner-city residents were shunted to distant and unfinished suburbs, reported the *New York Times*. There were no public hearings or voting. The press was banned from reporting about ties between officials and developers. Details of demolition and redevelopment were closely guarded. Like other Chinese cities, Shanghai has been built on stifled voices.

In the years to 2025, China's lead over India in urbanization will widen. McKinsey expects China's city population to be close to a billion people, or about 64 per cent of the total by then. India's will inch up to 37 per cent or about half a billion. China will have many more cities but Beijing and Shanghai will continue to remain powerhouses. China's urban consumption will rise five times to nearly $3.5 trillion, while India's will grow six fold to over $1 trillion.

India's attitude towards urbanization was ambivalent at Independence. Mahatma Gandhi glorified the (non-existent) ideal village, with modern amenities and well-informed people. But Jawaharlal Nehru saw backwardness and ignorance in rural hamlets, their vitality sapped by British rule. B.R. Ambedkar, the father of India's Constitution, thought villages were a 'cesspool, a den of ignorance, narrow-mindedness and communalism'. He saw salvation for the whole of India in 'reviving our towns, building our industries, in removing as much population as we possibly can from our villages to towns'.

Unlike China's restrictive *hukou*, Indians have a fundamental right to live and move freely in the country, so city populations have grown unchecked. The last census (in 2001) estimated India's slum population at 41 million (12.5 per cent of urban people). Wrong policies and inefficiency have aggravated urban misery. The World Bank says that between 1964 and 1991, Mumbai *reduced* the amount of space that could be built up on a plot of land when other cities all across the world were encouraging vertical growth. (Though Shanghai's population has doubled, space availability per person has increased from 6 to 22 sq. metres). Properties are traded in cash to avoid high stamp duties. Rent control laws have frozen a third of Mumbai's housing stock. Only one in ten houses has a legal title, so there is little redevelopment.

In Delhi, the agency charged with city development itself has turned a speculator profiting from short supply; for instance, when it offered 5,010 flats at a discount via a lottery, there were 800,000 applicants, or 160 for each flat. Allotment was frozen after allegations of fraud (that the police later found to be false). The government has summary powers of acquisition. The terms of compensation are such that farmers feel cheated. The result is litigation and delay. At one stage, nearly 60 per cent of commercial construction in the city was against the master plan and therefore illegal. Among the offenders were India's largest mobile phone company and a bunch of fashion designers. Four journalists accused the chief justice of being in league with mall developers—they were hauled up for contempt of court. A minister candidly admitted that if most people in the city had become lawbreakers, the law itself must be defective. A new one was hurriedly notified that encouraged high rises and allowed mixed use of space (some kinds of commercial activity in residential areas).

Much of the mess is created by money, or the lack of it. Chinese cities have much more financial autonomy. Earlier, under a policy known as 'eating out of one pot', revenue was consolidated and spent with central approval. After reforms the fiscal contracting system or 'eating out of separate kitchens' was introduced. Local governments enter into fiscal contracts of say five years. This guarantees income to the central government and encourages city managers to become entrepreneurial. They get to keep the extra cash and compete with each other to attract investment. They become helping hands, not grabbing ones.

But Indian cities are starved; after octroi (tax on goods entering municipal limits) was abolished, property tax is the main source of revenue. It is undertapped as most cities do not even have a full list of properties in their domain. In Delhi, property tax covers just 16 per cent of revenue expenditure, in Mumbai 24 per cent and in Hyderabad 48 per cent. An average citizen in Mumbai pays just $28 a year by way of property tax; in Delhi he parts with a jaw-dropping $7 (Delhi's collection *fell* after it moved to a new method of assessing the tax). Another study of thirty-six large cities found they had collected only a quarter of their possible income. Two states have reneged on their commitments and abolished the tax after taking incentives from the Central government; in Punjab two-thirds of the properties are exempt. Clearly, city governments seem to have become dangerously addicted to doles, becoming comfortable underperformers, giving low-quality services and underpricing water supply, sanitation and waste collection.

In 2008, American cities issued municipal bonds worth $400 billion. But India made its first issue for just $28 million in 1998, to finance a water supply and sanitation project. Revenue for ten octroi posts was pledged to assure investors—the issue was oversubscribed. In 2002, another state made the country's first pooled bond issue to retire the debt contracted by thirteen municipalities for water supply and underground drainage. Since then, nearly $350 million has been raised in fourteen municipal bond issuances. But the instrument is yet to catch fancy, despite being given a tax-free status in 2007. Investors are wary of poor finances, and city governments prefer to avoid the scrutiny of creditors and the discipline of markets.

'Our cities and towns are not an acceptable face of a rapidly modernizing and developing economy,' the prime minister's laments are now creating the first stirrings of change. Contracts have been awarded for projects worth $22 billion in water supply, sewerage, roads, metro rail, garbage disposal, house construction and public bus services.

Perhaps India's planners need to take a few lessons, if not from 'adversarial' Shanghai, then certainly from the exceptional story of Jamshedpur. More than a hundred years ago, Tata Steel acquired a lease on this 64 sq. km industrial township. Today, drinking water is available for longer in Jamshedpur than pretty much anywhere else in India. Its quality is better than the national average; unsurprisingly, the daily average consumption is double the official norm. There is a call centre where people can post complaints about water supply problems, power outages, carcasses lying on the road, dug up streets and fallen trees. The city is run with corporate efficiency; in 2004, it outsourced its municipal services to a company called Jusco. 'I believe it is the best managed town in the country,' claimed the steel company's head honcho. Sadly, in 2006, the city's lawmakers wanted to convert it into a municipality to get urban renewal aid from the Centre. 'This is creating anxiety because the citizens of Jamshedpur are used to a certain quality of life—water, power, roads and clean air—that is not found in any other part of this country.' The company moved the Supreme Court which told the lawmakers not to proceed with their plans till it decided the suit.

At a population of just 0.7 million, Jamshedpur's problems are not comparable to that of a large Indian city. Yet it is a template, and given good governance, an exception which could become the rule.

Roads Have an Ideology—They Are Capitalist!

Inaugurated in 2008, the Hangzhou Bay Bridge is a 36 km link with six lanes on either side. The S-shaped bridge cost $1.7 billion and nine years to build. It cut the distance between Shanghai and the port city of Ningbo by 120 km, halving the travel time. The Chinese are justifiably ecstatic about building the longest sea-crossing bridge in the world.

Exactly one year later, in June 2009, the Worli–Bandra sea link was thrown open in Mumbai. Indian media exulted, and Indians were ecstatic, but the celebrations were a bit out of proportion to the length of the bridge—a rather modest 5.6 km. The bridge had had a turbulent history and took eight years to build. Fishermen and environmentalists had objected. There were several changes in design. Costs had risen many times to $355 million.

In north India, the execution of the Delhi–Gurgaon expressway was not as smooth as the seamless connectivity it now provides between the two cities for about half a million vehicles a day. The 28 km toll road had to brave delays in land acquisition, clearances from seventeen government departments, shifting of utilities and religious structures. The cost of the project overshot by more than 70 per cent and there was a two-and-a-half-year delay, including some caused by VIPs unable to find time to inaugurate the project.

In south India, the Bangalore–Mysore infrastructure corridor is still two years from completion ten years after the original deadline. It has seen five changes of government since the project agreement was signed in 1997. There have been challenges from environmentalists and citizen groups. Legislative changes, difficulties in land acquisition, political tussles over alignment, accusations of land grab by the developers, charges that the administration has bent the law and legal cases would qualify the inter-city road project as the Mother of Controversies.

Emperor Sher Shah Suri is the father of India's roads—he built the Grand Trunk Road 450 years ago. It spanned the breadth of India from current-day Bangladesh to Pakistan. At every 6 km was a sarai or rest place for caravans. Centuries later, Adam Smith would call roads 'the greatest of all improvements', but Sher Shah Suri had figured it all out for himself. He realized that roads promoted commerce and generated revenue for the state. Medieval India's Mughal empire was dotted with *kos minars* (towers every 3 km) as markers of distance. After the British vanquished the Mughals and occupied India, they relaid the

Grand Trunk Road with a slight change in alignment between Kolkata and Varanasi in central India. This 'work of great magnitude' was carried out by the Department of Public Works, which was formed by the British in 1849, after annexing Punjab.

But much of the good work came to a standstill after India's independence. There was no highway construction during the first Five-Year Plan in the 1950s. In the third, the entire (and amazingly paltry) addition of 179 km over five years was in Assam. In the 1960s, the primary responsibility for road building was transferred to the states. Within their borders, they have built 130,000 km—as big as China's national highway network—of passable quality. As early as 1961, the Bombay Road Congress had proposed 1,600 km of expressways, but that was ignored. The inability to build highways and expressways was aggravated by the failure to maintain them.

In China, the Silk Road became an exchange for ideas, invention and trade with Xinjiang, the current ethnic flashpoint, as the clearinghouse. The 11,000 km, 2nd century BC road was actually a string of routes to Central Asia, West Asia and western Europe. The Han Emperors used the road to build military alliances in Central Asia against the pastoral nomads of Mongolia. Buddhism also travelled to China through this route. But the road went into decline with the revival of Islam and the isolationist policies of the Ming rulers. West Europe also discovered an alternate sea route to Asia via Africa's Cape coast. Though the Silk Road is nostalgia now, the Chinese have tried to revive it as a railway called the Eurasian Continental Bridge, a substitute for the Trans-Siberian Railway. The first leg was inaugurated in 1992, and the second railway line in December 2009.

China built the first modern highway in 1913. At the time of the Revolution, it had over 80,000 km of road, but none of it was designed for speed; only a third was surfaced. Ironically, China's new communist rulers saw cars and highways as a 'capitalist' relic, to be shunned. Inspired by the Soviets, they wanted to aggressively build railways; no one thought there would be as many cars as now 'even after 100 years'!

When Deng Xiaoping opened up the economy in 1978, China had plenty of uneven tracks but nothing that came even close to expressway standard. But an unshackled economy demanded roads: coal had to be transported from the north to feed power plants on the coast, and liberated farmers wanted to sell their produce in towns. A milestone was the construction of the Beijing–Tianjin–Tanggu highway in 1987 (known as JingJinTang highway after the last syllables of the cities it connects). It was China's first competitively bid road project. Built with a loan from the World Bank, the 143 km stretch was completed in 1993. A five-hour ride—which could take up to a full day in bad weather conditions—was slashed to just two.

China's highway construction took off in earnest in 1992. The plan was to connect all cities with more than half a million people with expressways. The original length was 30,000 km, later expanded by a sixth, at an investment of $150 billion. There were to be twelve highways, five of them north–south and seven east–west. True to Chinese-style execution, all but 3 per cent had been done by 2004.

Of Roads, by Roads, for Roads

Halfway across the globe, America was showing the way to the world. In 1993, it completed I-105 in Los Angeles. This was the last link in the 68,000 km interstate highway system, which was President Dwight D. Eisenhower's antidote to the Great Depression. It was modelled on the German autobahns. Carmakers like General Motors were ardent advocates—their exhibit 'Futurnama' at the 1939 New York World Fair had drawn huge crowds, tantalizing people with the prospect of zipping about uninterrupted on 'entry-restricted' highways. But the various lobbies—farmers, truckers and big city folk—could not arrive at a compromise, and Eisenhower had to bash their heads together. He created the Highway Trust Fund with taxes on petrol, tyres and trucks. The post-war economic boom and surge in car ownership helped. Finally, the earthmovers rolled in 1956 when Eisenhower signed the Federal Aid Highway Act.

The massive reconstruction effort should have been completed in sixteen years, but true to democracy's pitfalls, it took thirty-seven years to finish the originally planned length. With federal aid, the US built 76,400 km of highways by 2004. They have unleashed productivity, fed the country's obsession with cars, promoted suburbanization—and depleted inner cities.

Prime Minister Atal Bihari Vajpayee tried to do an Eisenhower in India; predictably, the road-bumps were similar, but the jolts were more spine-crunching. The world had imposed harsh economic sanctions on India after the 1998 nuclear tests; the Asian financial crisis aggravated the distress. Like Eisenhower, Vajpayee needed to devise an antidote. On 6 January 1999, he laid the foundation stone for converting the Bangalore–Hyderabad highway into six lanes. It was the beginning of his government's flagship national highway development programme.

The media was sceptical. The *Indian Express* dismissed it as a whim; according to its report, not much thought could have gone into crafting such a game-changing programme, because the prime minister's office had simply called up the highways ministry and asked it to prepare a feasibility report 'by this evening'. The next day, an ambitious programme, on a hitherto unprecedented scale, was launched! Whatever the veracity of that report, the fact is that there were no ponderous deliberations. Taking after the US, a tax was imposed—first on petrol and then on diesel—to raise the cash.

During his first full term in office, Vajpayee added more highways than the country had built in half a century. One set of highways, called the Golden Quadrilateral, would connect the four biggest cities. The other would run north–south and east–west to connect cities at the extremities. 'Nowhere in the world had such a huge project been attempted in such a short time and with so little funds,' wrote Deepak Dasgupta, the first chairman of the National Highways Authority of India. The agency had been specially created to cut through the usual bureaucratic sloth that paralyses public works in the country.

Prime Minister Vajpayee made a retired army engineer his highways minister. Major General B.C. Khanduri brought a military discipline into road construction. He monitored projects closely; 'You are not only making money, you are building a nation,' he told contractors. By the time he left, nearly half the Golden Quadrilateral was done and contracts awarded for the rest.

The Vajpayee government suffered a shock defeat in 2004. With its driving political patron vanquished, the national roads sector wasted away for the following five years. The new minister was from a regional party that had little interest in national politics. The courts chided him for changing the chairman of the highways authority five times in just two and a half years (such was the ill will for him that he was not made a minister when the government was voted back to power in 2009).

The change in government coincided with a switch in the mode of highway financing. The Vajpayee government had awarded cash contracts, but the preference now was for privately financed toll roads. To sweeten such investments, the government offered a capital subsidy of up to 40 per cent, but went a tad too far in trying to 'protect' public interest. The model concession agreement was designed to promote efficiency and check greed, except that the technical criteria it prescribed disqualified many Indian contractors. Their owned funds had to be at least two times the project cost. Cross-holdings among various consortiums had to be very low (5 per cent) to duck conflict of interest clauses. A road concession could be forfeited if traffic exceeded the target for three years in a row, but the contractor failed to expand capacity for the higher-than-expected traffic growth. The model agreement ignored the reality that a road is not stretchable like elastic; it has to reckon with land acquisition and utility shifting difficulties. Contractors protested, but a suspicious government saw that as arm-twisting tactics to secure unfair gains. Inevitably, the whole mess landed in the courts; no contracts could be awarded in the first eight months of 2008. When auctions were resumed, the financial crisis had changed the world. Of the sixty projects auctioned, bids were received for nineteen and only ten were awarded.

The highways authority too has not covered itself in glory. The World Bank found systemic deficiencies upon reviewing six of the thirty contracts. In one case 90 per cent of the alignment had been changed after award of contract. There was a gap of up to nine years between preparation of detailed blueprints and completion of projects. The World Bank was vexed with the poor safety record; on a 36 km stretch, its review team identified 350 high-hazard locations.

In India, land acquisition is the most common impediment to highway development. The law gives the government summary powers. Acquisition cannot be contested if due process has been followed, only compensation can be. While large factories and economic zones have attracted severe protests, roads have still got off lightly because wide swatches are not required. Cutting of trees is another touchy issue. Often the gods themselves come in the way. A temple of goddess Kali sat smack in the middle of a relaid stretch of Grand Trunk Road; the contractor wanted to shift the temple, but the people were unwilling. They believed that mysterious ailments would strike their village if the goddess was removed. Writing in the *New York Times*, Amy Waldman called the makeover of the national highway system a metaphor for a country struggling to modernize itself kilometre by kilometre, 'goddess versus man, superstition versus progress, the people versus the state'.

Satyendra Dubey, an engineer from the prestigious Indian Institute of Technology, was a project manager on Bihar's section of the Golden Quadrilateral. He had blown the whistle on shoddy work and corrupt practices. When his bosses did not take notice, he wrote to the prime minister directly. Unfortunately, his identity was leaked out. A year after he wrote that letter, on 27 November 2003, he was shot dead. A newspaper campaign stirred an outcry across the country; the prime minister deployed central investigators. A witness to the murder went missing; two people taken for questioning killed themselves. Seven years later three persons were convicted for killing Dubey while robbing him; his brother alleged a cover-up. Little wonder that several activists have called India's road projects a hotbed of mafia, crime and corruption.

Toll-ways of Growth

'Democracy sacrifices efficiency'—many road builders in America and India may quietly agree with the Chinese official who made this billion-yuan pronouncement.

China's highway construction target has been expanded to 85,000 km by 2020. This project is called 7918: seven capital radials, nine north–south highways and eighteen east–west corridors. They will connect all large cities with smaller ones. Deadlines in China are like records—meant to be broken. 'No other country can compete with China when it comes to expansion speed of road building,' says a professor at the Highway College in Xi'an.

Roads flatter the value of the land they pass through. There has been much debate on who should enjoy a rightful share of this latent bounty. Should original landowners get a slice of this road-inflated gain? In China, the authorities have settled this question unambiguously; in their scheme, the state has an almost unequivocal right to tap into this equity. For instance, the municipality financed the Outer Ring Road of Changsha by leasing strips of land 200 metres wide on either side of the highway. Thirty-three sq. km was transferred to Ring Road Investment Corporation, of which nearly a third was finished land with infrastructure access and development approvals. Half of the $730 million financing came directly from leasing rights.

Land leasing was introduced experimentally in 1987; it caught on after Shanghai and Beijing adopted it. From 2002 onwards auctions, rather than private negotiations, have been mandated for transparency. Land is acquired by shifting state-owned enterprises to the outskirts of cities. Landholders are often paid fifty to sixty times less than the future value. But protests by excessively dispossessed peasants are now threatening to spin out of control.

China has also made tolling something of a religion. It reportedly has 70 per cent of the world's toll roads. The model was pioneered by the Hong Kong tycoon Gordon Y.S. Wu, a civil engineering graduate from Princeton who founded Hopewell Holdings. He built China's first modern superhighway between Guangzhou and Shenzhen in 1991 on a thirty-year concession. After an investment of $1.34 billion, it opened in 1997, but not before Hopewell had run out of money and the Chinese government had to do the rescue act.

China's tolls are said to be the highest in the world relative to its currency's buying power. They range from 4.2 to 10 cents a km. (By contrast a 28 km expressway connecting Delhi with a satellite city costs 1.4 cents a km, though another charges 7 cents a km for a 6 km drive). Illegal exactions are not uncommon; in February 2008, the National Audit Office detected $3.1 billion in illegally collected tolls, either as overcharges or charges for non-tolled roads.

The proliferation of toll booths has also slowed down traffic. Trucks have taken to overstuffing to spread the cost over a larger load. This has taken a toll on the roads themselves. Safety has been a casualty—with 2.6 per cent of the world's traffic, China had 26 per cent of the globe's fatalities in 2002, the highest in the world. India has since breached that record. According to the World Health Organization, there were 114,000 deaths on Indian roads in 2007, or thirteen a day. The *People's Daily* reported a little under 82,000 deaths on Chinese roads that year.

The prevalence of tollways does not mean that private investment is the main source of financing. An Indian study found that China spent $78 billion on roads in 2006 (next only to power and irrigation); a little over a tenth came from the state budget, a third were bank loans, and half the money was 'self-raised funds' (including land leases) of local governments. Only 1 per cent came from foreign investment.

Even the United States has depended primarily on state funding to build its roads. But India is charting a unique path by relying on private money.

In his second term, Prime Minister Manmohan Singh is keen to make amends. He has given the highway portfolio to Kamal Nath, a minister with a can-do image, who earned his spurs as a tough trade negotiator. Against an earlier average of 4 km, the minister has set an ambition of 20 km of roads to be constructed a day, but has achieved only half the target in his first year. A special division has been proposed for expressway construction with a target of 17,600 km (India hardly had any until now). The revised model concession agreement takes on board the concerns of investors and lenders. If projects fail on toll viability, they could be awarded as cash contracts. Road developers in a consortium can cash out to operation and maintenance contractors after completion of construction. Earlier, their stake could not fall below 26 per cent. This could free up almost $2 billion of equity funds for them, which can be redeployed in new projects. One hundred and fifty land acquisition cells have been proposed. The highways authority will have ten regional offices to liaise with state governments who have the critical wherewithal, much more than the Central government, to build roads or stall them. A shelf of projects is always available for auction. The aim is to get 60 per cent of the projects privately financed as toll roads.

Until not so long ago, India boasted of a larger road network (3.4 million sq. km) than China's, albeit most it was rural roads. China has evened that score. Today, 40 per cent of Indian villages are not connected, although according to the original plan, all villages with more than a thousand people should have had a road link by now. But the deadline was pushed back by two years. Only 53 per cent of the target has been achieved. The quality of roads is said to be good—the World Bank and Asian Development Bank are keeping an eye. But there are not enough contractors who meet the grade. Local governments too lack execution ability.

*

The hare was whistling softly in the evening breeze: 'Country roads, take me home'. His roller blades seemed to glide effortlessly over smooth expressways. The tortoise had to stop ever so often to shake pebbles out of the holes in the soles of his shoes—huff, crunch, puff; huff, crunch, puff . . .

Indian Rail: Squandering a Quarter-Century Lead

China has added 20,000 km of railway tracks over the last two decades. This is equal to the entire network of Japan or the UK. India has done a pitiful 860 km in the same period.

China Rail's investment in 2009 alone was double that of the previous year; at $88 billion, it was ten times that of Indian Railways.

China will spend $513 billion on just its railways in the next three years; this is higher than what India's Planning Commission has in mind, over five years, to plug the entire infrastructure deficit in the country.

*

India got its first rail service in 1853, a full quarter century before the Chinese did. At 3.35 pm on 16 April, to the roar of a twenty-one-gun salute, three locomotives named Sultan, Sindh and Sahib hauled 400 guests in fourteen carriages between Bori Bunder in Mumbai and Thane on the outskirts. The 33 km journey took an hour and fifteen minutes. A London newspaper said the 'opening of the Great Indian Peninsular Railway was of much greater importance than the victories in the battlefields of Plassey, Assaye and Gujrath'.

More than 150 years have gone by, but Indian Railways have always behaved like a government monopoly. Most trunk routes were laid by private operators before Independence under what is now described as the BOT (build, operate and transfer) model. They were guaranteed minimum returns by the colonial British government. Exorbitant price gouging compelled the government to take over construction, financing and operation in 1924.

Twenty-three years after the opening of the Great Indian Peninsular Railway, in 1876, a British firm named Jardine Matheson built China's first railway line. The concession was for a road between Shanghai and Woosung on which a 23 km narrow gauge track was laid. The reigning Qing dynasty rejected it as an iron monster offensive to the gods. The rails were torn up and shipped along with engines and carriages to the island of Formosa where they were dumped in the sea. China Rail's recovery after that aborted beginning is nothing short of a celestial miracle.

China had just 22,000 km of railways at the time of the Revolution. India had two and a half times as much. But China caught up swiftly in the following decades. It rehabilitated its tracks and substantially expanded them. Although there was a marked slowdown in investment during the 1980s, the railway ministry devised a contract system to overcome the capital shortage. It handed over operations and maintenance to regional railway administrations, with targets and incentives for breaching them. The ministry gave trains on rent and made all investments. Efficiency improved, revenue increased and investments rose. By 1991, China Rail had substantially expanded its network to 58,000 km, just 4,000 km less than India. At 1.5 billion tons it was hauling five times more. While passengers in China were just a quarter of those in India, they were travelling much longer distances. In net terms, both India and China were logging up 315 billion km of passenger miles.

Chinese railways took a modern turn with a 1991 law. China converted the railway ministry from a service operator into a supervisor and regulator. The law allowed partnerships with provincial and city governments. Of 86,000 km of track, more than 10,000 are now owned by these joint ventures. Industrial enterprises are allowed to have rail services within their premises. The first private line of 70 km is currently being built with money from insurance companies and pensions.

The new law asked the state to control investment and pricing.

The ascetic and the revolutionary: As independent nations India and China were midwifed differently. Mahatma Gandhi abhorred violence. Mao Zedong believed that political power grows out of the barrel of a gun. (*above*) Gandhi on fast to force communal peace in January 1948, a few days before he was assassinated. (*left*) Mao proclaims the founding of the People's Republic at Tiananmen Square in Beijing on 1 October 1949. (AP Images)

'The last Englishman to rule India': First prime minister Jawaharhal Nehru's self-description because of his western breeding. Nehru loved heavy industry and Soviet-style planning but seeded India's software industry through institutes of technology. Nehru in October 1949 with Indian students at the Massachusetts Institute of Technology. Indians are the largest overseas student community in the United States. (Photo Division)

'The goddamn woman': President Richard Nixon had choice epithets for Prime Minister Indira Gandhi for defying the US and carving Bangladesh out of Pakistan in December 1971. Nixon regretted that he had 'really slobbered over the old witch' during her visit to the US the previous month to canvass support. (*left*) Walking Gandhi to her limousine at the White House. (AP Images) (*below*) Gandhi announcing in Parliament on 16 December 1971 the surrender of Pakistani forces in Bangladesh. (Photo Division)

The dragon and the eagle: Nixon made diplomatic history in February 1972 when he visited China and ended the Communist country's twenty-three-year isolation. (AP Images)

Capitalist roader: After Mao's death 'paramount leader' Deng Xiaoping freed China's economy from ideological restraints and made it the world's workshop. Mao suspected Deng's economic policies and had purged him twice during the Cultural Revolution. Deng reviewing the armed forces on 1 October 1984, the thirty-fifth anniversary of the People's Republic of China, in a Hongqi convertible. (AP Images)

The ice breaker: India and China have quarreled just once, in 1962, in their long history. Indians have not forgotten that shock defeat. In December 1988, Rajiv Gandhi became the first Indian prime minister to visit China in thirty-four years. In conversation with Deng Xiaoping. (indiatodayimages. com)

Mango diplomacy: China lifted the ban on Indian mangoes, agreed to expand trade ties and put discordant political notes on mute during Prime Minister Atal Bihari Vajpayee's visit in July 2003. Despite the goodwill generated, the border dispute remains, as Deng described it, 'a mound of stale rice buzzing over with flies'. Industrialist Anand Mahindra asks a question during an interaction with the prime minister in Shanghai. (PTI)

Natural allies: President George W. Bush saw India as a counterweight to China. Braving opposition, he gave it a sweetheart nuclear deal. Prime Minister Manmohan Singh was so touched that he controversially told Bush, 'The people of India deeply love you.' Bush found Singh 'serene and calming'. Singh hugs Bush during a visit to Washington in September 2008 to stitch up the nuclear agreement. (PTI)

The panda's handshake: China sees Africa as a market for its exports and a supplier of oil and minerals. Western countries have accused it of cozying up to murderous regimes and ignoring human rights abuses. President Hu Jintao welcoming Zimbabwe President Robert Mugabe to the Africa summit in Beijing in November 2006. (AP Images)

The splittist: China accuses the Dalai Lama of fomenting separation. The spiritual leader of Tibetan Buddhists who fled to India in 1959 to escape Chinese repression says he wants autonomy, not independence. At a press conference at Japan's Narita airport in April 2008, before the Beijing Olympics, the Dalai gestures that he is not the devil China makes him out to be. (AP Images)

Silent tears: A Tibetan Buddhist monk breaks down at a temple in Lhasa before foreign journalists on an official visit in March 2008 as part of a publicity exercise ahead of the Olympics. Tibet, observing the forty-ninth anniversary of the 1959 uprising, had broken out in violent protest that month. (AP Images)

The steamroller: The first train arriving at the new railway station in Lhasa, the capital of Tibet, on 2 July 2006. The Qinghai–Tibet railway line is the highest in the world and an engineering feat. Tibetans feel it will bring in more Han immigrants and undermine their way of life. (AP Images)

Terrifyingly gorgeous: An engineering marvel, the Three Gorges Dam could become an environmental disaster. (*above*) Water discharge in Yichang city. (AP Images) Lacking checks, the Chinese leadership can attempt grand projects with tragic consequences like the Great Leap Forward that is estimated to have claimed 30 million lives. The one-child policy will make China older before it gets richer.

Dragon head: Chinese cities closer to Hong Kong got initial priority during the Deng era, but Shanghai's attributes could not be long ignored. The city has more skyscrapers than Manhattan—making the point that whatever the Americans do, the Chinese can do bigger. A cruise ship at Shanghai port. (AP Images)

Socialism with Chinese characteristics: China's capitalism is predatory. Much of its enterprise is in state control or owned by party organs and their bosses. Italian–American artist Arturo DiModica with a replica of Wall Street's Charging Bull at the Bund in Shanghai, May 2010. (AP Images)

Cultural Revolution!: Mao's attempt to reassert his authority caused social turmoil in China for ten years from October 1966. Those dreadful memories have lost their sting. Even nostalgia is now on sale. A singer dressed as a Red Guard performing at Beijing's Red Classic restaurant. (Reuters)

Socialist badge: Like the politician's homespun cotton attire and the Gandhi topi (cap), the white Ambassador car was India's 'official' car, a symbol of public sector sloth. (*above*) Installation art by Hetal Shukla: an Ambassador car dressed like a polar bear at the Kala Ghoda festival in Mumbai, February 2008 .(PTI)

Olympian dream: The 2008 Beijing Olympics was an impressive event that India can only aspire to replicate. Delhi chief minister Sheila Dikshit at the Bird Nest stadium in May 2008. (PTI)

Hurdle race: Delhi's preparation for the Commonwealth Games in October 2010 has been fitful, making the organizing committee quite anxious. Commonwealth Games Federation president Michael Fennell visiting the Games village with chiefs of missions to assure themselves. (PTI)

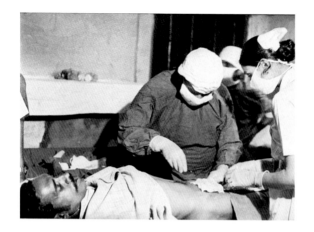

Unkind cut: People were sterilized forcibly during the mid-1970s in India but the government paid the price for that attempt at social engineering. (*left*) A vasectomy operation from that period. (HT Media)

This land is my land: Seizure of land by the government for dams and industrial development has become a touchy issue in India. (*right*) Chiranjeevi, Telugu superstar turned politician, addressing people who lost land to a special economic zone in a district adjoining Hyderabad, in September 2008. (*below*) The funeral procession of Kanu Sanyal, founder of the Naxalite movement, who killed himself in March 2010. Naxalites (Maoists) want to overthrow the state and have a large following among dispossessed tribals. (PTI)

Terror target: The idea of India is under threat from fanatical religious groups and communist extremists. (*left*) The Babri Masjid in north India demolished by Hindu fanatics on 6 December 1992. (indiatodayimages.com) (*below*) Pakistani terrorists lay siege to Mumbai's landmark Taj Mahal Hotel on 26 November 2008. (HT Media)

Socialist act: Competition in the manufacturing industry has brought the car, priced as low as $2,500, within the reach of many Indians. It has also given people like Urmila Bhatia of Navi Mumbai, the first owner of the Tata Nano in her area, a reason to pose for the cameras. (PTI)

Enterprise on wings: Indian entrepreneurs have developed global ambitions. Communities like the Parsis, one of whom founded the House of Tatas, have enterprise in their DNA. The CEO of Tata Steel B. Muthuraman, Tata group chairman Ratan Tata, Corus CEO Jim Leng and Corus chairman Phillippe Varin putting their hands together in London in October 2006 to announce Tata Steel's takeover of Corus, a British steel company. (PTI)

Trust deficit: India likes cheap Chinese railway, power and telecom equipment but worries about embedded spyware. Huawei Technologies, which has a research and development centre in Bangalore, is suspect because of its People's Liberation Army origins. (PTI)

'Monkey money': That is how the CEO of Arcelor described Indian steel magnate Lakshmi Niwas Mittal's hostile 2006 bid for the Luxembourg-based company. The difficulty of doing business in the country forced Indians like Mittal to look abroad. French workers in 2009 protesting Arcelor–Mittal's decision to scrap 1,400 jobs. (AP Images)

Greased tracks: China Rail had a smaller network than India's until two decades ago. Now it is the busiest in the world. The first of China's 200 km an hour train service leaving Shanghai for Suzhou on 18 April 2007. The top train speed in India is 140 km an hour. (AP Images)

Hidebound: The Indian Railways is the only infrastructure sector in the country to be virtually untouched by reform. Sonia Gandhi, chairperson of the ruling alliance with then railway minister Lalu Prasad Yadav at the commencement of construction work on the eastern India stretch of a heavy-duty railroad. Progress has been glacial. (PTI)

Soft power: Movies and film songs have been India's best calling card, giving it an introduction to millions of people who have never been to the country. Bollywood, as India's film industry is called, is the most prolific in the world. There have been many co-productions with Hollywood, including *Chandni Chowk to China*, a box office disaster, whose star Akshay Kumar is seen here at the film's European premiere in London in January 2009. (PTI)

Wear it, don't eat it: India has not sustained the productivity gains of the 1960s in high-yielding varieties of rice and wheat. Genetically modified seed has made India the second largest exporter of cotton, but people are wary of GM food. Environment minister Jairam Ramesh experiences protests against Bt Brinjal first-hand. (PTI)

Discount dilemma: American discount store Wal-Mart buys huge quantities of cheap Chinese goods for sale abroad and also sells merchandise at everyday low prices to 7 million customers a week in China. (*above*) Buyers crowd a newly opened Wal-Mart store in Shanghai in July 2005. (Reuters) But the Communist Party of India (Marxist), which has an ideological affinity to the Chinese Communist Party, does not want Wal-Mart in India (*below*), and nor does the Bharatiya Janata Party, at the other end of the political spectrum. (PTI)

While competition was prohibited, enough commercial freedom was given to the eighteen regional railway administrations (which are like the sixteen zones of Indian Railways). The regional units were given incentives to deliver profits. Today, employees down to the level of station master make a deposit depending on rank. If commitments made are not met they lose the deposit. They can get twice as much by exceeding the targets. If there is a major accident they forfeit the incentive. This has made China Rail one of the safest in the world, despite being the busiest. India, on the other hand, had to create a $3.6 billion safety fund after a series of horrific train accidents.

The British had given India a clear edge in railways, but it was rapidly squandered in the early decades of independence. While China's railways became a locomotive of its economy, India's remained a drag. Their performance was so poor in the '70s that Prime Minister Indira Gandhi had to sack the entire board in one shot. India's railways have the dubious distinction of delaying a third of the 190 infrastructure projects that are behind schedule. Neither have they woken up to their promise as a sunrise industry. This is one transport sector that is virtually untouched by reform. They remain a department of the government. The tradition of presenting a separate budget in parliament, a practice that began in 1925, continues. It is an annual opportunity for the railway minister to play politics and sprinkle largesse on favorite constituencies. In the 1990s, when reforms spurred the rest of the economy, the Railways grew at an anemic 1.8 per cent a year.

'More than being run better, the railways need to be run differently'— this was the common sense prescription from a landmark study on India's infrastructure, conducted by an economist who later became the deputy governor of the Reserve Bank of India. Indian Railways needs leaders, not just managers, it said. It rightly noted that the railway board is an operating team of line professionals, wholly engaged in keeping the network humming. But all its members, including the chairman, rise on the basis of 'seniority', or number of years in service; merit or performance plays a rather limited role in the elevation to the top jobs. Surely that's not the best way to choose the CEO of an entity with yearly revenue of $19 billion, it asked. Of greater concern is the very short stint at the top—the chairman has a tenure which is half that of the minister; both are birds of passage, without an eye on the long term.

In India management is still by function—there is a board member for mechanical, electrical, traffic, finance and so on. In China Rail, management has been constituted along two main lines of business: freight and passenger.

The study concluded that Indian Railways should cease being a department of the government and become a company—the Indian Railways Corporation, with a board to run it. The CEO should be chosen from among the best talent available; modern systems of accounting need to be adopted, the cost of social obligations should get transferred to the government budget, and prices should reflect costs— all very sensible suggestions. While acknowledging that 'privatization was neither feasible nor desirable', it wanted Indian Railways to hive off all activities not related to their main line of business. The ministry reacted by holding a series of seminars where unions, managers and politicians vented their opposition. The report was ignored. Today, far from shedding non-core activities, a rabble-rousing railway minister wants it to build 522 hospitals and diagnostic clinics, sixty schools, eighteen medical colleges, five sports academies, an indoor stadium, museums and more staff quarters!

Hurtling at 200 km Per Hour

China's response to the non-core conundrum was diametrically opposite. Realizing that running trains does not equip it to run schools, China Rail has handed over 400 hospitals and 900 schools to local governments. Sticking to knitting, China Rail has extensively shed other non-core activities as well. The plants that make engines, wagons and coaches have been hived off into joint ventures with multinational companies; from Alstom, Kawasaki, Bombardier and Siemens to General Electric, EMD and Toshiba, China's railway vehicle units have stitched up alliances with firms the world over. It has also created three enterprises for container services, special freight and parcels. Staff engaged in activities like quarrying, cement-making and real estate have been transferred to more than 6,000 so-called 'Decos' (diversified economy companies). Two state-owned companies, one operating a 653 km heavy-haul coal line from Shanxi province to the east coast, and another that introduced China's first 200 km-an-hour passenger line between Guangzhou and Shenzen, are listed on the stock exchanges. To flatten the organization an entire management layer has been abolished, raising productivity considerably.

Typically, China Rail has not shed its pursuit of knowledge, which continues to be a 'core' activity. It retains an impressive network of research institutes and specialist universities, to help it absorb the latest technology. In the words of a Chinese official, 'After being digested by us . . . we don't completely copy it, according to China's situation, we recreate it.'

China's railway expansion is driven by a 2003 blueprint, which has received an extra dollop of cash in the state's massive post-Lehman stimulus program. By 2020, China intends to have 120,000 km of rail, on the assumption that the economy would be four times bigger, 60 per cent of people living in cities would like to travel faster, and the services component of GDP would increase relative to manufacturing.

China Rail is now the biggest freight carrier in the world after US railroads and the largest mover of passengers. There is no other rail system that is as busy. Passengers have to book in advance, especially during festivals. A quarter of China's network has double tracks, is electrified and has automatic signals that allow trains to follow each other in shorter intervals of five to eight minutes. India has a similar share, except it has virtually no automatic signals, creating delays. China has raised the axle load of wagons to 25 tons; India is not far behind, but its wagons are heavier, so they carry less. Today, China's network does 3.3 billion tons, nearly four times more than India.

For fifty years—until 1995—China had kept fares on a leash, hiking them just three times. There were long queues and frayed tempers. After the lid on fares was removed, passenger services have improved dramatically. Sixty per cent of China Rail's fleet is air-conditioned, compared to India's 10 per cent. Chinese trains routinely run at 200 km an hour; the travel time between Shanghai and Beijing, a distance of 1,300 km, is five hours. There are eight corridors with 8,000 km of track with speed up to 250 km an hour, marketed as China Rail High Speed. There are trains that do 350 km an hour as well. Compare that with the average speed of Indian passenger trains, which is 55 km an hour. The fastest run, at 150 km an hour, is between Delhi and Agra, a small distance of 200 km.

India has been rudely jolted out of its slumber by China's line to Tibet, which is a marvel of strategic technology. It was inaugurated a year ahead of schedule in July 2006. The 2,000 km track gives Chinese troops quicker access to the disputed border areas with India—invoking fears of a 're-run of 1962', when the Chinese war machine had outflanked an utterly underprepared and under-resourced Indian army.

Re-inventing the Wagon-Wheel

'Trains cannot be run for charity,' wrote Mahatma Gandhi in 1947. He was annoyed with the rampant practice of fare dodging. Many Indians regard cheap—even free or 'ticketless'—rail travel as something of a right. Since India gives a huge subsidy on passenger fares, it is forced to recover losses from freight rates that are among the highest in the world. Government ministers seem to endorse such irrational policies— one of them loudly proclaimed: 'No privatization, no retrenchment and no increase in passenger fares.' To recover costs, Indian Railways are packing more people into coaches, making train travel quite uncomfortable. The country's lawmakers—who otherwise support the lopsided fare structure—have been scathing about the lack of sanitation and the bad quality of food.

There is hardly any spectacular project that Indian Railways can showcase. Perhaps the only one which can barely qualify to queue up against the Chinese is Konkan Railway. It had been on the drawing board for 100 years, stymied by technical challenges and opposition from environmentalists. 'Where there is a will there is a railway, otherwise there is only a survey'—saying this, a daredevil minister teamed up with a veteran railway engineer to get it going. The 760 km project, which cuts through densely forested hills along India's west coast, was finally a reality in 1998. Unfortunately, Konkan Railway is a can-do exception to India's stillborn railway projects.

Take the case of the high-speed heavy-haul 6,600 Dedicated Freight Corridor between Kolkata, Delhi and Mumbai. Its cost has more than doubled to $13 billion since it was proposed in 2005. Negotiating with landowners in 3,200 villages and fifty-one districts will not be easy, with a minister who has vowed that she will not acquire land by coercion. Execution in private partnership could have sped up progress, but the government will not let go.

Yet Indian Railways have gained whenever they have attempted even modest reforms. In 1989, the container business was housed in a separate company and listed on the stock exchanges. This is one of the services where private players have been allowed to enter. In 2001, catering contracts were outsourced to another subsidiary, whose ambitious employees decided to get into the business of selling tickets. The subsidiary now sells 300,000 tickets, a third of all sold every day.

The mother ship too has embraced change, albeit grudgingly. Its computerized ticketing system, allowing passengers to buy and cancel from anywhere in the country, is one of the most extensive and sophisticated systems in the world. In 2004, a minister known for his rustic instincts thought he would revamp the railways by 'milking the Jersey cow'. He surprised everybody by his turnaround strategies. He set stretch targets, dusted up old advice, tore up narrow departments and made quick payback investments. Running faster, longer and heavier trains, he got the same network to carry 50 per cent more in five years' time.

But even his charm could not work on multinational corporations, who have not taken a fancy to Indian Railways in quite the same manner as they have in China Rail. A $6 billion tender for two diesel and electric locomotive plants in the minister's constituency attracted just one bidder each—GE and Siemens. Three others dropped out as they found the terms of the contract unfavourable.

In the end, however much one pumps up India's piffling successes against China's spectacular achievement on rails, this is one fable whose end is almost foretold.

*

The tortoise started the race twenty-five years earlier than the hare. His British relatives had fed the tortoise rather nourishing food, keeping him young, strong and swift, against a hare which was a weak toddler. But then the fable turned on its head: it was not the hare but the tortoise who became overconfident. Thinking he was far ahead in the race, the tortoise went to sleep. The hare, gathering strength with every stride, overtook the sleeping tortoise, leaving him far, far behind. The best that the tortoise could now do was step quickly on the hare's paw-marks and follow him.

The Wright Cousins of India–China

India's J.R.D. Tata and China's Feng Ru can be called the Wright cousins of Asia.

JRD (as the second generation founder of India's industrial conglomerate was fondly called during his lifetime) was twenty-four years old when he passed out of Bombay Flying Club. He always cherished the blue and gold aviator's certificate that he got on 10 February 1929, with 'No. 1' stamped on it. 'Right from childhood I have been mad about flying and anxiously waited for the day when I would fly myself,' said the first licensed Indian commercial pilot. As in business, so in flight, JRD was always known for his acute sense of fair play. In 1930, he was competing for the Aga Khan trophy and 500 sterling in prize money—his task was to fly solo from Karachi to London. In Alexandria (Egypt), he ran into fellow-competitor Aspy Engineer, who was flying in from London to Bombay. Engineer was stranded for want of spark plugs. JRD could have easily ignored Engineer's predicament, but he chose to give him spark plugs from his own plane. Eventually, Engineer won the competition by a few hours. 'I am glad he won,' said JRD, 'because it helped him get into the Royal Indian Air Force.' (Aspy Engineer went on to become the second chief of independent India's Air Force.)

JRD's contemporary Feng Ru was just as addicted to flying. In September 1909 he is said to have built an aircraft all by himself at Kitty Hawk in North Carolina, just six years after the Wright brothers' flight. Sadly he died three years later in Guangzhou when his plane crashed during an exhibition. Sun Yat-sen anointed him China's 'aviation pioneer'.

Civil aviation in China took off as joint ventures. CNAC was a partnership with an American firm that was later taken over by Pan Am. Another airline was in collaboration with Lufthansa (whom the communists ejected later). CNAC survived the Japanese occupation, flying a difficult supply route known as the Hump over the Himalayas to India—it became a lifeline during the Second World War, when the Japanese cut off the road to Burma. CNAC later shifted to Hong Kong after its Shanghai headquarters was bombed during the war.

At the time of the Revolution in October 1949, China's aviation facilities were tattered. Its thirty-six airports, cratered and mined by Nationalists and Communists in the civil war, could not receive heavy aircraft. It took a year before civil aviation could resume in the country. At that time the two airlines, one wholly owned by the government and another a joint venture with the Soviets, were merged into the Civil Aviation Administration of China (CAAC), which was effectively under the control of the military.

During those years China was isolated. It had diplomatic and trade relations with few non-communist countries. There was no national carrier to speak of. Air miles travelled (1,956) in per capita terms were a quarter of India's. Total international routes flown were about 5,000 km. The industry was hit by Mao's disastrous political experiments; in the decentralization drive of the Great Leap Forward, the national airline was broken up into regional bureaus, each responsible for air connectivity to multiple provinces. The Cultural Revolution of the 1960s with its violent protests, killings and attacks on intellectuals dented business; air traffic slowed and even shrank in some years. China also lost a supplier of long-range aircraft when it fell out with the Soviets. Relief came with membership of the United Nations (1971) and the thaw in relations with America (1972). China acquired a fleet of Boeing 707s, but the airline industry had to wait a while since Deng's reforms were directed initially at agriculture and special manufacturing zones.

Perhaps the first recorded civil flight in India took wing in 1911, when a French pilot flew a 10 km stretch between Allahabad and Naini in north India. One year later, a British airline began a regular service between Karachi and Delhi, as an extension of the London flight. But it was JRD—a qualified pilot and entrepreneur extraordinaire—who began a regular service from Karachi to Bombay with his maiden flight in October 1932, carrying 25 kg of mail. Neville Vincent, a Royal Air Force pilot and JRD's business partner, flew the inaugural Bombay–Madras route. Just four months earlier, the two of them had set up Tata Aviation Service (which later became Air-India).

The aircraft was a Puss Moth, a primitive machine. There were no aids in air or on the ground; the airport in Bombay was a mud flat that would disappear under water during the monsoons. The aviation regulator commended the airmail service in its annual report, for not a single delay or missed flight!

Tata Aviation Service went public a year before India gained independence. Two years later, in 1948, it became Air-India International, in which the government took a 49 per cent stake with the right to buy another 2 per cent. At that time there were eight airlines in India, and their problems were the same as now: cut-throat competition, mounting salary bills and high jet fuel prices. An official committee that enquired into their troubles suggested a voluntary merger, which was initially rejected by the players. But the government had its way—in 1953 they were merged into Indian Airlines. The government also exercised its 2 per cent option to take majority control of Air-India. India's airline industry had been nationalized—but the government had the wisdom to let JRD continue as chairman of Air-India. Under his leadership, it became one of the best airlines in the world. Its mascot, the little bowing Maharaja with an upturned martial moustache and elaborate turban, became an iconic brand in world aviation. Air-India was quick to adopt the latest technology and became the first all-jet airliner. When his biographer referred to his quest for excellence, JRD replied, 'Not excellence, perfection. If you aim at perfection you will attain excellence.'

Air Pockets of Nationalization

Even as China stymied and India nationalized their aviation industries, the world's pioneering market, the United States, was booming. The period after the end of the Great Depression was one of phenomenal growth, albeit in controlled conditions. The Civil Aeronautics Bureau regulated fares to ensure profitability, disregarding costs. Discounts were disapproved except for students and families. The industry was deregulated in 1978 with an eye on innovation, efficiency and profitability. The Federal Aviation Authority was set up—it controlled flights in and out of airports, gave licences to crews and technicians, certified the airworthiness of planes and equipment, and monitored maintenance. A wave of competition was unleashed as interstate airlines competed with national carriers. Fares fell to levels that barely covered operating costs. A number of bankruptcy filings followed, including from Pan Am, TWA and America West.

Sadly at that time Indian aviation was hit by violent air pockets of nationalization. A hands-off state had done well in the early years of its ownership, leaving the management largely free under a visionary JRD. But it was too good to last, as the ills of nationalization were unsheathed under a new government in the late '70s. Since JRD was seen to be too 'friendly' with the outgoing regime, he was unceremoniously sacked on prime time news. Nobody had had the courtesy to inform him beforehand; JRD found out only when his successor came to replace him. Air-India never quite recovered from that blow.

More than a decade later, it was the turn of another newly-elected prime minister to use Indian Airlines in a dirty political fight against his outgoing adversary. There had been loud murmurs about slush money in an aircraft deal; just before the elections, Indian Airlines had suddenly switched vendors, placing a large order for fourteen aircraft with Airbus Industries, even though Boeing had qualified after a six-year grind. As it was, several charges of corruption had rung loud in a vicious election campaign, unseating the incumbent prime minister. So when one of the new aircraft crashed, the new prime minister grounded the entire fleet, implying that a corrupt deal had been done to buy 'unsafe' aircraft. It was a cynical but politically effective ploy to tarnish his predecessor's image and burnish his own 'Mr Clean' credentials. As politicians raked mud, Indian Airlines lost $1.5 million every week; this sorry state of affairs continued for nine long months. Eventually, an enquiry blamed 'pilot error' for the crash, and the thirteen remaining Airbus aircraft were quietly reinducted. But by then the damage was done. (In an entirely unrelated sequence of events, the 'Mr Clean' prime minister was ejected from office after one of the briefest stints by an elected politician in India.)

As India's aviation industry hit political turbulence, China was grappling with challenges of restructuring. In 1985, Vice Premier (later Premier) Li Peng was put in charge; he made a young technocrat the head of CAAC. Airport regulation was separated from airline operation, a policy that India was to implement two decades later. Local governments were encouraged to invest in airports—in six years they built forty-six. Airline operations were hived off into six companies, each responsible for their profits and losses. These included the Big Three: Air China, China Southern and China Eastern (the other three were China Northern, China Northwest and China Southwest). All were state-owned. There was no bar on governments, departments and state enterprises setting up airlines. By 1994 there were more than forty of them, some with less than five aircraft. Many airlines were losing money. Massive investments had increased China's seat capacity by five times, while India's had gone up by just 40 per cent.

The second half of the 1990s saw aggressive competition, price undercutting, overcapacity, poor scale economies, high debt and low profitability. Superfast highways and railroads edged out air travel over shorter distances. In 1996 the new civil aviation law upgraded rules for registration of airlines, mortgage of planes, airline security and carrier liability, but left out issues relating to competition, route allocation and fare regulation. Though there were strict norms for giving licences, state entities were able to use their clout to wangle them. By the turn of the century, Beijing had to step in again with a restructuring plan where ten airlines were collapsed into three corporations.

In India, the pendulum was swinging away from state control. Four hundred pilots of Indian Airlines struck work during the Christmas season of 1990. The public mood turned ugly as the strike extended for five weeks; an angry government roped in fighter pilots and hired planes from the Soviet Union. Within two years the nationalization law was abolished, and private operators were allowed to compete with state carriers. But the early rush of private operators ended in a few resounding failures; while the first to shut shop was a murky operator whose top honcho was allegedly shot in a mafia gang war, a couple of others went belly up when revenues fell far short of their extravagantly luxurious services.

But one private airline was rapidly colonizing the Indian skies. Jet Airways was set up in 1992 by an entrepreneur who had built a thriving business in West Asia selling tickets for a number of international airlines. There were allegations about him being a frontman for questionable Middle Eastern money, but these were never substantiated. The Jet Airways' founder was known to have influential friends in high places. While his role can never be conclusively proved, there were several media stories at that time about how he had aborted stiff competition from the Tatas and Singapore Airlines.

JRD, the father of India's civil aviation, was no more, but his nephew was keen to reclaim the Tatas' heritage. Fortuitously, the Singapore prime minister visited India around this time, and wanted his airline to invest in the country. The Indian prime minister was willing, and nudged the Tatas to do a deal with Singapore Airlines. The joint venture agreement was signed with much fanfare. But it had to contend with India's fractious politics; the civil aviation minister delayed consent saying Indian airports were not ready for another entrant. Then it was election time—the incumbent government was defeated, and the opposition took over. 'Foreign airlines over my dead body,' the new civil aviation minister declared. The government virtually called it a threat to national security. 'Would you like an airline owned by China in your domestic sector?' the civil aviation secretary asked rhetorically at a press conference. 'What if there is a war tomorrow?'

A bizarre new law was made to kill the Tata–Singapore Airlines deal. Foreign airlines were barred from making an investment in local carriers, even as foreign financial investors could hold up to a 49 per cent stake. Overnight, a qualification to run an airline had been made a disqualification in India. In a last ditch effort, the Tatas dropped Singapore Airlines as a partner to comply with the norms. Yet the civil aviation minister in a new government—the third since the Tatas had pitched to re-enter the airlines business—asked for six weeks to decide. In distress, the Tatas killed the project, much to Jet Airways' relief.

A Twenty-first-Century Roller Coaster in the Skies

The aviation industry has been sky-surfing a dangerous roller coaster for the last decade and a half. The dot com bubble of the 1990s created a surge in travel demand, especially in America, but the internet bust and the 9/11 terror attacks threw it into a tailspin. Another wave of bankruptcies followed, prominent being those of US Air and United

Airlines. A new breed of low-cost airlines like JetBlue (established in 2000) has encouraged mass air travel and quick weekend getaways. These no-frills airlines have halved average business class fares.

The years from 2003 to 2007 spelt sunshine for India's aviation industry. Cargo grew at 10 per cent a year and passenger traffic at double that. As state airlines withered, about a dozen private ones bloomed, grabbing three quarters of the 40 million passengers. Jet Airways finally got to feel the heat from robust private players. Kingfisher Airlines, launched by a flamboyant liquor baron and positioned like Virgin Airways, is neck-to-neck with Jet Airways today, both holding a quarter of the market.

India's first low-cost airline got off to an inauspicious start in 2003, as its inaugural flight caught fire. But it was a small one, which was quickly controlled without much damage. Six years later, India has, expectedly, proved to be low-fare country. Jet did a hostile takeover of a low-quality airline, making it a low-fare adjunct. Even Kingfisher, who once swore by a full-frills service, has followed suit. Intense competition forced fares down by half during this period.

Profit, wafer-thin at the best of times, vanished in 2008, due to the economic slump and a spike in jet fuel prices. Airport charges, at one time almost twice the international average, have further increased as facilities are being expanded and upgraded. Taxes have nearly crippled the business, inflicting $2.5 billion in losses. Dubiously, India's aviation industry made a quarter of the world's airline losses in 2008, on just 2 per cent of the global traffic.

Private airlines have been thrashing about to cut costs. One morning in October 2008, Jet Airways staff discovered that they had been laid off when pick-up cars failed to arrive at their homes. Eight hundred young airhostesses and flight attendants, some fresh out of college, staged a noisy and tearful protest before TV cameras, attractively attired in their yellow cabin uniforms. The impact was sensational; viewers were appalled, politicians jumped in to grand-stand, forcing Jet Airways to backtrack. A few months later, the private airlines themselves threatened—but dare not execute—a cartel-like strike to ask for lower taxes on jet fuel (currently the tax is as high as 30 per cent in some states). The turmoil continued as Jet Airways pilots disrupted air services with a two-day strike. They were followed by restive action at Air-India, the fast-sinking government carrier, which was in the sick bay with losses of over $1 billion. With 32,000 employees it has a staff to aircraft ratio of 209:1, perhaps the highest in the world. It ran out of cash with an ill-timed purchase of aircraft, forcing it to beg for a taxpayers' bailout.

The last decade has been a rough roller coaster for Chinese airlines too. Hit hard by the Asian financial crisis (1998) and the SARS epidemic (2003), they rebounded with characteristic aggression, piling up huge amounts of debt in building large fleets. At over 1,200 aircraft, China's 2008 fleet was three time's India's size and carried five times as many domestic passengers, but still only a third of all the people who fly in America.

As if the global slump was not enough, China had to weather vicious snowstorms, Tibetan protests, the Sichuan earthquake, record fuel prices and the yuan depreciation. China Eastern lost $2.2 billion, Air China $1.3 billion and China Southern $700 million in 2008. The government bailed them out with cash, fuel tax rebates and airport charge waivers. But private airlines have had to fend for themselves. Okay Airlines, China's first low-cost carrier, had to suspend flights for some time in 2008. East Star Airlines went bankrupt after the regulators vetoed a restructuring plan. A provincial government took over United Eagle Airlines.

But the current difficulties are a blip on the radar, as the roller coaster is likely to turn up again. China's fleet is expected to more than double to 2,800 aircraft by 2026; it will take delivery of three new aircraft every week for the next five years, creating capacity at a 'frightening' rate. It has ambitions of building its own seventy-seat commercial aircraft for which it has already taken orders. 'It is the will of the nation and its people to have Chinese large aircraft soar in the blue sky,' said Prime Minister Wen Jiabao at the launch of the Commercial Aircraft Corporation of China. That may not be an idle aspiration, since China has experience of manufacturing aircraft parts for Boeing, and has a joint venture with Airbus for final assembly of planes.

India too is finally overhauling its dilapidated airport infrastructure. Delhi and Mumbai have large private airports, although the government is persisting with an archaic policy which allows only one airport in these metropolises. This will have to change, as equivalent mega-cities like London, Paris and New York have several airports. Gateway airports in two more metros are being expanded and upgraded in public–private partnership. The government is revamping thirty-five city airports, all of which should create a vibrant tourism industry, the ultimate salve for a wounded aviation business. Some artificial constraints remain; for instance, local carriers cannot fly overseas unless they have a five-year track record, but incoming foreign airlines are not similarly restricted. This has allowed fledgling foreign operators to take away international market share from domestic carriers. But by far the most crucial reform is needed in a mindset which looks upon air travel as a 'rich man's preserve' and taxes fuel at nearly 30 per cent, when every sensible recommendation is to cap that at 4 per cent. This is the ultimate air pocket for India's aviation industry.

Airbus has predicted that China's aviation industry will grow at 7 per cent until 2020, the second fastest; India should be the fastest at 10 per cent. In this modern industry of the skies, the Indian tortoise is a twenty-first-century character, agile, privatized and entrepreneurial, full of energy and adrenaline. Unlike in the traditional fable, it is not seen as a hopeless loser. The Chinese hare is a swift behemoth. But both are fighting headwinds, and the endgame is quite a bit in the blue yonder.

No Contain(er)ing China's Growth

Malcolm P. McLean began life as a driver. In 1937, he spent a whole day waiting at a port in New Jersey for cotton to be loaded from his truck to a ship. Those days, loading and unloading of cargo, detention in warehouses and handling by batches of port workers was very expensive. Travel schedules were uncertain, with considerable risk of damage and theft. McLean figured there had to be a better way of carrying cargo on a ship. A brainwave hit him: put the cargo in standard sized boxes, or containers, which would neatly slot into storage holds, like bricks stack up in a wall. His calculations showed him that the cost of loading a medium-sized ship would drop from $5.83 a ton to just 16 cents. On 26 April 1956 a ship owned by McLean called *Ideal X* left Newark for Houston with fifty-eight box trailers. It was the world's first container-laden ship. His company, Sea-Land Industries (now part of Maersk) revolutionized the shipping industry, eased global trade, enabled just-in-time manufacturing—and later, made China the workshop of the world.

China has 18,000 km of coastline against India's 7,500 km. China also has 1,300 ports, against India's 200. China's merchant fleet, at over 3,300 ships (2008), was the fourth largest in the world, after Greece, Japan and Germany. India has only 872 vessels, of which less than 300 are engaged in overseas trade. Clearly, China is a bigger seafaring nation. But containers landed in the two countries at about the same time, almost to the date. In September 1973, the first container landed at Tianjin port in China, and two months later, in November, American President Lines unloaded the first container at Kochi port in India. Five years later, a regular container service started between India and Australia. Coincidentally, in that very month, *Ping Xiang Cheng* set sail with 162 containers from Shanghai to the same destination.

Curiously, India's railways, not its shipping lines, caused the early spread of containers within the country. In hindsight, that was understandable; India had a bustling domestic economy, but rather insignificant trade with the world. So the railways began dabbling with containers as early as 1966; these were five-ton boxes, smaller than the international norm, handled through an improvised inland container depot. Two decades later, Indian Railways set up Container Corporation (Concor), a somewhat unexpected act of enterprise. Concor took up the job in earnest, setting up a string of fifty-nine inland container depots, starting with the capital city. This allowed shippers to complete customs formalities without having to travel to the port; it also conserved scarce real estate at the waterfront.

As usual, India began well but soon let go an early lead. Even as Concor whipped up the market, other players were kept out for nearly two decades. The first private container service (by Innovative B2B Logistics Solutions) started as late as 2007; today there are sixteen of them holding 15 per cent of the market. They would have got more if they did not have to negotiate the thicket of unequal concession agreements and stiff usage fees for the incumbent's well-located dry ports. Indian Railways does not allow anybody to haul container trains; experts have lamented for long that India's logistics cost, at 13 per cent of GDP, could fall to a far more efficient 9 per cent if private operators are allowed greater play.

Containers finally took off in India's shipping lines in the '90s, once the economy opened up. Today, nearly a third of India's overseas cargo travels in containers. The rising share of manufacturing in India's predominantly services economy should keep up the momentum. The tendency to transport even bulk cargo in boxes to avoid damage and theft should help.

Having begun together, China has catapulted into another league—again understandably, since manufactured exports are the bedrock of its economy. This also explains why China's shipping companies, not its railways, have engineered the container revolution there. Few economies have been as transformed by an explosion in container traffic as China has. 'Low transport costs help make it economically sensible for a factory in China to produce Barbie dolls with Japanese hair, Taiwanese plastics and American colourants, and ship them off to eager girls all over the world,' says economist Marc Levinson.

In an uncharacteristic lag, China Railway Container Transport Company was set up as late as 2004 (a good fifteen years after Indian Railways set up Concor). At one level, this shows the small role that the hinterland economy played in China's early decades of growth. But having started late, China is playing furious catch-up. It plans to set up eighteen inland depots as manufacturing moves inland with wages rising in coastal areas (the traditional engines of growth). Seventy per cent of inland container traffic now originates in China's mid-west.

Over the last decade, China has been the driver of sea-borne container trade, which doubled to $4 trillion in 2008. China handles more than a fifth of the world's container traffic at 102 million units, fourteen times more than India. Seven mainland China ports are among the top twenty container terminals. Having displaced Hong Kong, Shanghai is vying with Singapore for the top slot. Chinese companies are also among the world's leading container operators. China Ocean Shipping Company or Cosco ranks sixth with 141 container ships, and China Shipping Container Lines is at seventh place with 122 ships. Together they own half as many containers as the world leader, Maersk Line of Denmark.

The global financial crisis almost choked the boom in container traffic overnight. Container volumes dropped at double the rate of overall sea trade. But China used the crisis as an opportunity to launch another furrow of its 'escape velocity' investments. Shanghai went ahead with developing the Yangshan deepwater port, flattening a rocky island in deep waters, to accommodate large tankers and container ships. The plan is to have thirty terminals, capable of processing 15 million containers a year, by 2020.

China's plans for its shipbuilding industry are just as ambitious. Traditionally, the industry has chased lower wages—from the West to Japan to South Korea, which has 40 per cent of the market. China, which is close behind, intends to beat the rest to the finishing line by 2015. It has fifty-eight shipyards and is building the world's biggest in the Yangtse delta near Shanghai.

India has employed its cheap labour to become a world leader at the other end, in ship breaking. But Alang, said to be the world's biggest breaking yard, is often panned for environmental damage and appalling work conditions. In 2006, the Supreme Court denied entry to *Clamenceau* after it was found with 500 tons of asbestos. In 2009, *Platinium II* got into a similar flap. Despite low wages and a string of institutions that supply skilled people to the world's shipping industry, India is a bit player in shipbuilding (1 per cent of world order book in 2007). But ambition is rising with an $11 billion national shipping plan. The state-owned Shipping Corporation of India plans to acquire seventy-six ships by 2012. Tax treatment for shipping companies has been brought in line with international practice (with tonnage tax). A cruise shipping policy was announced (2009) to promote tourism. Two world-class shipyards are being set up on either coast. Today there are twenty-eight shipyards, many owned by private firms like ABG and Bharti Shipyard. Giant conglomerates like Reliance Industries and Larsen & Toubro, known for their execution ability and engineering skills, have entered the business too. India could yet put up some fight here.

Ports of Good Hope

Ports have been top priority in China's development plans for two decades (since 1991). The ministry of communication was in complete control initially; it kept the revenue and made all investments. In 1987, dual control was introduced. Local governments were made responsible for human resources. The ports could retain a part of profits for development, but project proposals had to be vetted by the government.

By 2002, China had decentralized port governance, separating the administrative from the enterprise function. Thirty-eight major ports were converted into companies. China now follows the landlord port model, which is in vogue the world over. Governments do not directly invest in or operate ports. Administration is by port bureaus answerable to city governments. Port corporations are financially independent. They keep profits, pay taxes, award concessions to operators, and plan business strategy. But the ministry of communication decides how best to use deep-water coastal lines, while provinces plan for the rest. There are national layout plans to integrate the ports with regional transport networks, avoid duplication and unhealthy competition. The ports have been divided into five clusters according to eight freight categories. It's all very methodical, efficient and ambitious.

In India, ports were traditionally government-owned. They were run as trusts—supposedly for the public good—and not as enterprises for profit. A law dating back to 1948 gave complete job security to dock workers and was highly protective of their rights. This resulted in rampant overstaffing—in Kolkata, thirty-two workers were employed in moving a container from ship to shore; in Mumbai, on average twenty-eight workers would de-stuff a container. Unions had a vice-like grip on port operations and productivity suffered. While a worker at the port of Rotterdam did 50,500 tons in 1998, the average in India was 1,400 tons. A ship would have to wait more than five days before it was attended to; turnaround time was twelve days. Workers had to be bribed to hurry up—customs officials were also on the take. A 1999 study estimated the cost of all these inefficiencies at $1.5 billion.

Things began to improve after 1990. Jawaharlal Nehru port, India's largest container port and ranked twenty-ninth in the world, began to turn around ships in two days. Waiting time too fell from five days to ten hours. Another port, Ennore, converted itself into a corporation (2001), although it was the only one to have done that. Eight years later, the finance ministry was still exhorting five other port trusts, including Jawaharlal Nehru port, to convert and shed 49 per cent in a public listing. As happens so often in India, an enabling law was stuck in parliament.

P&O Australia Ports was the first private investor in Indian ports. It was awarded a thirty-year concession in 1997, but as usually happens with public–private partnerships, the deal was dogged by controversy. The terminal was built (at a cost of $183 million) within two years, beating the deadline for completion. By 2005, traffic handled was more than double the capacity initially estimated. The terminal turned in an annual return of 80 per cent, against the stipulated 20 per cent, making it one of the most profitable ports in the world. This ignited a blame game; the extravagant profit was blamed on poor oversight by TAMP (Tariff Authority for Major Ports), the tariff regulator. The concession was awarded to P&O as it had made the highest offer of royalty, which was passed on to customers. Critics argued, with some justification, that royalty should have been a charge on profits. The anti-corruption police suspected collusion. The policy has since been revised; tariffs are capped and partially indexed to wholesale prices. Concessions for terminals are now awarded on the basis of royalty (as a charge on profits) and revenue share.

Unlike in several other areas, the Indian government has been rather bold in crafting a liberal overseas investment policy for ports. India allows 100 per cent foreign ownership in all aspects of port operation from construction to support services. In 2006, it did not block DP World, a subsidiary of Dubai Ports, from operating a container terminal at Jawaharlal Nehru port, despite concerns that it could set uncompetitive rates and divert traffic to Dubai. In the US, the same company had got a frosty reception on security concerns sparked by its Middle Eastern origin; following Congressional outcry, it had to offload P&Os terminals there. But DP World operates five terminals in India, making it the largest single container operator. It has also won a concession for a hub port near Kochi at the very southern tip of India. In the absence of such a port, large vessels were skipping India—traders had to catch them at Colombo, Singapore and Dubai through feeders. This delayed consignments by forty to fifty hours, and added to cost.

An aggressive private ports policy could have made Gujarat the fastest-growing state in India, and this has inspired other coastal states to mimic its port-led development. Free from legacy and pricing issues, they have discovered that nothing prevents their 'minor' ports from becoming bigger than the so-called major ports. But Indian ports dwarf in comparison with their Asian peers. In 2006, Singapore port handled 28 million container units, eight times more than Jawaharlal Nehru port. There was a similar gap in various material handling devices, whether quay cranes, rubber tyred-gantry cranes or rail-mounted ones. Total costs in India were higher by a sixth.

When all is said and done, it does appear that the Indian government has been quicker off the block in building ports (as opposed to its lethargy in power, for instance). Cargo has been growing at the rate of 11 per cent, with major ports getting as much traffic as they can handle. An aggressive $13 billion investment in 226 projects is targeted by 2012—half of them have been awarded. Two-thirds of the investment is to be privately raised. Competition for concessions is acute, with some bidders quoting a revenue share as high as 50 per cent. The intention could be to get a foot in the door and wangle concessions later (learning from the concessionaire for Delhi airport!).

*

The hare was dressed up like Admiral Cheng-ho, a Ming dynasty eunuch whose nine-mast ships were much bigger than what Christopher Columbus had sailed in to discover the New World. In the early 1400s, Cheng-ho had taken his armada of ships and 30,000 men as far as Africa on seven naval expeditions. The tortoise was happy moving at his own pace, not willing to take on the hare in admiralty exploits.

Power Games in China, Enron in India

'Political power grows out of the barrel of a gun,' said Mao Zedong. His successors believe it flows out of the chimney of a thermal power plant. They echo Lenin more than Mao—'Communism is Soviet power plus the electrification of the entire country,' Lenin had said.

Mao was a peasant leader, a non-technocrat who worked his rhetoric on masses to devastating effect. His successors today—fully seven out of nine members of the Politburo Standing Committee, the highest decision-making body—are engineers who can plot differential equations to grow China. President Hu Jintao's engineering thesis was on hub hydropower stations and he was assigned to construct one. His predecessor Jiang Zemin was an electrical engineer. Premier Wen Jiabao is a geologist. Zhu Rongji, the previous premier, was an electrical engineer. Li Peng, the prime minister before him, was a hydroelectric engineer. His son and daughter, the so-called princelings, were both in charge of power plants. In non-religious China, engineers are priests, and electricity the votive offering.

China is now the second largest producer of electricity after the United States. In 2008, it had 790 GW of installed capacity, five times more than India's. That year alone it added more capacity than India has struggled to do over five years. There are no power breaks in China (well, actually there are, as we will see a bit later).

Chinese power reforms began around the mid-'80s, when a state monopoly was dismantled. Non-central government investors were allowed entry, independent producers could sell to the grid, returns were guaranteed and tariffs were raised to create a power construction fund. About $20 billion a year was raised during this phase.

India followed six years later, in the crisis year of 1991, when its foreign exchange reserves fell to a paltry $1 billion. Among a fully messed-up economy, the power industry was especially sick. Even by the lax accounting standards of those times, a fifth of the electricity was not being billed because of transmission losses and plain theft. The tariff structure was utterly lopsided, with shops and factories subsidizing cheap (often, absolutely free) power to farms and homes. Over and above that, the government was shelling out $3 billion to cover losses. Strangely, such an ill sector was hastily thrown open to foreign investors; what followed was a scandal that has haunted India's power industry ever since.

It started with the charismatic Rebecca Mark of Enron striding in with a $3 billion deal for the Dabhol power project. Enron had friends in high places in America, being one of the biggest contributors to President George W. Bush's election campaign. A smitten, inexperienced government caved in to Mark's hardsell, and signed a contract in a matter of days, ignoring the complexity of a project that depended entirely on imported fuel and largely on imported equipment. A subsequent enquiry damned the government: 'Neither the balance sheet and annual accounts of Enron, nor any information about its activities, area of operation, its associates etc. was obtained by the government then, or later.' Enron was accused of inflating costs, including a declared amount of '$20 million to educate people in India', which was just a euphemism for paying bribes!

Little wonder that Enron produced power at twice the cost of its nearest competitor. Its electricity was seven times as expensive as the cheapest power available in the area. Therefore, it made economic sense to pay a shutdown penalty to Enron than buy its power. But an over-eager government had taken the unprecedented step of guaranteeing revenues and return on equity to the American company. Activists screamed in protest; since 'Article 293 of the Indian Constitution limits the power of the state to guarantee loans, there is no provision to guarantee revenues to a third party'. To rub it in, the Pakistan government rejected Enron's request for a similar counter-guarantee. Worse was to follow, as the imported turbines of the power plant turned out to be faulty. Finally, Enron was forced to abandon the project, which many have called the most massive commercial fraud in India's history. (Ironically, a decade later, Enron collapsed in an accounting scandal, driving its CEO to suicide. It was accused of manipulating California's deregulated electricity market, which saw the state face rolling blackouts.)

But Rebecca Mark wasn't the only American power woman to come buzzing. President Bill Clinton's Energy Secretary, Hazel O'Leary, a millionaire utility company executive from Minnesota, came in 1994 with an entourage of seventy-six top-notch investors. (As an aside, her group came in a chartered plane that was once hired by pop star Madonna.) A subsequent audit ticked her off for spending $700,000 of American taxpayer money on that trip, even though it generated investment pledges of $25 billion spread over sixty projects. India's power industry those days was unusually scandal prone, whether the slush related to electricity or not.

Those were heady days when rash projections were made about installed capacity rising to 220 GW by 2007. (India is still struggling at a third lower than that.) If a memorial were erected to India's early attempts at attracting foreign investment, epitaphs would have to be written to such US giants as Enron, Cogentrix and AES.

Meanwhile, Chinese reforms took off in earnest after the electricity power law was enacted in 1996. The ministry of electric power was abolished. Its commercial operations of generation, transmission and distribution were converted into a state-owned corporation. The regulatory and financial functions were transferred to a regulator. Competition was introduced on a limited, experimental basis in 1999 when demand fell in the aftermath of the Asian financial crisis. The state behemoth was broken up into five independent power-generating companies (the Big Five). Two grid companies were also carved out. But control has remained largely in state hands. Private investors are allowed only in power generation, except in some rural areas where private distribution companies have been established. State-owned enterprises have a 90 per cent market share in power production, a little more than the Indian public sector's 87 per cent share. The largest state-owned power producer, China Huaneng Group, is two and a half times the size of India's National Thermal Power Corporation.

Despite the strides made by China, eighteen provinces faced power shortages in the summer of 2008. 'It is impossible for any factory, if they rely on public utilities; they cannot survive,' said a worker in Guangdong, which is China's manufacturing hub for exports, home to appliance makers like Midea, Galanz and Kelon.

But China's power cuts spring from a very different malady. Unlike in India, China has got plenty of power capacity. Unfortunately, its producers are caught between a rock and a hard place, as the government has capped power tariffs while liberalizing coal prices. Many independent producers have run into the red; they would rather back down their plants than suffer more losses. Downtime at coal-fired plants is mounting year after year.

Power Thieves at the Taj Mahal

It is difficult to believe, but Indian planners may have eventually crafted better policies than their Chinese peers (although Indian implementation remains a tale of massive false starts): they realized that utilities have to be healthy enough to pay power producers, otherwise, investor interest would fizzle out like it did in the 1990s. Unlike China, all three areas in electricity in India—production, transmission and distribution—are now open to private investment.

Two states have completely privatized their distribution utilities, while some others have given franchises over smaller areas. Private trading is allowed and two trading exchanges have been established.

But reality has lagged far behind the expansive promises of policy. An eastern state jumped the gun and allowed four private companies to do the last-mile supply. AES, an American company, was among the early adventurers. It quit after a very unhappy experience. Another provincial leader from South India was always an overzealous reformer. He was hailed as the poster boy who broke up the bleeding state utility into three parts for generation, transmission and distribution, converted them into companies, and hiked farm tariffs. His intentions were right but the timing was wrong. Rains failed the state that year and farmers were squeezed between lost crops and bloated power bills. They voted him out.

India's capital city tried a different tack. It was grappling with industrial thieves who stole half its power. Losses were as high as 63 per cent in one of the suburbs. The utility was sold to three private companies, with a somewhat mixed track record. The network has been upgraded, theft is less and subsidy bills are down. Yet the summer of 2009 saw extended power cuts. Private owners shied away from costlier power in the spot market. Harried customers cried foul, but at least there was some focus on profitability.

Looking back over nearly two decades of turbulence, there has been plenty of activity, but little movement. Indian state utilities are still losing money—nearly $7 billion at the last count. Half of them had a negative return on net worth. Power supply is 10 per cent short of demand and the gap rises to 12 per cent during peak hours. A third of the power supplied is lost or stolen nationally, though most utilities have improved their performance.

Accounting now is less inaccurate, billing has improved, nearly 90 per cent of consumers are metered, and all states (barring one in the North-East) have regulators to determine tariffs. Agricultural states continue to supply free power to farmers, and one charges a ridiculous half a cent for each unit. But at least such political freebies are now explicitly shown on the balance sheet, rather than hidden or papered over.

Electricity thieves can now be thrown in jail. The Taj Mahal, among the wonders of the world, actually boasts of a nearby police station that exclusively deals with power theft. But at the national level, this continues to be a challenge.

The Indian government is also trying to make up for lost time by a rather unique initiative. It is auctioning shell companies which have all the permissions and fuel arrangements in place. Nine such 'pay and immediately begin playing' kind of plants are being set up near coal mines or on the coast, with new boiler technologies that reduce greenhouse gas emissions. Four have already been auctioned, though there is some concern about three of the projects going to just one industrial group.

There was a shortage of equipment at one time, with only one state-owned domestic supplier. Now four multinational corporations have set up joint ventures. The central regulator has set a price cap of Rs 8 (17 cents) a unit for bulk power, which when distributed, sells for a third more. This is three times the rate that Enron was charging. Distribution companies get away with this, because they blend these spot rates with cheaper power obtained on long contracts. The average price of traded power has more than doubled in three years An official who drafted the 2003 law says: 'The consumer is hostage to an interconnected chain of monopolies.' Sensing big profits, many private players have entered the field of power generation, making initial offers of equity and juicy promises. Many of these plants are based on imported coal, and could come to grief if the rupee depreciates in value.

India's lax execution capability gets aggravated in hydro projects as they are in remote and difficult areas. Obtaining forest clearances, winning over the project-affected people, getting long-term finance, and installing transmission lines to evacuate the power has not been easy. The relatively young Himalayan terrain also springs geological surprises. Though hydro power production has increased from 5 billion units a year to 670 billion, its share in the total has fallen from 44 per cent in the late 1960s to 26 per cent now.

While India grapples with capacity creation, China continues to potter around an unfinished pricing policy. Prices there do not fully reflect costs. Different rates apply to homes, farms, industrial and commercial users. The government is scared of increasing prices and stoking inflation. A sharp regional imbalance is another problem. Demand is heavy in the industrial coastal regions of the east and southeast, while 80 per cent of coal exists in the northwestern provinces. The west–east power link has sparked resentment among residents in the west, who believe they will get pollution and high-priced goods in exchange for the cheap power they supply to the east.

China's power sector is also weighed down by climate change concerns. Coal-fired plants supply more than four-fifths of its electricity. Today, it is the largest consumer of coal in the world, with the dubious distinction of being the largest emitter of sulfur dioxide, a respiratory irritant and the cause of acid rain. To cut down emissions, China will have to retire old, inefficient power plants. It made an attempt early this decade and failed. Provincial governments that own most of the small plants, are not keen on shutting them for fear of displacing workers. New plants are under a directive, backed by penalties and incentives, to use clean-burning 'supercritical' technologies.

'Turning a deep chasm into a thoroughfare ... till a smooth lake rises in the narrow gorges. The mountain goddess ... will marvel at a world so changed,' wrote Mao 'Wordsworth' Zedong, in an uncharacteristic display of sentimentality over the Three Gorges dam, when it was still an idea in 1958. China is once again waxing lyrical about hydropower, on which most of its new investments are focused. It is also taking to wind power with a gale-like intensity. 'Three Gorges on the land' is a giant wind farm coming up in the Gobi desert. About half a dozen such mammoth wind farms are planned. Large power companies are now required, by law, to generate at least 3 per cent of their power from renewable sources by 2020. China is set to achieve 30 GW by 2010, ten years in advance. That is three times India's current capacity of wind power, though India's Suzlon has become a global player in the business.

*

The turbo-charged hare was miles ahead of a sputtering tortoise. But the tortoise's master had replaced more faulty batteries in the last lap than ever before (no single industry in India has seen as many policy changes as the power sector in the past two decades). Would this give the tortoise enough fresh charge to begin closing the gap with a powered-up hare?

Five

SOCIAL INFRASTRUCTURE

Land Ahoy!

The Tatas are icons of corporate governance in India. Their oldest steel plant in communist-dominated east India has not struck even for a day in eighty years. People usually woo the Tatas for investments in their areas. But not the farmers of Singur, where the Tatas and their thirty vendors planned to manufacture the ultra-compact Nano. The farmers were angry with the state government for forcibly acquiring a thousand acres at cheap rates. Under prevalent norms, the Tatas should have paid $19 million upfront as *salaami* or lease premium, and over half a million dollars every year for the ninety-year lease. Instead, they paid a token amount, rising up to $4 million a year in the last thirty years of the lease. But the prospects of the car factory had pushed up land prices; industrial plots were selling for five times the price that had been paid to holders of single-crop land. Most of the 9,000 farmers felt severely shortchanged. Opposition politicians stoked the fires of unrest. The factory building was put under siege. Eventually, an angry Tata management abandoned the plant, taking the project to another state.

In hindsight, the Tatas should have negotiated directly with the farmers instead of being hands-off.

Earlier, a dozen people were killed in police firing in another restive area of east India. Tribals had come armed with bows, arrows and axes to protest the levelling of land for steel and chrome washing mills. Simmering protests had also broken out across other projects involving land, from Raigarh in west India to Jhajjar and Dadri in the north.

India was paying the price of a deeply prejudiced and outdated policy for acquiring land.

India's land acquisition law is a colonial import. It was enacted in 1894, consolidated from several laws framed over the previous seventy years. Its aim was to cheaply promote British commercial interests, specially the expansion of the railways. Independent India made the mistake of holding on to this rather old piece of legislation. The state could force people to give up their land for a 'public purpose', including the development of industrial estates. In the early years of free India, private land was massively acquired for dams, canals, steel mills, hydroelectric plants, petroleum refineries, fertilizer units, paper mills, cement factories, defence installations, railway workshops, technical institutes and metal-bashing facilities. Soviet-style industrial townships like Durgapur, Bhilai and Rourkela were established. New provincial capital cities like Chandigarh, Gandhinagar and Bhubaneswar were constructed from scratch.

Protests were quelled by a determined government which claimed it was acting for the 'greater good' of the community, especially since most of the assets were publicly owned. But in a landmark judgment in 1962, the Supreme Court questioned the 'public purpose' behind the acquisition of land for a private textile-machinery manufacturer. It castigated the government for acting like a 'general agent' for companies. The government responded by changing the law: land could now be acquired for private companies as well. There was some merit in such a heavy-handed action. Some amount of coercion is often necessary on defence and security issues, or for the alignment of roads, pipelines and railway tracks, or for the extraction of minerals. Otherwise, you run a real risk of endless litigation, as Indian land records are poorly kept, title is uncertain and plots are dispersed over a large number of small holders. For these very reasons, the courts have not defined 'public purpose', saying it is an evolving concept. So land acquisition can be challenged if it is shown to be bad in law, or where procedures have been flouted, or there is fraud, or public purpose is actually disguised private interest.

India is not the only country which exercises force to acquire land. In the famous Kelo vs City of New London case, the Supreme Court of Connecticut (USA) said if the acquisition of a privately-developed economic project created jobs, improved tax collection and revitalized a depressed area, then it could be called 'public purpose'. That judgment created quite a stir and many US states rushed to protect private property. Michigan said land could not be acquired and transferred to another private entity for economic development, or to increase taxes. If done to eliminate economic blight, a higher standard of proof would be necessary. New Hampshire said private property could not be acquired and handed over for private development or private use, directly or indirectly. Florida required 60 per cent approval by the legislature.

These provisions are still in force in both the US and UK.

The Farmer Shareholder

If India is to grow in double digits, it has to transfer a lot of land from agriculture to new industrial parks and cities. India has always wanted to copy China's success with coastal special economic zones (SEZs). These special zones are enclaves where India's income tax and customs laws do not apply, with the objective of super-conducting exports away from the thrall of a degrading infrastructure. Almost every Indian businessman worth his salt has jumped in with an application (many critics see this as a thinly veiled attempt to grab land). As of August 2009, ninety-eight SEZs were operating, although six times as many had been approved.

Predictably, Indian SEZs are atomized versions of China's huge zones. The biggest one in China was set up in 1988 over 3.4 million hectares. But many of India's smallest ones are just well-appointed buildings with satellite connectivity and assured power to run computer software outfits. Many of the larger ones are as yet stillborn.

Perhaps Indian lawmakers should take a few lessons from China's ravaged efforts here. Some reports suggest that 200,000 hectares are taken from rural folk every year with little or no compensation. China also has no rural property rights; 750 million rural residents lease land, but are at the mercy of local officials if they are evicted for infrastructure or industrial purposes. They cannot borrow against this leasehold land. Between 1992 and 2005, 20 million farmers were thought to have been evicted; between 1996 and 2005, more than 21 per cent of arable land was taken away for non-agricultural use; 87,000 riots were reported in 2005, up 50 per cent from 2003.

Mercifully, not every effort to acquire land in India has ended in grief. In fact, there are a few heart-warming instances of sensitive administrative action that ended in a win–win for industrialists and farmers.

'Land is owned by the people. They should be taken into full confidence,' says Prabhakar Deshmukh, who was once the District Magistrate of Pune in west India. Bharat Forge, a leading forgings manufacturer, wanted to acquire 5,000 hectares for a $5 billion automobile SEZ which could create 120,000 jobs. Some of India's biggest motorcycle and truck makers are based in Pune. They have spawned a large number of ancillary suppliers. Though the government could have used force, Deshmukh was against third-degree methods. He opened up with farmers—the last discussion lasting about ten hours—and paid them a negotiated price. Bharat Forge pledged to train and employ each displaced youth. Tribals who had lost land were given built-up houses with hospitable compounds. Fifteen per cent of the acquired land was converted into industrial plots and returned to farmers at cheap rates. A thousand farmers actually pooled these plots into a joint stock company owning 250 acres of industrial land, which was leased to the SEZ for a steady income.

Ironically, just a few hundred kilometres from where Tata's Nano car factory met a sorry end, there is a shining story of a large steel plant. The company negotiated directly with 700 farmers to buy 450 acres of land. The remaining 4,300 acres was fallow government land. Farmers were paid half in cash, with an option to get the rest in shares of the company. Each land seller was also promised a job in the mill.

Moved by blood and tears, the Indian government is keen to reform its land acquisition law. It wants to step in only after a private developer has bought 70 per cent of the land directly from sellers; coercive policies will apply only to the 30 per cent who are holding out. Apart from higher compensation, sellers will have the option of getting at least a quarter of the payment in shares or debentures. Special courts will settle disputes. The original owners will share in the spoils if the property gains in value—although how they will be traced, and for how long this should be valid, is not specified. There is a provision for an 'obligatory social impact assessment' if more than 400 families get displaced. But many of these proposals have not found favour with a parliamentary committee.

But reformers want more. Seventy per cent of the number of landholders should say yes, as against getting a quick okay from a handful of large owners accounting for 70 per cent of the land, they say. Land use should be changed from agriculture to industry well before the acquisition, allowing land-losing farmers to 'skim the cream'. Auction value should be 'discovered' like it happens in an 'open offer for shares' on the stock market. Farmers should go to a village registry and tender their land in, and the highest price paid to any single seller should be paid to all of them. Cropped land should be acquired only if there is no other alternative. Excess land should be returned to sellers (and not vest with the government, as now) and landowners should be given the option to lease out rather than sell.

*

Shrill slogans rent the air—'Down with land grabbers, down, down. We will die but not give up our ancestors' land'. Thousands of farmers were angrily shouting and waving placards. As the hare raced past this restive group, his eyes misted up with the memory of his family's travails in his village; he remembered how they had to give up their land for the Three Gorges Dam. The hare slowed down, wistful and sad, but stayed at a safe distance from the fracas. Soon the tortoise came along; sensing their anguish, he went right up to the group of agitating farmers and joined their struggle. His mind told him to continue racing, but his heart was beating with their pain. 'Sometimes,' the tortoise said under his breath, 'it is good to think with the heart and not the mind.'

Everything Else Can Wait, but Agriculture

India was in the grip of a severe drought in August 2009. 'It is going to be more like the 2002 situation,' said the weatherman—that year,

India's rainfall had fallen to a twenty-seven-year low. Worried investors now sold stocks—but in less than a week, the Bombay Stock Exchange Sensex bounced back to gain 500 points. Investors ignored the dire drought warning, but cheered a new code to lower taxes. The markets were also excited by an official US statement that the recession was ending. An Indian minister added to the celebration, saying the economy would grow at 6 per cent. The markets rapidly forgot the bad news in agriculture.

There was a time when a drought would have meant double-digit inflation, plummeting stock markets, widespread unrest, and India queuing up before the US with a begging bowl. In those days, India's food insecurity used to be about 'no dollars in the treasury and no grain in the granary'. Now India's got both—over $250 billion in reserves, and millions of tons of grain in warehouses. So this time, there was no panic, just a quiet confidence that India would be on top of the situation.

The previous year's harvest was reassuring. There was record production of wheat, rice, coarse cereals, pulses, oilseeds and cotton. This had protected Indians from shortages that had sparked riots from Bangladesh to Haiti in 2008. But here's the paradox: farmers were producing in record quantities, yet were themselves in debt. India did not have to import food, but its farms may have become a basket case.

'Everything else can wait, but agriculture,' India's first prime minister Jawaharlal Nehru had famously said. But like a lot of political rhetoric in India, real action had to wait for a big crisis. Weakened by the 1962 China and 1965 Pakistan wars, India faced two successive droughts in 1965 and 1966—at one time it had just two weeks of wheat stock. The country had to swallow its pride and queue up under America's Public Law 480 (PL 480) to import 21 million tons of wheat. A newspaper in Alabama rubbed salt into the country's wounds saying 'New Indian Leader Comes Begging'. President Lyndon B. Johnson made India feel even smaller, as he released ships month by month, when India wanted an annual commitment.

United by this indignity, India's politicians and scientists launched a frontal attack on low crop yields. Norman E. Borlaug was a scientist experimenting with hybrid dwarf varieties of wheat in Mexico. C. Subramaniam, India's dynamic new agriculture minister, ordered an experimental planting of these Mexican seeds. They yielded 5,000 kg a hectare, five times the output from Indian varieties. Subramaniam gave permission for direct farmer trials in 150 fields; he even sowed the hybrid seed in the lawns of his bungalow in New Delhi. In 1966, India imported 18,000 kg of seed from Borlaug; by 1968, the wheat harvest increased to 17 million tons from 12 million in 1964. Grain production scaled over 100 million tons for the first time; India grandly called this turnaround its Green Revolution. More big labels followed. Operation Flood in 1970 spurred milk production. An Oilseeds Mission doubled production over a decade. The poultry revolution was silent, powered by rising incomes; the annual availability of eggs per person increased from seven in 1961 to forty-two now.

But after the first flush of success, grain production levelled off. Unfortunately, a ballooning subsidy bill continued to remain sticky. Every player in the agriculture chain had got addicted to freebies, most of all politicians who saw free water, fertilizer and power as an easy ticket to win elections. To this day, subsidies continue to scorch India's agriculture. $25 billion are doled out as subsidies every year, but just a fifth of this is spent on building rural infrastructure, although study after study shows that investments are far more productive than subsidies.

Orient Craft is a large exporter which holds camps for poor people in garment-making. To be eligible for training—and a subsequent job—a candidate has to have a 'below poverty level' (BPL) card. Theoretically, that means the cardholder is consuming fewer than 2,400 calories and earning less than $1 a day. But don't be surprised to visit a camp and find many of the trainees looking rather well fed, some even sporting gold ornaments. If you were to ask them about their family's vocation, someone is likely to say 'my father runs a TV repair shop'. How, you might ask, did they get a BPL card then? Simple—the district is pampered with misplaced largesse because it is the constituency of the chief minister's son. In any case, the district is unlikely to be impoverished since 80 per cent of it is irrigated. There are perhaps millions of similar examples of 'below poverty line' cardholders who 'leak' away India's bloated subsidy bill into utterly undeserved mouths and hands.

Here's another ludicrous 'fact'. The number of BPL cards issued in two southern states is actually equal to their populations! Theoretically then, every person in those provinces, including wealthy politicians and industrialists, lives on less than a dollar a day. In reality, a huge number of these cards are fake, allowing local 'operators' to salt away the subsidies into personal bank accounts. An attempt was made in 1997 to reduce food subsidies by targeting them to the absolutely poor. It did not make much headway. Social action groups that champion India's new food security law say entitlement should be universal, as targeting tends to exclude the really poor. That's how bogus and wasteful India's subsidy architecture is, which has kept yields and agricultural enterprise at unhappily low levels (half of China's, for instance, but that story is coming up later).

Yet India's farmers can be driven like entrepreneurs if there is money to be made. When Pepsi wanted to enter India in 1989, a left-leaning government (that was the only kind that existed in India in those days!) asked it to do something special for the country's agriculture, a sort of quid pro quo to access the consumer market. A local competitor, who obviously wanted to thwart Pepsi's entry, raised the bogey of India needing 'silicon chips, not potato chips'. The heat was on Pepsi. It set up a 650-ton-a-day tomato paste plant in Punjab, Asia's largest at that time. Pepsi contracted thousands of farmers, supplied them with new varieties of seeds, introduced deep chiselling and seed-bed planting techniques, extended the harvest season from twenty-five to seventy days a year and started winter cultivation in greenhouses. Yields leapt from 16 to 54 tons a hectare. Tomato paste was followed by potato, chilly, barley, corn, basmati rice and peanuts. Pepsi even began to develop citrus orchards to feed its Tropicana fruit juice brand.

There are a few more scattered tales of enterprise. D.B. Desai, a plant breeder, is better known as the Robin Hood (or pirate, depending on which side of the fence you are on) of biotechnology. He sold a homegrown variety of genetically modified cotton seed, much before Monsanto's legal species was authorized. It was like giving an unauthorized drug to a patient. It could have been dangerous. But these pirated seeds produced cotton that resisted pest attacks like the legal versions do. The regulators wanted to burn the crop. The government was scared about a showdown with farmers, who would have none of it. Today, several pirated or locally engineered crossbred seeds have created a cotton revolution in the western state of Gujarat. Monsanto's legally authorized Bollgard seeds have only added to the success story.

In fact, Gujarat shows what Indian farmers can achieve if backed by a bold leader. Narendra Modi is a controversial politician. His opponents call him the Hitler of Gujarat's anti-Muslim pogrom. But his admirers call him a model chief minister, the kind who can lead India from the front. In just five years, he increased the number of check dams in the state by ten times. Such quantum jumps are unheard of in India's sluggish political systems. An elated columnist likened it to a blockbuster film, calling it *'chak de* (go for it) check dams'. Modi can also take credit for a simple, but effective, innovation. He separated the electricity for village households from that meant for irrigation pumps, thereby assuring eight hours of continuous, high-quality power supply for tube wells. Farmers have to pay more, but are happy their motors don't burn out any longer.

Gujarat's agriculture has grown by 12 per cent against 1.5 per cent in communist-ruled West Bengal. 'Gujarat can show to the rest of the country that agriculture is not a 2 per cent growth story,' says scientist Ashok Gulati who heads the International Food Policy Research Institute in India. Gulati also makes a difficult-to-connect comparison with China. 'To understand India's agriculture, you must know its culture,' he says. 'Eighty-five per cent of Indians will not eat beef, because they are Hindus. And at least 12 per cent will not eat pork because they are Muslims. So chicken will be the main source of meat, which is a very efficient converter of feed. That also means India will not need to import large amounts of grain—something that China has to do.'

But China Is Acres Ahead ...

'I do not envy China. I want to emulate China'—that's what India's finance minister said in a moment of candour. But China is streets— or should we say acres—ahead of India. With 12 million less hectares under wheat and rice, China manages to produce much more. Its fields give 6 tons of rice a hectare, three times India's yield. Its wheat fields are twice as fecund. Even as China extracts bumper harvests, its appetite for pork, poultry and beef has been growing, forcing it to import millions of tons of Brazilian soya bean as animal feed.

A travel down Chinese history since the 1949 revolution shows a greater sense of purpose in its leadership. When the communists seized power, China was a feudal nation. Ten per cent of landlords owned 80 per cent of the land, renting out farms at exorbitant rates. These lands were ruthlessly taken away, without compensation, and distributed among poor peasants, who were first grouped into Soviet-style cooperatives of around 200 households. Output improved handsomely as the state set targets and paid higher prices for excess production.

But food production collapsed in the attempt to play 'industrial catch-up' with the West during the Great Leap Forward. Farmers were regrouped into large communes of around 5,000 families. This sapped their enthusiasm and encouraged free riders. The primacy given to steel production in backyard furnaces added to farmers' woes, resulting in the Great Famine which killed 30 million people. Communes were quickly disbanded, and production was back in the hands of twenty to thirty 'family teams'. Crop yields had barely begun to recover when the Cultural Revolution emasculated the gains all over again. A dejected peasantry was ready for Deng Xiaoping and reforms.

Anhui was a poor but politically vibrant province in 1978, about the time that Deng ascended to power in Beijing. Eighteen peasant families there had taken an unusual risk. They had secretly parcelled land among themselves, in a primitive flirtation with the idea of private property, when Deng stumbled upon this 'model'. He was in the midst of consolidating his grip on power by 'trying to cross the river by feeling the rocks'. The Anhui experiment gave Deng an idea, and the household responsibility system was born. He called it 'a great invention of Chinese farmers'. It allowed individual households to grow and sell whatever they liked, after meeting a (low) quota set by the state. The animal spirits of Chinese farmers were let loose. Cereal production rose and 150 million people moved out of poverty, considered the most dramatic fall in poverty rates in history. By the early '90s, 80 per cent of grain was freely traded against the 5 per cent when reforms began.

A flurry of reforms followed; trading in agriculture machinery, pesticides and plastic film was privatized. Chemical fertilizers came off the state hook in the '90s. By the time China joined the WTO in

2001, it had cut farm tariffs to a simple 21 per cent. That year it also abolished agricultural taxes over five years. Soon individual households were given thirty-year cultivation rights. It's the closest China has come to private property for farmers.

As incomes rose in the countryside, cottage entrepreneurs sprung up to meet the demand for other products. In his book on Chinese enterprise, Yasheng Huang, a professor at Massachusetts Institute of Technology, talks about a farmer in impoverished Anhui who built a business selling sunflower seeds (a popular snack) employing over 100 people and making a million-yuan profit in 1986. As farmers were no longer tied to land, they set up small manufacturing, distribution and service industries. These town and village enterprises, or TVEs, quickly expanded to a quarter of the GDP. Just one more flourish for China's buoyant agriculture!

... And India Should Take the Tractor by the Tail

India's early reforms were solely confined to industry, trade and investments. Since the 1991 collapse was triggered by a foreign exchange crisis, agriculture was literally ignored. Even a slight move, to lower fertilizer subsidies by increasing prices, backfired. A politically singed government had to lower fertilizer prices again. From then on, chastened politicians stuck to the status quo in agriculture, keeping alive a regime of super-high subsidies and quotas against global trade. Even within the country, agricultural commodities were not allowed to freely cross state boundaries. The whole setup remained hidebound and archaic.

Being a founding member of the WTO, India signed the agreement on agriculture in 1994. But it took another seven years to abolish import quotas, replacing them with high tariffs. Yet it remained paranoid about cheap imports. A 'war room' (it was officially called that!) was set up to monitor 300 'sensitive' imports. 'We may have to declare war against surges in imports and dumping,' said a visibly nervous trade minister. All fears were unfounded and the 'war room' was speedily disbanded. Contrary to imagined fears, India was not swamped by cheap agricultural imports. As for exports, India treated them as a residual activity, to be done if there was enough food at home. Such an on–off–on–off policy kept India an underperformer in the export market. Once again, its policymakers had betrayed unnecessary fear and timidity in making agricultural policy.

Finally in 2002, ten years after industrial and investment policies were liberalized, clamps were lifted on private trading, storage and movement of farm produce within the country. The right-wing government was keen to oblige traders, its natural constituency. But the communists protested, complaining the liberalization would lead to 'reckless profiteering'. Four years later, when commodity prices spiked despite free imports, politicians took knee-jerk action to ban futures trading in wheat and rice—though price manipulation had not been established except in the case of some thinly-traded commodities.

It is only now that eighteen states have allowed private traders to buy directly from farmers, rather than through regulated market places. India's granary states of Punjab and Haryana have yet to fully adopt this law, thwarting an efficient linking of producers, traders and consumers. In West Bengal, the ruling communists like to directly control upcountry wholesale grain markets.

'Indian agriculture is not supply-driven, it is demand-driven,' says Ashok Gulati. He has been championing the cause of agriculture liberalization for over two decades. He can rattle off example after example where India's farmers have responded with astounding enterprise. Take the case of maize. His estimates had shown that India would touch 18 million tons by 2020. The farmers beat him by a solid twelve years—India produced 19 million tons in 2008, charged by unexpectedly strong demand from the poultry sector.

Similarly vast gains are possible if India learns from its own best practices. India's eastern state of Assam can treble its maize yields, while a clutch of other states can double their rice output. Central India could more than quadruple wheat produce. (These estimates are made by the same officials who display far less guts in making policy that can get all of this done!)

The eastern state of Bihar was once India's Wild West. Ruled by a notorious political family for fifteen years, extortion and kidnapping became its major industry. Fed up with these shenanigans, the people elected a clean, respected engineering graduate, Nitish Kumar, as their new chief minister. His rule brought about a sea-change in Bihar.

Village councils were freely elected, roads are being furiously built, and thousands of criminals have been jailed. Reaching out to a gathering of 2,000 farmers, Kumar promised to spend a billion dollars to create a 'rainbow revolution' in farming, fisheries and milk production. The state has all the ingredients in place: fertile soil that has not been damaged by chemical fertilizers, plenty of water and hardworking people. But its average wheat yield is half of what Punjab achieves. Therefore the potential is huge and Bihar, along with other eastern areas, could be the platform for the next Green Revolution in India.

The time has also come to pick up another big idea that could drive a generational change in Indian agriculture but which has been lying in the political dustbin for over a decade: organized retailing. The entry of large corporate groups into grocery retailing has been marked by acrimony. In an unusual axis, both right-wing politicians and communists see them as a threat to India's mom-and-pop stores. The heat is so intense that foreign retailing giants like Wal-Mart have been banned from investing in front-end retailing. Through truncated arrangements with Indian grocery chains, they can only do what is called 'cash-and-carry business', that is, sell to small businesses in quantities of invoice value as low as Rs 1,000 ($22). Not all states allow them to buy from farmers. As against this, Wal-Mart in China buys fresh fruit, vegetables and cereals directly from farmers for sale in stores that attract 7 million consumers a week. This programme started in 2007; by 2011, Wal-Mart intends to rope in a million farmers. It also has eleven purchase bases in seven provinces covering 10,000 hectares. Wal-Mart helps farmers adapt to markets, ensure food safety and check water pollution.

Here is yet another opportunity for Indian leaders to shed their timidity and emulate China (as India's finance minister had candidly desired to do).

China's tenancy reforms are also more dynamic than India's. Even though land is owned by the state, China is creating a market for lease rights. In 2009, it allowed farmers to sell cultivation rights to other farmers or corporations. China squared up to a reality in the countryside, where young and able-bodied farmers have migrated to factories in the coastal areas, leaving land in the care of the very old or the very young. (Of course the Chinese story is marred by the state's expropriation of land. So farmers are fighting for ownership rights, instead of mere lease rights. But that's another tale, to be told at another place.)

China's encouragement of the lease market holds another mirror to India. Eighty per cent of Indian farms are less than two hectares each. Farming in India is becoming unprofitable because of small holdings, low productivity and high cost. While ownership of large tracts should perhaps continue to be banned to discourage distress sales by farmers, consolidation of holdings—and investment—can be made possible by lifting the thirty-month limit on leases (beyond which land belongs to the tiller).

Across the country, hardworking farmers are willing to learn and experiment. An exploding television network could be used to demonstrate best practices. But what is missing is innovative programming. India's largest tobacco and agri-business company has already shown how to hook 4 million farmers to the internet, through its 6,500 internet kiosk-cum-trading centres, known as e-choupals (village meeting places), across 40,000 villages. Today, 10 per cent of India's weather insurance is sold through e-choupals.

*

The tortoise turned a stricken, pleading face to his Master. 'Oh Master, we have been a "debating" society for far too long now. Please, Master, we need to become a "mobilizing" society now. Please free me Master, untie me, so I can join the race against the hare. Otherwise, I will never catch up with him.'

Meanwhile the hare kept bounding ahead, secure about his generational lead in this lane.

(S)Killing a Growth Story

'India Desperately Seeking Talent', said a headline in *Businessweek*. With the economic boom, the article said, companies are scrambling to find—and keep—skilled Indian workers. It spoke of the predicament of Larsen & Toubro, a big engineering firm. Despite a hike in salary to recruit engineers, the company was losing them to better-paying software firms, multinational rivals and companies in West Asia.

'Everyone is growing fast and India is facing a skill shortage,' complained L&T's combative chairman.

That was in November 2005, when India notched up one of its highest ever growth rates of 9.5 per cent. Murmurs about a dearth of skills, serial job-hopping and salary spikes grew louder as the economy pushed ahead at the same rate for two more years. MBA students at India's premier institute got a 40 per cent jump in placement salaries; foreign recruiters paid 25 per cent more. Industry bodies cried about a shortage of shop floor workers. 'This is the biggest problem in India,' said a hapless finance minister at the 2007 Wharton Leadership Lecture.

China was waging a similar battle. 'Perhaps more than any other country, China epitomizes developing Asia's skills crisis,' said the Asian Development Bank in 2008. The *Economist* spoke about how terribly few China's 4,000 general medical practitioners were for its urban health plan, which would need 400 times as many. The *New York Times* chronicled the lament of factory executives across China 'being forced to give double-digit salary hikes in order to find young workers at all skill levels'. A bicycle factory worker in Shenzen had increased his wage by 50 per cent in just six months. Shanghai was short of more than a million finance professionals.

China has always been good with mass education. More than a hundred years ago, when it was still a monarchy, an imperial decree was issued for a system of modern schools across the country leading up to the university. The traditional examination system was abolished. Today, nine out of ten Chinese are literate, and in the college-going bracket there are virtually no illiterates, a result of the primacy given to schooling.

But unlike early schooling, higher education was ravaged during the Cultural Revolution of 1966. Universities were closed down. Teachers and students were sent to villages for 're-education'. There were beatings, torturings and killings as Maoists tried to purge 'bourgeois' influences. Age limits and entrance examinations were done away with in an attempt to be 'egalitarian'. Graduate courses were shortened and examinations abolished.

Once Mao was gone, China's reformist leaders moved quickly to fix the mess in higher education—this was done even before the economic reforms of 1978. Entrance examinations returned; professional standards and expertise became respectable again. The thrust on heavy industry meant a bias for technical skills, many of which were learnt from Soviet teachers. The curriculum was highly specialized; even senior high school students were supposed to major in either the sciences, humanities or social sciences.

Ever since then, there have been no half measures in Chinese education. Today, Chinese students spend twice as many hours doing homework as do their American peers. It insists that even primary school teachers in math and science have degrees in those subjects. China launched an 'action plan' in 1999 to decisively plug its skills deficit. It was so resolutely implemented that the 15 per cent enrolment rate was achieved eight years before the target date. The next milestone of 19 per cent by 2010 has also been crossed. Doctoral students are growing faster than undergraduates. The number of college and university students exceeds India's by more than half.

Ironically, some of India's ills can be blamed on the excellence-oriented education policy fostered by Jawaharlal Nehru, the country's first prime minister. His focus was on elite institutions that could supply the skills needed by the 'temples of modern India'—its dams, power plants and steel mills. Inspired by the Massachusetts Institute of Technology, the first of many Indian Institutes of Technology came up in a former British prison in Kharagpur near Calcutta. The first of several Regional Engineering Colleges was founded in south India. The sprawling All-India Institute of Medical Sciences was built in New Delhi. Unfortunately, such a singleminded pursuit of excellence may have led to the neglect of mass education—a constitutional requirement to 'universalize' primary education within ten years after Independence was breached. Nehru was the prime minister through that failed decade for India's illiterate children (India has recently passed a law making universal primary education a 'legal right').

India's zeal to propagate high quality education may have forced the country to make an error from which it has yet to recover: expensive higher education was made virtually free for every student, rich or poor. Even today, at Delhi's Jawaharlal Nehru University, the annual tuition fee is just $6, payable in two instalments. The yearly library fee is less than 15 cents. The government picks up the rest of the tab.

To be fair, India has seen a massive expansion in higher education in the last sixty years. Today, there are 378 universities, up from a mere twenty at the time of Independence. There are a little more than 18,000 colleges; 11 per cent of India's youth studies in them. Women are close to the halfway mark where the student population is concerned. While this may seem impressive, it is half the Asian average and a fifth of the level in rich countries. The numbers also conceal wide disparities. In more than half of India's 604 districts, the college-going rate is 'abysmally low'. It is half the national average among the lower castes, tribals and the rural youth. The share of women drops to a fifth in the backward provinces. Youth in the relatively prosperous south and west have a greater likelihood of being in college.

But these achievements are dwarfed by India's challenges. The university regulator has found that only 1.3 per cent or 245 colleges make the grade. Almost two-thirds of the universities and 90 per cent of the colleges are rated below average. To strain this already creaking system, collegegoers are growing at double the population's pace because of the bulge in lower age groups. The numbers would have been even higher if there were more institutions to take them in—or if the dropout rate had not doubled between the tenth standard and college (a 'relief' which is actually a crisis).

(S)Killed By Politics

Unlike the boon it has proved to be elsewhere, India's democracy has been a bit of a curse here. Even sixty years after Independence, higher education is being used as an instrument of political mobilization. Take the case of an old world politician like Arjun Singh. As education minister, he tried to make capital for his Congress party (and many say, for his own dwindling stock in the establishment) by reserving 27 per cent of the seats in government-funded institutions for 'other backward caste' (OBC) students, provoking a violent backlash from other communities. A shaken government had to concede that the number of 'general category' seats would not be reduced. Instead, it pledged to create new seats to accommodate the OBC students.

The politics of patronage has ravaged India's higher education like little else has. 'The university system in India is the collateral damage of Indian politics,' claims a highly regarded research paper. The

education ministry makes more than a hundred key appointments. It
has an annual budget of $7.5 billion to play around with, of which a
fifth is for the university system. Even the prime minister of the
country is helpless: 'I am concerned that university appointments,
including that of vice-chancellors, have been politicized and have
become subject to caste and communal considerations. There are
complaints of favouritism and corruption.' Fifteen vice-chancellors
were appointed in a tearing hurry just days before the last elections.
Newspapers reported that the search committee must have scanned
fifty-six applications a day to meet the deadline. Twelve of the
universities did not even have an office, campus, students or faculty!

There have been other excesses. In 2004, the Supreme Court scrapped
112 private universities that a small state government had approved in
just one year. That did not stop the Central education minister from
subsequently conferring 'deemed' university status on thirty-six
institutions, more than the number conferred in the first thirty-five
years of Independence.

In Kolkata, the Marxist government has a stranglehold on educational
institutions. Under pressure from the communist-controlled teachers'
union, it denied autonomy for close to forty years to the prestigious
Presidency College, whose alumni include Nobel Laureate Amartya
Sen and renowned filmmaker Satyajit Ray. A study across ten universities
shows that teachers are invariably on strike, more than the students.

Campus politics got charged up after the voting age was lowered
from twenty-one to eighteen. Students are seen not only as voters but
also as vote-getters. Student elections have become a springboard to a
full-time career in politics. A Supreme Court committee 'was appalled
by reports of chaos, lawlessness and crime, not only during student
elections but as a permanent condition'.

Ideological excesses have been less of a concern in India, except for
the seven years during which India was ruled by a right-wing coalition.
Its ideologically active education minister revised textbooks to reflect
Hindu cultural nationalism. Courses in Vedic astrology got state
support. (Incidentally, his website described him as a person whose
'high-brow mind reeks of decency'.)

The business of education also provides Indian politicians a
'respectable' and 'noble' veneer behind which profits and patronage

can be pursued. Four-fifths of engineering, medical and management education is in private—or should we say political—hands. Access to cheap or free land, ready demand and tax-free status make it commercially attractive, and the aura of 'service to society' makes it politically attractive too. The current President of India, its civil aviation minister, highways minister, agriculture minister, and top opposition leaders all manage successful educational trusts.

Unfortunately, privately-run professional colleges are generally low on quality. A 2005 McKinsey study found that only 10–15 per cent of the 350,000 engineers who graduate every year (and who had applied for a job with a multinational corporation) were fit for direct employment without further training. That forces prospective employers to spend huge sums on re-training the rest. Take the case of Infosys Technologies, which is among India's top three software firms. Its newest acquisition is a 337-acre campus modelled on the Parthenon, built at a cost of over $400 million. It runs up a training bill of $180 million a year—more than 1 per cent of the Indian government's annual payout to universities. $5,000 is spent on a sixteen-week programme for each recruit. Even though it hires the best talent, four in a hundred fail to qualify in the test that follows.

China has to grapple with a quality problem as well. A 2005 McKinsey study found that only a tenth of the candidates for jobs at multinational corporations had the right skills. Their main shortcoming was the ability to speak in English. Engineering graduates were well-versed in theory but lacked practical skills.

China's overdrive has also produced graduates who do not fit into the job market. A year after being hit by the global recession, the Chinese government was straining to keep the 6 million new graduates engaged. It was giving loans for start-ups, persuading city governments to relax residency norms, reimbursing fees to those joining the army or opting to work in remote areas, and promising tax breaks and loans to employers who would take them on.

China is pushing for another Great Leap Forward in research. The 'thousand talents programme' aims to bring 2,000 key personnel—foreign-educated Chinese scientists, academics, financial experts and MBAs—back home over the next five to ten years. Some people are sceptical: unless intellectual property rights are stringently enforced, top-quality talent may remain aloof. Some of the returnees may also be of questionable pedigree; for instance, this thrust may have created a peculiar problem of academic fraud. Chen Jhi was one of China's brightest scientists at Jiao Tong University in 2006. His computer chip was hailed as a national triumph, until it was discovered that the chip was a Motorola device whose logo had been replaced. The same year a professor at Beijing's elite Tsinghua University was removed for faking his academic achievement and work experience. Following a string of such instances, the government announced a law to punish scientific misconduct.

'Bamboo Shoots after a Spring Rain'

Quality is now getting attention from the Chinese government. The top nine universities have been given liberal grants to achieve world-class status. The 211 Project will create 100 institutions focusing on research. Unlike in India, Chinese students have to pay virtually full fees though they are supported with scholarships and loans. Foreign universities are also allowed to set up campuses in local partnership. Private institutions are thriving 'like bamboo shoots after a spring rain'. Education shares are allowed on stock markets—Hualin University in Guangzhou is an example.

A benchmark index of world universities has been created, against which Chinese universities can measure themselves. The index is based on academic research, publications, citations and exclusive international awards like the Nobel Prize. India had two in the top 100 engineering list, China had three.

India's economic reforms of 1991 were not particularly propitious for its universities. The World Bank, somewhat ambivalently, asserted in the 1990s that higher education 'should not have the highest priority claim on incremental public resources' of developing countries. With finances under strain, the government was looking for corners to cut. It put higher education into the category of 'non-merit' subsidies, as the benefits to the recipient were more than to society. But now the government is making amends with 6,000 special schools across the country to provide a quality benchmark. Thirty new universities will be established, with deprived states getting priority.

Nearly two decades after setting industry free, India is also readying to unshackle higher education. Sam Pitroda, the inventor–entrepreneur who pioneered India's telecom revolution despite being born to a carpenter, and Prof. Yashpal, a scientist, have done the thinking. Pitroda sees private investment as a fallback option because the government cannot foot the entire bill. Universities 'obviously must not be driven by commercial consideration', he says. His National Knowledge Commission makes a strong case for generous scholarships and easy bank loans. Foreign students attracted to India by a much lower cost of living and fees could perk up the market. India's trade ministry agrees with him, wanting to drive up services exports.

In lawyer Kapil Sibal India has an education minister who is eager for change. He wants the best foreign universities to locate in India without too many conditions. Currently 160,000 Indian students study abroad. This number is next only to China's. Their cost has been variously estimated at $4–7 billion a year, money that could be invested in India if comparable facilities were available.

Kaushik Basu, India's Chief Economic Advisor, was earlier a member of a high-ranking government committee on education reform (when he was concurrently a professor at Cornell University); he raised a storm by suggesting an end to college licensing. Education for profit is fine, he says. Colleges should be free to charge any fee so long as they declare information that enables students to make an informed choice, and misinformation is severely punished. That would leave the government free to concentrate on those disciplines that have little investor interest. He wants star professors to get multiples of standard salary. Rather than spreading money thin, the government would get better bang if it chose twenty of the best for funding every three years by rotation to be developed as centres of excellence. 'Our main aim must be to nurture excellence instead of spending a disproportionate amount of energy trying to curb the lack of it,' Basu says.

Wealth Is Health

China and India share an undesirable trait that is unique among countries—rising incomes have not resulted in improved health care. It is a bizarre impact of the rapid privatization drive in both countries.

A majority of India's 1.3 million nurses wants to work in cities or migrate overseas. Its 645,000 doctors suffer from the same bias. In any case, their numbers pale compared to China's 2 million doctors.

*

Fourteen-year-old Rida Shaikh became India's first swine flu victim in early August 2009. By then a large number of people had been infected. Saturated television coverage whipped everybody into a state of panic. The mini metropolis had only one government-validated testing lab. Scared private doctors began referring even those with mild symptoms to that solitary facility. Two days later about a thousand people had queued up—beyond the hospital lab's ability to cope. At noon a scuffle broke out; the police had to be called in to restore order.

As the virus multiplied, the decibel levels on India's two dozen hyperactive twenty-four-hour television news channels reached a frightening frenzy. Containment and isolation of potential patients ceased to be an effective strategy. The virus had to be mitigated on a mass scale. If only Indian cities had neighbourhood community health centres, like there were in rural areas, people could have been screened for infection and only the severely affected would have been referred higher up for intensive treatment. The feeling of helplessness among people upset even the prime minister's cardiologist. 'The anarchy that characterizes urban health care was so painfully evident during the swine flu epidemic,' said Dr Srinath Reddy, who also heads the Public Health Foundation of India.

A similar health catastrophe had hit the diamond-exporting city of Surat fifteen years earlier. A bubonic plague killed fifty-two people and forced 300,000 migrant workers to flee. Panic-stricken people across the country could be seen walking around with surgical masks on. The antibiotic tetracycline vanished from pharmacies, travellers skipped the country and air cargo restrictions affected trade. The World Health Organization estimated India's loss at $1.7 billion.

The World Economic Forum's latest Global Competitiveness Ranking places India at a modest forty-ninth among 134 countries. In business sophistication its position is twenty-seventh, which is almost sparkling. But then it's dragged down by health and primary education, where India's rank is excruciatingly low, at 101.

Sixty-two years after Independence, India's public health care system, with some exceptions, is generally dismal. The Integrated Disease Surveillance Programme, required to watch the outbreak of diseases in districts, does not have enough epidemiologists. Over 10,000 village clinics do not even have a nurse or midwife, and half of them lack a male health worker. About 800 primary health centres have no physicians. Over half the required number of gynecologists, pediatricians and surgeons are missing. The network of district laboratories to test pathogens is yet to be established. 'Public health needs regular, reasoned and rational review, not sporadic, shrill and sensational scrutiny,' rues Dr Reddy.

China was similarly found wanting, in candour and readiness, when the SARS epidemic hit in 2003. The disease, which causes respiratory failure, rapidly spread within China, and then to Hong Kong and elsewhere. Over 300 people died on the mainland. Chastened by that experience, China set up an information system for disease control and prevention, said to be the largest internet-based reporting system in the world. Cases detected have to be reported within twenty-four hours. In recent decades new outbreaks of animals infecting humans have been reported at the rate of one a year. China is particularly vulnerable. Meat-eating has increased with prosperity. The pig population has grown a hundredfold, while the poultry population has multiplied a thousand times in just four decades.

Eating habits of both countries have changed with prosperity. The Chinese now consume less cereal, like Indians, and more meat and cooking oil. Fat intake has almost doubled among rural folk. Calorie intake has remained unchanged over two decades but increased television viewing and less physical activity has made more Chinese fat or obese. Indians are following these trends. The latest survey shows calorie intake has fallen but 13 per cent more fat is making its way into the Indian belly.

India now has the highest number of diabetics in the world while China leads in hypertension. Salt intake among the Chinese is double the recommended level. China also has the largest number of smokers followed by India. India still has age on its side, but every tenth Chinese is above sixty years.

The average Chinese can now expect to live up to seventy-four years, ten years longer than an Indian. For every one five-year-old baby that dies in China, three die in India. Childbirth is six times more lethal for Indian mothers than for those across the border. Many more people will die of infections in India, while more people will succumb to chronic illnesses in China.

Economic growth has not spread cheer uniformly in both countries. In India, there is a clear rich–poor and urban–rural divide. In China too, where you live determines how you live. A Shanghai resident can expect to walk on this planet for thirteen more years than a fellow citizen in the poorest province. Migrant rural women in Shanghai run a thirty times higher risk of dying than resident women. About 140 million people move in search of better prospects annually. Those that leave the villages tend to be young and able. If they return, it is because illness or injury has made them incapable of working. So migration means the export of good health and the import of ill health for villages.

A Giant Leap Backwards

As India tried to balance its budget, it cut public spending on health to under a per cent of GDP by 2000. Public hospitals slashed expenditure on new equipment and beds by 75 per cent of the 1991 level. 'User fees' were slapped on poor patients; while these deterred them from seeking hospitalization, the extra money added no more than 2–3 per cent to state budgets during the 1990s. It is no wonder that India's health care system has become one of the most privatized in the world. Only 10 per cent of Indians have any kind of medical insurance. Out-of-pocket expenses were 81 per cent of total spending at last count, higher than the US's 55 per cent and the UK's 13 per cent, according to the World Health Organization.

Those attending international conferences on 'medical tourism' in India cannot grasp India's health care crisis. There they are told that India's health care market is just 20 per cent smaller than the UK's. There are glowing reports about India's cut-rate cardiac surgeries that cost $4,000 against $50,000 in the US, at a slightly higher success rate too. Or about the rising business of air ambulance services—365 airlifts a year in Delhi alone. But health experts take a dim view of these fancy statistics. They accuse the private sector of ignoring public health goals. An official survey actually gives truth to their claim. In eight districts in as many states, the private sector supplied three-quarters of the dental, mental, orthopedic, vascular and cancer care. But most of the clinics were in towns. In thirty-five villages, there were virtually no private doctors or nurses.

China too has suffered from the malaise of health care privatization. Hospital administrators are spurred by the extra commission they earn from drug sales. There is voluminous evidence to show that expensive drugs are needlessly prescribed. 'Too difficult to see a doctor, too expensive to seek health care' has become a common refrain. Studies show that out-of-pocket expenses have risen eighteen times since 1980 and account for nearly half of the total spending now. Annual health expenditure has grown a full 2 per cent faster than China's double digit GDP. Many Chinese households find medical treatment simply unaffordable.

China is now taking a giant leap 'backwards'. It has admitted that a market-oriented health care system is a 'wrong concept'. It has vowed to spend $124 billion over three years on new facilities, training thousands of health workers and insuring more than 90 per cent of the people. Leading the charge will be Zhu Chen, China's new health minister, the first non-party member to be appointed to such a high post in thirty-five years. 'You can't make heaven overnight. You need to have a step-by-step approach,' says the man who got his doctorate in hematology, gene cloning and DNA sequencing from France, and once spent time as a 'barefoot doctor' In the countryside.

Zhu's got his job cut out. Urban residents, farmers, and even poor people who cannot pay will be covered by three distinct types of insurance schemes. Essential drugs will be heavily subsidized. All children will be born in hospitals and vaccinated. Health archives of all citizens will be set up.

Characteristically, the Indian government's response has not been as dramatic. It has set a modest target of increasing health expenditure to 2–3 per cent of GDP in three years. As against China's orchestrated, military-like campaign, India's 'attack' is made up of small, scattered tactical strikes, led by politicians and entrepreneurs who can think 'out of the box'. As with almost everything else in India, the hope is that these grassroot strikes will gather geometric momentum and create an 'organic, bottom-up multiplier' which could ultimately be more robust and efficient.

An interesting innovation is the use of health motivators known by the acronym Asha, which means 'hope' in Hindi. An Asha volunteer gets incentives for immunizing children and persuading mothers to deliver in hospitals. Wherever primary health centres work, people seem to prefer them to private clinics. But drug availability remains a major concern, as also chronic absenteeism among medical officers.

'India will become the world's first country where health care will be dissociated from bank balance,' says Dr Devi Prasad Shetty. Coming from anybody else, that would have sounded like an empty boast. But Dr Shetty is the pioneer of inexpensive heart surgeries that cost just $2,000 a pop. The buzz is that at thirty a day, his hospital in Bengaluru performs the largest number of heart surgeries in the world with an amazing success rate of 95 per cent. American Insurance Group and JP Morgan have already invested in his 'Wal-Mart approach to health care'.

For a monthly insurance premium of 60 cents per person, Dr Shetty will provide medical consultation, discounted tests and a variety of surgeries to 3 million possible patients in his home state. The scheme relies on the power of numbers: the rest pay for the 2.5 per cent who get operated every year. Another state in south India has brought 18 million extremely poor families within the ambit of a similar scheme. The idea is catching on. The central government now wants to provide health cover to 60 million families below the official poverty line. So far a twelfth of the target has been met. Eventually it will cover all informal workers; as usual, implementation will be the big challenge.

Today, only one in five Indians has got any kind of health insurance. But these pilot efforts show that universal health coverage is possible. These 'out of the box' ideas could succeed where private health insurance is failing. While it has grown seventeen times over the last two decades, private health insurance is confined to the fringes. Only the very fit are provided cover and there is no protection beyond sixty-five years.

Gujarat is India's leading industrial state but lags in social indicators. At one time it had just seven obstetricians serving a rural population of 32 million, against 2,000 who practiced privately. That was quite understandable, since private earnings could be five times higher than what the government was paying. Along came Amarjit Singh, a government health commissioner, who outsourced child deliveries to private doctors on contract for a $40 fee. Only sixty-four mothers died during 400,000 deliveries, against an expected 1,600. 'If we keep the pace we can do better than China,' says Singh. The prime minister, the Gujarat government and the World Health Organization have applauded his bold move.

At the other end of the spectrum are people who fear such private partnerships will wreck the public health care system. For them, the South Indian state of Tamil Nadu shows the way. It has a dense network of public health facilities. All primary health centres are open round the clock. Graduate doctors are appointed on contract and trained in disciplines like anesthesia, obstetrics and radiology. The death rate of mothers is half the national average—for infants it is lower by a third. The state's drug supply system brooks no shortages. It is a model for the rest of the country. Several of these examples show that the government apparatus can be cranked up if health becomes an active political issue and if women are empowered.

*

Both the hare and the tortoise fell ill at the same time. The hare had been gorging on salted meat. He had become heavier, his head was splitting and his blood pressure had spiked. He came upon two hospital buildings, one built by the Emperor, another by the village merchant. Both were equally modern and efficient. He went into the Emperor's hospital.

Behind him, a heavier, ruddier tortoise had become short of breath. He had been gorging on sweets. He too stumbled by two hospital buildings. The spanking and expensive one had been built by the village merchant, and a dilapidated one was being run by his Master. The tortoise huffed and puffed to the run-down hospital, but the doctor was on leave and the nurse had taken the day off.

Both recovered and resumed their race. The tortoise's pockets were much lighter than before. The poor fellow was now short of cash, not breath.

Epilogue

FIFTY FIFTY?

I began researching this book with a clear question in mind: who could win the economic race between China and India? I was also working with a set of fairly crystallized notions. For instance, the world was clearly in awe of China's stamina, ambition and speed. It was understandably spellbound by China's unwavering focus and execution. It was willing to overlook China's flaws—its totalitarian state and grinding poverty—giving it the benefit of doubt legitimately due to a gritty pioneer. But I equally suspected that the world could be overestimating the value of China's economic surge. I questioned whether an exploding GDP would rinse it clean of all ills. I was convinced that China's rise could be capped unless it mutated into a reasonably free and transparent country.

On the other hand, I began with the notion that the world was underestimating India's strengths. It was seeing all the warts in its democracy—the endless delays, corrupt public figures, the inefficient state, the crumbling urban edifice, illiteracy, poverty, violence, separatism, terrorism—but missing the institutional strengths of a liberal democracy, constitutional freedom, independent media, evolved judiciary, individual enterprise, throbbing civil society and blossoming opportunities. I was convinced that India was being erroneously benchmarked against visible symbols of developed western democracies; since India lacked gleaming skyscrapers, fancy airport terminals, smooth expressways and smartly uniformed policemen, the West thought India was a failed state.

But having done a deep dive into their respective legacies— encapsulated in the book you have just finished reading—I have bobbed back to the surface with a new, subtly refracted perspective. To begin with, I now believe that my core question was framed somewhat incorrectly. It's not about who will win; instead, it is more about who will *lose* the economic race between China and India.

Frankly, I now believe that the world has *underestimated* China's drive and ambition. If there is one country which can slice through the umbilical cord between democracy and prosperity, it is China. China's supremely energetic drive to materially empower its people—with rising incomes, education, health, infrastructure and economic options— could well allow it to 'calibrate' the manner in which it opens up its civil society. Quasi-free but rapidly prosperous citizens may be far less 'dissatisfied' than liberal intellectuals are willing to concede. Some social scientists even argue that 'private freedoms'—the ability to own property, earn money, consume without impediment and generally determine how one's family lives—are far more important than 'public freedoms' like free speech and politics, which are quite 'dispensable'. Once this is layered up with a culture of compliance with authority and deeply cherished nationalism, you could have the makings of a society which may not fit the classical western bill of freedom and democracy, but could well be as positive and productive. Yet China could still lose this race if its ambition morphs into naked aggression, its confidence degenerates into arrogance, its determination turns into ruthlessness and its focus ignites into a fury against adversaries. An overbearing, intolerant, Soviet-inspired China could still lose this race.

As against this, I am grappling with the shocking realization that India's democratic strength may have been *overestimated* by the world. There are two pillars of India's democracy: its constitutional state and its vibrant civil society. Unfortunately, while its civil society is soaring with genuine aspirations, its state is deeply dysfunctional. Almost all the ills plaguing India spring from its apologetic, unambitious state. India's civil leaders, across levels, appear tired and defeated. Many seem like handwringers who use the excuse of democracy to cloak their own doubt and disbelief. As is evident through this book, India needs new leadership, bolder governance and modern policies, especially in those sectors which strike at the root of poverty—agriculture, health, education and infrastructure. As someone asked graphically, 'Who will do a Teddy Roosevelt for India?' Indeed, without such fresh, confident leadership, India will lose the race.

So what's my final wager now? I would say it is 'advantage China' on velocity and momentum, and it's 'odds on India' as the institutional favourite. But the ultimate outcome is still anybody's guess—it's Fifty Fifty.

SELECT BIBLIOGRAPHY

Ablett, Jonathan, Baijal, Aadarsh, Bose, Anupam et al, 'The "Bird of Gold": The Rise of India's Consumer Market', McKinsey and Company, May 2007, 5–16.

Agnihotri, V.K., *Indian History*, New Delhi: Allied Publishers, 2008.

Agrawal, Raamdeo, 'A Trillion Dollar Opportunity', *Business Standard*, 20 September 2009, 13.

Ahiya, Chetan, 'Time to Address the Fiscal Problems', *Economic Times*, 19 October 2009, 10.

Ahluwalia, Montek Singh, Speech by the Deputy Chairman, Planning Commission at the 53rd Meeting of the National Development Council, 29 May 2007 [Internet]. Available at http://planningcommission.nic.in/plans/planrel/53rdndc/dchndc53.doc.

Ahmed, Ehsan, Li, Honggang and Barkley, Rosser, Jr., 'Nonlinear Bubbles in Chinese Stock Markets in the 1990s', *Eastern Economic Journal*, 32 (1), Winter 2006, 1–18.

Aiyar, Swaminathan, 'Benefits of Port Liberalization', 2008 [Internet]. Available at http://www.cato.org.

_____, 'Hidden Benefits of the Brain Drain', *Times of India*, 29 November 2009, 20.

_____, 'How India Beat China in Auto Exports', *Times of India*, 27 September 2009, 24.

Akbar, M.J., 'BJP, Left Face Existential Dilemma', *Times of India*, 17 May 2009, 14.

Allen, Franklin, Chakrabarti, Rajesh and De, Sankar, 'India's Financial System', 27 October 2007 [Internet]. Available at http://ssrn.com/abstract=1261244.

Altbach, Philip G., 'The Giants Awake: The Present and Future of Higher Education Systems in China and India', in *Higher Education to 2020*, Vol. 2, OECD Publishing, 2009.

Annamalai, E., 'Nativization of English in India', *Journal of Language and Politics*, 3 (1), 2004, 151–62.

Anonymous, 'Aiming High', *The Economist*, 24 October 2009, 13–14.

_____, 'An Analysis of the BRICs Phenomenon', *Contemporary International Relations*, 14 (9), October 2004, 1–32.

_____, 'BRICs, Emerging Markets and the World Economy', *The Economist*, 18 June 2009 [Internet]. Available at http://www.economist.com.

_____, 'China Takes on Boeing and Airbus', *The Economist*, 15 May 2008.

_____, 'China's Place in the World', *The Economist*, 3–9 October 2009, 9.

_____, 'A Dragon of Many Colours', *The Economist*, 24 October 2009, 15–16.

_____, 'English Beginning to be Spoken Here: The Language Business in China', *The Economist*, 15 April 2006.

_____, 'India Desperately Seeking Talent', *Businessweek*, 7 November 2005.

_____, 'Land Reform in China: A "Breakthrough" or a Damp Squib?' *The Economist*, 16 October 2008.

_____, 'The Long and Winding Road to Privatization in China', *Knowledge@Wharton*, 10 May 2006 [Internet]. Available at http://knowledge.wharton.upenn.edu/article.cfm?articleid=1472.

_____, 'Nationalization Rides Again', *The Economist*, 14 November 2009, 36–37.

_____, 'The New Champions', *The Economist*, 20 September 2008 [Internet]. Available at http://www.economist.com.

_____, 'Overkill', *The Economist*, 24 October 2009, 9–11.

_____, 'The Price of Cleanliness', *The Economist*, 24 October 2009, 7–8.

_____, 'Recession Elsewhere, But It's Booming in China', *New York Times*, December 2009 [Internet]. Available at http://www.nytimes.com/2009/12/10/business/economy.

_____, 'The Rich Scent of Freedom', *The Economist*, 24 October 2009, 14–15.

_____, 'Round and Round it Goes', *The Economist*, 24 October 2009, 5–6.

_____, 'Singur: Myth and Reality', *People's Democracy*, 50, 10 December 2006 [Internet]. Available at http://pd.cpim.org/2006/1210/12102006_edit.htm.

_____, 'Sore Points', *The Economist*, 24 October 2009, 11–12.

_____, 'Tug of Car', *The Economist*, 24 October 2009, 6–7.

Archer, William, *India and the Future*, London: Hutchinson, 1917.

Bajpai, G.N., 'Development of the Securities Market in India', in Jahangir Aziz, Steven Dunaway and Eswar Prasad eds. *China and India: Learning from Each Other's Experience: Reforms and Policies for Sustained Growth*, Washington DC: IMF Publications, 2006, 93–113.

Balan, Sridhar, 'Book, Booker, Bookfest', in Ira Pande ed. *India 60: Towards a New Paradigm*, New Delhi: HarperCollins, 2007, 274–82.

Barry, Sautman and Yan, Hairong, 'Friends and Interests: China's Distinctive Links with Africa', *African Studies Review*, 50 (3), 2007, 75–114.

Basu, Kaushik, 'Asian Century: A Comparative Analysis of Growth in China, India and other Asian Economies', BREAD Working Paper No. 209, 2 March 2009 [Internet]. Available at http://ipl.econ.duke.edu/bread/papers/working/209.pdf.

Beech, Hannah, 'The World of China Inc.', *Time*, 7 December 2009, 26–31.

Bhambhri, C.P., *The Foreign Policy of India*, New Delhi: Sterling, 1987.

Bijapurkar, Rama, *We Are Like That Only: Understanding the Logic of Consumer India*, New Delhi: Penguin Portfolio, 2007.

Bloch, Julia Chang, 'US China Policy: New Realism in a New Century', in Paau

Danny and Yee Herbert eds. *Return of the Dragon: US–China Relations in the 21st Century*, Frankfurt: Peter Lang, 2005, 13–27.

Bozan, Jian, Xunzheng, Shao and Hua, Hu, *A Concise History of China*, Foreign Language Press: Beijing, 1986.

Bradsher, Keith, 'Green Power Takes Route in the Chinese Desert', *New York Times*, 3 July 2009.

Burke, Michael E., Cutshaw, Kenneth A. and Krishna, Rahul, 'The Legal System in India and China: A Comparative Perspective', *India Journal of Economics and Business*, September 2006 [Internet]. Available at http://www.thefreelibrary.com/The+legal+systems+in+IndiaChina:+a+comparative+perspective.-a0169310104.

Calder, Kent E., 'China and Japan's Simmering Rivalry', *Foreign Affairs*, 85 (29), 2006, 129.

Carter, Jimmy, Remarks at the Opening Ceremony, Seminar in Commemoration of the 30th Anniversary of the Establishment of Diplomatic Relations between China and the United States, *Foreign Affairs Journal*, Special Issue, 2009, 3–6.

Centre for Asia Pacific Aviation, *Aviation Outlook for China, Hong Kong and Macau*, May 2009.

Cha, Ariana Eungjung, 'In Aging China, a Change of Course: Looming Population Crisis Forces Officials to Rethink One-Child Policy, But Couples Hesitate', *Washington Post*, 12 December 2009 [Internet]. Available at http://www.washingtonpost.com/wpdyn/content/article/2009/12/11.

Chandra, Bipan et al, *India's Struggle for Independence*, New Delhi: Penguin, 1989.

Chaudhury, Dipanjan Roy, 'BRIC Aims to Create a Just and Equitable World Order', *International Affairs*, 55(1), 2009, 51–56.

Chaudhary, Shreesh, *Foreigners and Foreign Languages in India: A Sociolinguistic History*, New Delhi: Cambridge University Press, 2009.

_____, 'Will India Become an English Speaking Country?' in B.N Patnaik and S. Imtiaz Hasnain eds. *Globalization, Language, Culture and Media*, Shimla: Indian Institute of Advanced Study, 2006, 39–70.

Chen, Yang and Sanders, Richard, 'Institutional Constraints on Changes in Ownership and Control within Chinese Publicly Listed Companies', in Shujie Yao and Xiaming Liu eds. *Sustaining China's Economic Growth in the Twenty-First Century*, London and New York: Routledge, 2003, 117–32.

Chen, Zhu, 'Launch of the Health Care Reform Plan in China', *The Lancet*, 18 April 2009.

Chidambaram, P., 'India Will Become an Economic Power and Nothing Will Stop Us', *Knowledge@Wharton*, 3 October 2007 [Internet]. Available at http://knowledge@wharton.

Cohen, Jerome A., 'The PRC Legal System at Sixty', *East Asia Forum*, 1 October 2009 [Internet]. Available at http://www.eastasiaforum.org/2009/10/01/the-prc-legal-system-at-sixty.

Cohen, Stephen P., *India: Emerging Power*, New Delhi: Oxford University Press, 2001.

Conover, Tim, 'Capitalist Roaders', *New York Times*, 2 July 2006.

Crompton, Robert, Interview, 30 September 2009 [Internet]. Available at http://markschinablog.blogspot.com/2009/09/win-in-china-interview-with-robert.html.

Das Gupta, Monica, Desikachari, B.R., Somanathan, T.V. and Padmanabhan, P., 'How to Improve Public Health Systems: The Lessons from Tamil Nadu', World Bank Policy Research Working Paper No. 5073, 2009.

Dasgupta, Deepak, 'NHDP: Building a Success Story', *The Hindu*, 2 July 2003.

Dasgupta, Saibal, 'Harshad Mehta: A Legacy of Fraud', *Asiamoney*, 13 (1), 2002.

Dasgupta, Swapan, 'This Verdict Will Force Leaders to Think Nationally', *Times of India*, 17 May 2009, 14.

Dayal, Ravi, 'Wealth of Indian English Writing', in B.G. Verghese ed. *Tomorrow's India: Another Tryst with Destiny*, New Delhi: Penguin Viking, 2006, 297–308.

Department of Telecommunications, Government of India, *India Telecom 2009 Brochure* [Internet]. Available at http://www.indiatelecom.org/e-Brochure-conf.pdf.

Dixit, J.N., *India's Foreign Policy: 1947–2003*, New Delhi: Picus, 2003.

Drezner, Daniel W., 'The New New World Order', *Foreign Affairs*, 86 (2), 2007, 14.

Dreyer, June Teufel, 'The Evolution of Language Policies in China', in Michael E. Brown and Sumit Ganguly eds. *Fighting Words: Language Policy and Ethnic Relations in Asia*, London: MIT Press, 2003, 353–84.

Dubash, Navroz K. and Rajan, Sudhir C., 'India: Electricity Reform Under Political Constraints', World Resources Institute [Internet]. Available at http://www.wri.org.

Eckholm, Erik, 'The SARS Epidemic: China Admits Underreporting its SARS Cases', *New York Times*, 21 April 2003.

Edwards, R. Randle, 'Ch'ing Legal Jurisdiction over Foreigners', in Jerome Alan Cohen, R. Randle Edwards and Fu-mei Chang Chen eds. *Essays on China's Legal Tradition*, Princeton, NJ: Princeton University Press, 1980.

Epstein, Gady, 'Black Future', *Forbes India*, 20 November 2009, 66–67.

_____, 'Ponzi in Peking', *Forbes India*, 22 January 2010, 92–93.

Expert Group on Indian Railways, National Council for Applied Economic Growth, *The Indian Railways Report 2001: Policy Imperatives for Reinvention and Growth*, 2001.

Fan, Shenggen, Gulati, Ashok and Dalafi, Sara, in Ashok Gulati and Shenggen Fan eds. *The Dragon and the Elephant: Agricultural and Rural Reforms in China and India*, New Delhi: Oxford University Press, 2008, 3–9, 10–44, 465–88.

First Report Committee on Public Undertakings, 'Public–Private Partnership in Implementation of Road Projects by National Highways Authority of India in Respect of Delhi–Gurgaon Project', No. 934, 15th Lok Sabha.

Fong, Emily and Tsz, Yan, 'English in China: Some Thoughts after the Beijing Olympics', *English Today*, 25 (1), March 2009, 44–49.

Foroohar, Rana, 'Everything You Know about China is Wrong', *Newsweek*, 26 October 2009, 32–35.

French, Howard W., 'Shanghai's Boom: A Building Frenzy', *New York Times*, 13 April 2006.

Gadgil, D.R., *The Industrial Evolution of India in Recent Times*, London: Oxford University Press, 1946.

Garnaut, Ross, Song, Ligang, Tenev, Stoyan and Yao, Yang, *China's Ownership Transformation: Process, Outcomes, Prospects*, Washington DC: The International Finance Corporation and the International Bank for Reconstruction and Development/The World Bank, 2005.

Gewirtz, Paul, 'Legislative Supervision of Court Cases', International Symposium on Judicial Fairness and Supervision, Beijing, 10–12 January 2004 [Internet]. Available at http://www.law.yale.edu/documents/pdf/ENGLISH.pdf.

Goyal, Vatsal and Suman, Premraj, 'The Indian Telecom Industry', Consulting Club, IIM Calcutta, 21 October 2006 [Internet]. Available at http://www.iimcal.ac.in/community/consclub/reports/telecom.pdf.

Guha, Ramachandra, *India after Gandhi*, New Delhi: Picador, 2007.

Gupta, Anil K. and Wang, Haiyan, 'Why the Export Slump Won't Doom China's Economy', *Businessweek*, 20 April 2009 [Internet]. Available at http://www.businessweek.com/globalbiz/content/apr2009.

Government of India, *Economic Survey 2008–09*, New Delhi: Government of India Press, 2009.

Guruswamy, Mohan, 'Long Live Sibling Rivalry: Let There Be No War, Let Bhai-Bhai One Upmanship Last Forever', *Outlook*, 16 November 2009, 44.

Haldea, Gajendra, 'Candle-light Vigil', *Outlook*, 5 October 2008.

Hand, Keith J., 'Using Law for a Righteous Purpose: The Sun Zhigang Incident and Evolving Forms of Citizen Action in the People's Republic of China', *Colum J. Transnat'll*, 45 (1), 2006.

Harral, Clell and Sondhi, Jit, *Comparative Evaluation of Highway and Railway Development in China and India, 1992–2000, Lessons Learned and Transferability Issues*, Washington DC: The World Bank, March 2005.

Hathaway, Robert M., 'The US–India Courtship: From Clinton to Bush', in Sumit Ganguly ed. *India as an Emerging Power*, London: Frank Cass, 2003, 6–31.

Hecht, Jonathan, 'Can Legal Reform Foster Respect For Human Rights In China?' Congressional Executive Commission on China, 11 April 2002 [Internet]. Available at http://www.cecc.gov/pages/hearings/041102/hecht.php.

Hilgers, Lauren, 'The Growing Clout of Internet Justice', *Newsweek*, 23 November 2009, 13.

Huang, Yasheng, *Capitalism with Chinese Characteristics: Entrepreneurship and the State*, Cambridge: Cambridge University Press, 2008.

Huang, Yasheng and Khanna, Tarun, 'Can India Overtake China?' *Foreign Policy*, 1 July 2003 [Internet]. Available at http://www.foreignpolicy.com/articles/2003/07/01/can_india_overtake_china?page=full.

Hung, Veron Mei-ying, 'Judicial Reforms in China: Lessons from Shanghai', *Carnegie Papers: China Program*, No. 58, April 2005, 3–30.

Hu, Fred, 'The Effects of Stock Market Listing on the Financial Performances of the Chinese Firms', in Charles W. Calomiris ed. *China's Financial Transition at a Crossroads*, New York: Columbia University Press, 2007, 290–313.

India Infrastructure Report, *Land: A Critical Resource for Infrastructure*, 3i Network,

Infrastructure Development Finance Company, New Delhi: Oxford University Press, 2009.

Jaggi, Gautam, Rundle, Mary, Takahashi, Yuichi and Rosen, Daniel, 'China's Economic Reforms: Chronology and Statistics', Institute for International Economics, Working Paper 96.5, 1996, 1–31.

Jha, Prem Shankar, *The Managed Chaos: The Fragility of the Chinese Miracle*, New Delhi: Sage, 2009.

Kalish, Ira, 'China's Consumer Market: Opportunities and Risks', Deloitte Research Study, 2005, 1–22.

Kahn, Jeremy, 'India Cleans Up Its Act', *Newsweek*, 16 November 2009, 34–37.

Kapur, Devesh and Mehta, Pratap Bhanu, 'Indian Higher Education Reform: From Half-Baked Socialism to Half-Baked Capitalism', Presentation at the Brooking–NCAER India Policy Forum 2007 [Internet]. Available at http://www.ncaer.org/downloads/IPF2007/kapur-mehta.pdf.

Kellogg, Thomas E. and Hand, Keith, 'China Crawls Slowly Towards Judicial Reform', *Asia Times Online*, 25 January 2008.

Khanna, Tarun, *Billions of Entrepreneurs: How China and India Are Reshaping Their Future and Yours*, New Delhi: Penguin Viking, 2008.

Kissinger, Henry, 'Face to Face with China', *Newsweek*, 16 April 2001, 36–37.

_____, 'Major Experience of the Steady Development of Sino–American Relations Over the Past Thirty Years and its Global Relevance', Seminar in Commemoration of the 30th Anniversary of the Establishment of Diplomatic Relations between China and the United States, *Foreign Affairs Journal*, Special Issue, 2009, 19–23.

Kripalani, Manjeet, 'India's Madoff? Satyam Scandal Rocks Outsourcing Industry', *Businessweek*, 7 January 2009 [Internet]. Available at http://www.businessweek.com/globalbiz/content/jan2009/gb2009017_807784.htm.

Krishna, Srivatsa, 'China @ 60: Inspiring and Yet Worrisome', *Mint*, 5 October 2009, 7.

Kumar, Sudhir and Mehrotra, Shagun, *Bankruptcy to Billions: How the Indian Railways Transformed*, New Delhi: Oxford University Press, 2009.

The Lancet, 'Health System Reform in China: Emergence and Control of Infectious Diseases in China', *The Lancet*, 1 November 2008.

_____, 'Health System Reform in China: Emergence of Chronic Non-communicable Diseases in China', *The Lancet*, 8 November 2008.

_____, 'Health System Reform in China: Tackling the Challenges of Health Equity in China', *The Lancet*, 25 October 2008.

Lee, John, 'China's Africa Gambit', *Time*, 16 November 2009, 52.

Levinson, Marc, *The Box: How the Shipping Container Made the World Smaller and the World Economy Bigger*, Princeton, NJ: Princeton University Press, 2006.

Li, Cheng, 'Reclaiming the "Head of the Dragon": Shanghai as China's Centre for International Finance and Shipping', *China Leadership Monitor*, 28, Hoover Institution, Stanford University, 2009.

Liu, Melinda, 'China and the Fights within its Single Party', *Newsweek*, 5 October 2009, 29–31.

_____, 'China's Rare Earth Hoard', *Newsweek*, 5 October 2009, 17.

_____, 'Steal this Scientist', *Newsweek*, 23 November 2009, 38–39.

Liu, Zhi, 'Planning and Policy Coordination in China's Infrastructure Development', A Background Paper for the EAP Infrastructure Flagship Study, 1–36 [Internet]. Available at http://siteresources.worldbank.org/INTEAPINFRASTRUCT/Resources/855084-1137106254308/China.pdf.

Mahadevan, Suresh A., Wyatt, Philip, Anderson, Jonathan, Gupta, Navin et al, 'India: The Next Asian Tiger', UBS Investment Research, 22 September 2009, 1–16 [Internet]. Available at www.ubs.com/investmentresearch.

Mahbubani, Kishore, 'Understanding China', Foreign Affairs, 84 (5), September-October 2005, 49.

Mastercard Worldwide Insights, 'Dynamic Drivers of China's Consumers Market: The Middle Class, Modern Women and DINKs', 4th Quarter 2007, 1–21 [Internet]. Available at http://www.mastercard.com/us/company/en/insights/pdfs/2007/ChinaConsumerDrivers-S.pdf.

Maorang, Zhang, 'Rising Stars', Beijing Review, 52 (26), 2009, 10–13.

Mathur, Om Prakash, Thakur, Debdulal and Rajadhyaksha, Nilesh, Urban Property Tax Potential in India, National Institute of Public Finance and Policy, 2009.

McAleavy, Henry, The Modern History of China, UK: Morrison and Gribb, 1967.

McKinsey and Company, 'Addressing China's Looming Talent Shortage', McKinsey and Company Report, October 2005.

_____, 'Powering India: The Road to 2018', McKinsey and Company Report, 2008.

_____, 'Vision Mumbai: Transforming Mumbai into a World Class City', McKinsey and Company Report, 2003.

Mehta, Pratap Bhanu, 'Nationalism Is So 2000: As Economics Transforms Our Politics, Will We See a Smarter Idea of India?' Indian Express, 1 January 2010, 12.

Mehta, Vinod, 'No Hate Politics: This Is India', Outlook, 29 May 2009, 3.

Miles, James, 'A Wary Respect', The Economist, 24 October 2009, 3–4.

Mills, Elizabeth, 'Keep Friends Close but Enemies Closer: Changing Energy Relations between China and India', Harvard International Review, June 2009 [Internet]. Available at http://hir.harvard.edu/index.php/index.php?page=article&id=1888.

Ministry of Civil Aviation, Government of India, Report of the Committee on a Road Map for the Civil Aviation Sector, November 2003.

Ministry of Finance, Government of India, Mumbai: An International Financial Centre, Sage Publications for India's Ministry of Finance, 2007.

Ministry of Railways, Government of India, Indian Railways Vision 2020, December 2009.

_____, White Paper on Indian Railways, December 2009.

Mitta, Manoj, 'Bhopal Tragedy, Anti-Sikh Riots: Just Say Sorry, and Pay Up', Times of India, 5 December 2009 [Internet]. Available at http://timesofindia.indiatimes.com/india/Bhopal-tragedy-anti-Sikh-riots-Just-say-sorry-and-pay-up-/articleshow/5304212.cms.

Morse, Hosea Ballou, The Chronicles of the British East India Company Trading to China, 1635–1834, Oxford: Clarendon Press, 1926–29.

Mukherjee, Rudrangshu. A Century of Trust: The Story of Tata Steel, New Delhi: Penguin Portfolio, 2008.

National Knowledge Commission, Report to the Nation 2006–09 [Internet]. Available at http://www.knowledgecommission.gov.in.

Nayar, Lola, 'Bazaar Ping-Pong: Trade Is Growing but a Closer Look Finds India Chafing at Inequalities', *Outlook*, 16 November 2009, 50–51.

Nobrega, William, 'Why India Will Beat China', *Businessweek*, 22 July 2008.

Nobrega, William and Dhillon, Ruminder, 'White Paper: Why a Democratic India Will Outperform China', The Conrad Group, 2 May 2007 [Internet]. Available at http://www.conradgroupinc.com/index.php?s= why+a+democratic+india+will+outperform+china.

O'Neill, Jim, 'BRICs are Still on Top', *Newsweek*, Special Issue 2009, 44–45.

_____, 'The World, BRICs Dream and India', *SiliconIndia*, May 2006 [Internet]. Available at http://www.siliconindia.com/ magazine /articledesc.php ?articleid=AYT215 490556.

Pant, Harsh V., 'Indian Foreign Policy and China', *Strategic Analysis*, 30 (4), 2006, 760–80.

Parkash, Manmohan, 'Changing Lives: Building Railways in the People's Republic of China', Asian Development Bank, 2008.

Peerenboom, Randall, 'China's Long March toward Rule of Law', UCLA Asia Institute [Internet]. Available at http://www.international.ucla.edu/ asia/news/article.asp?parentid=2878.

Peerenboom, Randall and He, Xin, 'Dispute Resolution in China: Patterns, Causes, and Prognosis', *East Asia Law Review*, 4 (1), 2009 [Internet]. Available at http://www.pennealr.com/media/articles/vol4/ EALR4(1) PeerenboomHe.pdf.

Pei, Minxin, 'Why China Won't Rule the World', *Newsweek*, Issues 2010 Special Issue, December 2009, 16–18.

Pesek, William, 'India Shows Hedge-Fund Savvy with Huge Gold Buy', *Financial Express*, 6 November 2009, 7.

Phillips, Richard T., *China Since 1911*, London: Macmillan, 1996.

Poddar, Tushar and Yi, Eva, *India's Rising Growth Potential*, Goldman Sachs Global Economics Paper No. 152, 22 January 2007 [Internet]. Available at http://www.usindiafriendship.net/viewpoints1/ Indias Rising Growth Potential.pdf.

Powell, Bill, 'Five Things the US Can Learn from China', *Time*, 23 November 2009, 25–31.

PRS Legislative Brief, 'New Rules for Seizing Land', 19 May 2009 [Internet]. Available at http://www.indiatogether.org.

Qiao, Helen (Hong), *Will China Grow Old Before Getting Rich?* Goldman Sachs Global Economics Paper, 14 February 2006 [Internet]. Available at http://www2.goldmansachs.com/ideas/brics/book/BRICs-Chapter3.pdf.

Raja Mohan, C., *Impossible Allies: Nuclear India, United States and the Global Order*, New Delhi: India Research Press, 2006.

Ramesh, Jairam, *Making Sense of Chindia: Reflections on China and India*, New Delhi: India Research Press, 2005.

Ranganathan, C.V. and Khanna, Vinod C., *India and China: The Way Ahead*, New Delhi: Har-Anand, 2000.

Rao, Leena, 'Watch Out Baidu, China Clamps Down on Music Piracy', *TechCrunch*, 4 September 2009 [Internet]. Available at http://techcrunch.com/2009/09/04/watch-out-baidu-china-clamps-down-on-music-piracy.

Ray, Amit S., 'Managing Port Reforms in India: Case Study of Jawaharlal Nehru Port Trust, Mumbai', World Bank, 15 February 2004 [Internet]. Available at http://siteresources.worldbank.org.

Reddy, K. Srinath, 'Primary Lesson', *Frontline*, 29 August–11 September 2009.

Roach, Stephen S., *The Next Asia: Opportunities and Challenges for a New Globalization*. New Jersey: John Wiley, 2009.

Ross, Robert S., 'The 1995–96 Taiwan Strait Confrontation: Coercion, Credibility and Use of Force', in Robert J. Art and Patrick M. Cronin eds. *The United States and Coercive Diplomacy*, Washington DC: United States Institute of Peace Press, 2003, 225–73.

Salhotra, Bharat, 'Concession for Nava Sheva International Container Terminal', November 2007 [Internet]. Available at http://infrastructure.gov.in.

Sarkar, S., *Modern India 1885–1947*, New Delhi: Macmillan, 2001.

Saxena, Vijay K. And Verghese, T., 'Observations on Urban Ecology of Surat and Bubonic Plague Transmission in the City', National Institute of Communicable Diseases, *Current Science*, Vol. 71, 10 November 1996.

Schell, Orville and Shambaugh, David, eds. *China Reader: The Reform Era*, London: Vintage, 1999.

Seddighi, H.R. and Nian, W., 'The Chinese Stock Exchange Market: Operations and Efficiency', *Applied Financial Economics*, 14 (11), 2004, 785–97.

Shah, Ajay and Thomas, Susan, 'Policy Issues in the Indian Securities Market', in Anne O. Krueger and Sajjid Z. Chinoy eds. *Reforming India's External, Financial and Fiscal Policies*, New York and London: Oxford University Press, 2004, 129–73.

Sharma, Pranay, 'A Cure for Our Sinositis', *Outlook*, 16 November 2009, 46–48.

_____, 'India's Intention on Tibet', *Outlook*, 16 November 2009, 39–42.

Singh, Manmohan, Prime Minister's Address at the 150th Anniversary of University of Mumbai, 22 June 2007 [Internet]. Available at http://www.pib.nic.in/release/release.asp?relid=28780.

Singh, S., *India and China: Mutual Relations*, New Delhi: Anmol Publications, 2006.

Singh, Swaran, 'The China Factor in India's Look East Policy', in P.V. Rao ed. *India and ASEAN: Partners at Summit*, New Delhi: KW Publishers, 2008, 243–52.

Srinivasan, T.N., 'Development: Domestic Constraints and External Opportunities from Globalization', *Michigan Journal of International Law*, 26 (1), 2004.

Sripati, Vijayashri, 'Toward Fifty Years of Constitutionalism and Fundamental Rights in India: Looking Back to See Ahead (1950–2000)', *AU International Law Review*, 14 (2).

Subrahmanyam, K., 'Nehru and India–China Conflict of 1962', in B.R. Nanda ed. *Indian Foreign Policies: The Nehru Years*, New Delhi: Radiant Publishers, 1976, 102–30.

Subramaniam, Samanth, 'How Borlaug's Dwarfs Came to Stand Tall in India's Agronomy', *Mint*, 28 September 2009.

Sun, Yan, *Corruption and Market in Contemporary China*, Ithaca: Cornell University Press, 2004.

Swanson, K.C., 'China Stock Markets', *Institutional Investor*, 41 (9), 2007, 1–4.

Tata Motors, 'Nano: The Making of a Modern Classic' [Internet]. Available at http://tatanano.inservices.tatamotors.com.

Thakker, Puja and Reddy, K. Srinath, 'The Development of the Discipline of Public Health in Countries in Economic Transition: India, Brazil, China', in Roger Detels, Robert Beaglehole, Mary Ann Lansang and Martin Gulliford eds. *Oxford Textbook of Public Health*, Fifth Edition, London: Oxford University Press, 2009.

Tong, Tiger, *China Economy: The Frog Story*, Mumbai: IIFL, 3rd Quarter 2009, 1–21. URL: iiflcap.com.

Transport Coordinator, World Bank Office, *Tracks From the Past, Transport for the Future: China's Railway Industry 1990–2008 and its Future Plans and Possibilities*, Beijing: World Bank, March 2009.

Valentine, Vincent, *Recent Development in Maritime Transport and Challenges Ahead for Ports*, Trade Logistics Branch, UNCTAD, 18 September 2009.

Ven, Hans J. van de, *War and Nationalism in China 1925–1945*, New York: Routledge, 2003.

Waldman, Amy, 'Mile by Mile, India Paves a Smoother Road to its Future', *New York Times*, 4 December 2005.

Walker, Jim, 'And Then There Was None . . . China: Asian Economics Research', *CLSA Asia-Pacific Markets*, May 2005, 1–36.

_____, 'India: Embracing the Elephant', Asianomics Report, 14 September 2009, 5–132.

Wallerstein, Immanuel, 'The Decline of US Power', *Contexts*, 4 (2), 2005, 25–26.

Walsh, Bryan, 'A River Ran Through It', *Time*, 14 December 2009, 33–39.

Wang, Ping and Liu, Aying, 'Volatility and Volatility Spillovers in Chinese Stock Market', in Shujie Yao and Xiaming Liu eds. *Sustaining China's Economic Growth in the Twenty-First Century*, New York: Routledge, 2003, 150–63.

Weingroff, Richard F., 'Federal-Aid Highway Act of 1956: Creating the Interstate System' [Internet]. Available at http://www.fhwa.dot.gov/infrastructure/rw96e.cfm.

Wilson, Dominic and Purushothaman, Roopa, *Dreaming with BRICs: The Path to 2050*, Goldman Sachs Global Economics Paper No. 99, 1 October 2003 [Internet]. Available at http://www2.goldmansachs.com/ideas/brics/book/99-dreaming.pdf.

Wines, Michael, 'China's Economic Power Unsettles the Neighbours', *New York Times*, 9 December 2009 [Internet]. Available at http://www.nytimes.com/2009/12/10/world/asia/10jakarta.html.

The World Bank, 'Study of Capacity Building of the Electricity Regulatory Agency (SERC), PR of China', 2007 [Internet]. Available at http://www.worldbank.org.

_____, *World Development Report 2009: Reshaping Economic Geography*, Washington DC: World Bank, 2009.

Xiaoxia, Cui, 'An Understanding of "China English" and the Learning and Use of the English Language in China', *English Today*, 22 (4), October 2006, 40–43.

Yajun , Jiang, 'English as a Chinese Language', *English Today*, 19 (2), 2003, 3–8.

Yardley, Jum, 'Chinese Dam Projects Criticized for Their Human Costs', *New York Times*, 19 November 2007.

Yashpal, Report of the Committee to Advise on Renovation and Rejuvenation of Higher Education, New Delhi, 2008.

Yee, Herbert S., 'Into the New Century: Reconsidering the "China Threat" Factor in Sino–US Relations', in Paau Danny and Yee Herbert eds. *Return of the Dragon: US–China Relations in the 21st Century*, Frankfurt: Peter Lang, 2005, 111–34.

Yi, Wei, 'Taiwanese Foxconn Group Companies Fall Sharply on China Labour Protections', *Market Watch*, 13 December 2007 [Internet]. Available at http://www.marketwatch.com/story/taiwanese-foxconn-group-companies-fall-sharply-on-china-labor-protections.

Zakaria, Fareed, 'A Path Out of the Woods; We Need China to See that its Interests Are Aligned with America's, If Not, Things Could Get Very, Very Ugly', *Newsweek*, 152 (22), December 2008, 1.

_____, *The Post-American World and the Rise of the Rest*, New Delhi: Penguin, 2008.

Zarrow, Peter, *China in War and Revolution 1895–1949*, New York: Routledge, 2005.

INDEX